nstitute of
al Auditors

MW01691007

Congratulations on taking the next step toward pursuing The Institute of Internal Auditors' premier professional designation, the Certified Internal Auditor® (CIA®). By undertaking this important professional milestone, you are making a bold statement about yourself: You are communicating to your colleagues, your current and future employers, and your family that you take the internal audit profession seriously and that you intend to be one of the best in the field.

You've also made a smart decision to prepare for the CIA exam with The IIA's CIA Learning System®. When we created these study materials, our goal was to make the highest quality materials available to candidates around the world at an affordable price. We pulled together an amazing team of some of the world's best internal auditors and created a learning format that couples comprehensive printed materials with interactive online reinforcement software. We find that CIA candidates who take advantage of the resources in The IIA's CIA Learning System maximize their chances of passing the exam.

Congratulations again on making two important decisions — to pursue the CIA certification and to prepare for the exams with The IIA's CIA Learning System. I look forward to seeing you at an upcoming IIA conference with the *CIA* acronym behind your name!

Best of luck with your studies,

Richard F. Chambers

Richard Chambers, CIA, CGAP, CCSA, CRMA
President and Chief Executive Officer
The Institute of Internal Auditors

lobal Headquarters
47 Maitland Avenue
amonte Springs, FL
32701-4201 USA
+1-407-937-1100
+1-407-937-1101
www.theiia.org

Part 2 Study Checklist

Take advantage of all that The IIA's CIA Learning System has to offer and keep your studies on track by following this convenient study checklist. Once you have completed a step, mark your completion date in the space provided. This will provide you with a handy reference to where you left off.

Task	Completion Date
If you are planning to take the CIA exam, learn more details, apply, and register at https://global.theiia.org/certification/cia-certification.	
If this is the first time you've used The IIA's CIA Learning System, follow the link included in your online access invitation e-mail to set your login name and password. Specific instructions can be found on the previous page.	
Log on to www.LearnCIA.com and complete the online pre-test for Part 2.	
After completing your pre-test, use your results to create a customized study plan with the SmartStudy™ tool found in the Assess section of the online main menu.	
Study Section I, "Managing the Internal Audit Function," Chapters A-C of the printed or e-book reading materials. After each chapter, complete the corresponding online chapter quizzes and flashcards at www.LearnCIA.com.	
Section I, Chapter A: Strategic Role of Internal Audit	
Section I, Chapter B: Operational Role of Internal Audit	
Section I, Chapter C: Establish a Risk-Based Internal Audit Plan	
Study Section II, "Managing Individual Engagements," Chapters A-D of the printed or e-book reading materials. After each chapter, complete the corresponding online chapter quizzes and flashcards at www.LearnCIA.com.	
Section II, Chapter A: Plan Engagements	
Section II, Chapter B: Supervise Engagements	
Section II, Chapter C: Engagement Communications as a Process	
Section II, Chapter D: Monitor Engagement Outcomes	
Study Section III, "Fraud Risks and Controls," Chapters A-H of the printed or e-book reading materials. After each chapter, complete the corresponding online chapter quizzes and flashcards at www.LearnCIA.com.	
Section III, Chapter A: Common Types of Fraud and Fraud Risks per Engagement Area	
Section III, Chapter B: Assessing Response to Engagement Area Fraud Risks	
Section III, Chapter C: Determining Need for Fraud Investigation	
Section III, Chapter D: Process Review for Fraud Controls Improvement	
Section III, Chapter E: Detecting Fraud	
Section III, Chapter F: Culture of Fraud Awareness	
Section III, Chapter G: Interrogation/Investigative Techniques	
Section III, Chapter H: Forensic Auditing	
Go to www.LearnCIA.com and complete the Part 2 post-test.	
Go to www.LearnCIA.com and check the Resource Center for certification information, test-taking tips, feedback opportunities, and more.	
Go to www.LearnCIA.com and complete the Part 2 CIA Practice Exam.	

Are you planning on taking the CIA examination?
For details on how to apply, register, and enroll, visit
https://global.theiia.org/certification.

To create a more detailed and customized study plan based on your pre-test scores, log in at www.LearnCIA.com and select SmartStudy™ *from the main menu.*

The IIA's CIA Learning System®

Part 2: Internal Audit Practice

The self-study text for The IIA's CIA Learning System includes all sections and topics addressed in The IIA's 2013 CIA Exam Syllabus, which you can download from the online Resource Center or from The IIA's Web site. However, in some cases, the content for this learning system was reorganized to facilitate instruction and understanding. Refer to the Table of Contents for section and topic page numbers as well as a listing of all topics.

To get the most out of the course materials, complete the course in the order indicated below.

1. Begin by accessing the course at www.learncia.com.
2. Read the overview and return to the menu. Select Part 2 from the menu.
3. Complete the pre-test and view the report to help focus your study efforts.
4. Read each section and follow the Next Steps directions included at the end of the section.
5. Complete Part 2 as outlined in the online overview.

Study Support

The IIA's CIA Learning System includes online tools that are provided to support your study. These tools may be accessed at any time from the menu.

- Glossary—Refer to the glossary for definitions of terms used in all three parts of The IIA's CIA syllabus.
- Reports—Refer to the reports to review your most recent test scores and progress through the learning system.
- Resource Center—Refer to the Resource Center to access updates, test-taking tips, printable flashcards, related links, and reference material and to provide feedback to The IIA regarding the learning system.

The IIA's CIA Learning System® is based on the Certified Internal Auditor® (CIA®) syllabus developed by The IIA. However, program developers do not have access to the exam questions. Therefore, while the learning system is a good tool for study, reading the text does not guarantee a passing score on the CIA exam.

Every effort has been made to ensure that all information is current and correct. However, laws and regulations change, and these materials are not intended to offer legal or professional services or advice. This material is consistent with the revised Standards *of the International Professional Practices Framework (IPPF) effective January 1, 2013.*

Copyright

Acknowledgments

The IIA would like to thank the following dedicated subject matter experts who shared their time, experience, and insights during the development and subsequent update of the IIA's CIA Learning System.

Pat Adams, CIA

Terry Bingham, CIA, CISA, CCSA

Raven Catlin, CIA, CPA, CFSA

Patrick Copeland, CIA, CRMA, CISA, CPA

Don Espersen, CIA

Larry Hubbard, CIA, CCSA, CPA, CISA

Jim Key, CIA

David Mancina, CIA, CPA

Al Marcella, PhD, CISA, CCSA

Markus Mayer, CIA

Vicki A. McIntyre, CIA, CFSA, CRMA, CPA

Gary Mitten, CIA, CCSA

Lynn Morley, CIA, CGA

James Roth, PhD, CIA, CCSA

Brad Schwieger, CPA, DBA

Doug Ziegenfuss, PhD, CIA, CCSA, CPA, CMA, CFE, CISA, CGFM, CR.FA., CITP

The IIA's CIA Learning System is printed on 30% post-consumer waste recycled paper.

Part 2: Internal Audit Practice

Table of Contents

Part 2 Overview

Welcome to Part 2 of The IIA's CIA Learning System®. This part of the learning system focuses on managing the internal audit function at both a strategic and an operational level.

From a strategic perspective, the chief audit executive (CAE) must ensure the establishment of a risk-based plan for managing the function's activity. This will require that internal audit leaders can:

- Manage changes needed to implement and support the organization's strategy.
- Establish relationships throughout the organization to foster communication and cooperation.
- Assess and promote an ethical climate and good governance.
- Develop an appropriate system to measure the efficiency and effectiveness of the internal audit function and report performance to senior management and the board.
- Manage interactions with external auditors, regulatory bodies, and other internal assurance functions.

From an operational perspective, the CAE must ensure that the function is managed in a professional manner and that:

- Policies and procedures are in place to plan, organize, direct, and monitor internal audit operations.
- The function is administered to make the best use of internal audit resources.
- The function is staffed appropriately for its tasks.
- A risk-based audit plan is used to identify potential engagements and prioritize engagements.
- Management is informed about the effectiveness of the organization's internal control and risk management frameworks.
- The quality of internal audit work is monitored, assessed, and reported to management, and a quality assurance and improvement program is in place.

Those managing engagements must ensure that engagements are conducted in a professional manner—from planning through supervision and communication to monitoring engagement outcomes—and with a continuous awareness of risk.

Since fraud can be a considerable risk for many organizations, Part 2 concludes with a review of types of fraud, conducting engagements with awareness of the potential for fraud, and improving hard and soft controls for fraud activity.

The three sections of Part 2 explore these aspects of the internal audit function:

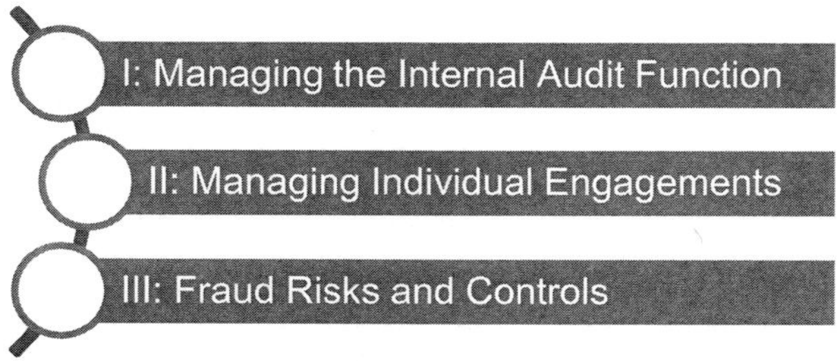

Section I: Managing the Internal Audit Function

This section is designed to help you:

- *Describe the role of internal auditing as a change catalyst in the organization.*
- *Describe managerial characteristics needed to manage reactions to change.*
- *Build and maintain networking with executives and the audit committee by understanding stakeholder needs and expectations of internal auditing.*
- *Organize and lead a team in mapping, analysis, and business process improvement/operational auditing.*
- *Assess and foster the ethical climate of the board and management.*
- *Educate senior management and the board on best practices in governance, risk management, control, and compliance.*
- *Communicate internal audit key performance indicators to senior management and the board.*
- *List steps to establishing an effective performance measurement process.*
- *Coordinate the internal audit activity's efforts with external auditors, regulatory oversight bodies, and other internal assurance functions to maximize audit coverage and minimize redundancies.*
- *Describe the purpose and contents of an internal audit manual.*
- *Review the role of internal audit within the organization's risk management framework.*
- *Direct administrative activities of the internal audit department.*
- *Interview candidates for internal audit positions.*
- *Report on the effectiveness of organizational risk management processes to senior management and the board.*
- *List audit procedures to be used and types of evidence to be gathered in order to support the soundness of risk management processes.*
- *Establish a framework for assessing risk.*
- *Describe major enterprise risk management (ERM) frameworks.*
- *Conduct assurance engagements, including the following:*
    - *Control self-assessment*
    - *External business relationships*
    - *Quality*
    - *Due diligence*
    - *Security*
    - *Privacy*
    - *Performance*
    - *Operational*
    - *Financial*
    - *Compliance*

- *Conduct consulting engagements, including the following:*
  - *Business process mapping*
  - *Benchmarking*
  - *Systems development life cycle review*
  - *Design of performance measurement systems*

The Certified Internal Auditor (CIA) exam questions based on content from this section make up approximately 40% to 50% of the total number of questions for Part 2. One of the topics is covered at the "A—Awareness" level, meaning that you are responsible for comprehension and recall of information. However, most topics are covered at the "P—Proficiency" level, meaning that you are responsible not only for comprehension and recall of information but also for higher-level mastery, including application, analysis, synthesis, and evaluation.

Section Introduction

This section traces the role of the internal auditing activity in developing and supporting an enterprise risk management (ERM) framework through the implementation of this framework through internal audit's own strategic plan and a risk-based internal audit plan. It emphasizes the role of the chief audit executive (CAE) in:

- Interacting with senior management and the board.
- Understanding what the organization does and its risk exposure and attitude.
- Assessing the adequacy of the organization's ERM framework.
- Managing the internal auditing activity in a strategic manner, which includes measuring and reporting internal audit performance and ensuring that resources are adequate to achieving performance objectives.
- Ensuring that the annual audit plan and individual assurance and consulting audits are aligned with risk management objectives.

Chapter A: Strategic Role of Internal Audit

Chapter Introduction

Strategically managed organizations recognize the need to operate not only as superficially connected functions but as fully integrated, often interdependent parts of a whole. Functional strategies must be aligned with the organizational strategy. The organization's risk management approach must be enterprise-wide.

The internal audit activity plays a critical role in assuring that the organization's resources are being used efficiently and effectively toward accomplishing organizational objectives and that the organization's ERM framework is adequate to controlling the variety of internal and external risks to which the organization is vulnerable.

The topics in this chapter focus on the strategic role of the internal auditing activity. In a strategically managed organization, internal audit management must also be strategic and must understand:

- What the organization does and how its functions interact to achieve its strategic objectives.
- How the organization is changing due to the influences of internal and external forces and how change affects the internal auditing activity.
- How the organization is responding to its mission, strategy, and environment—its structure, stakeholder needs, and the status of ethics and governance in the organization.

Topic 1: Initiate, Manage, Be a Change Catalyst, and Cope with Change (Level P)

The IIA has defined the "value proposition" of the internal auditing function as providing "assurance, insight, and objectivity." The term "insight" reflects internal auditing's role as a catalyst for change in an organization—improvements in efficiency and effectiveness that are based on internal auditing's observations and recommendations. To promote these changes, however, the CAE and auditing staff must understand not only their auditing tasks but the process of change itself.

In any competitive environment, change is constant. It is a reality for every organization, from giant multinationals to the simplest of organizations. While change can galvanize an organization and result in successful growth and other achievements, change can also pose great risks. The role of internal auditing is to support and facilitate strategic change while simultaneously identifying the potential for risks associated with the change and proposing effective controls for those risks.

Change can occur during an engagement, when the internal auditing activity recommends new controls or better implementation of existing controls. It can occur within the internal audit function itself, as changes in strategic plans call for different priorities or skills or changes in processes aimed at increasing efficiency. Change may also come from outside—from new regulations and amended existing regulations.

Whatever the source of change, the way in which individuals and groups react to change is often similar. They can feel threatened by changes, suspicious of the reasons for change, and stressed by the need to spend valuable time learning new processes. Within an organization, productivity and morale may decline.

These reactions to change are natural, but their negative outcomes can be controlled by anticipating and managing them. This requires:

- **Emotional intelligence.** This is an ability to understand and respect others' perspectives, accurately perceive their emotions, and skillfully convey one's own emotions.
- **Organizational awareness.** The CAE will need to secure buy-in of senior management and affected functions to implement change.
- **Honesty and transparency.** Dishonesty about motives for or impacts of change can undermine the process of implementing changes.
- **Strong communication skills.** Managers must be able to explain the problem that made the change necessary, the reason why this solution is the best response, and how the change will be implemented. Most importantly, managers must be able to listen. Through good communication, managers makes those affected part of the change. They can explain impacts and propose their own ideas. In this manner, the group begins to accept the change and becomes more invested in its successful implementation.
- **Monitoring the implementation.** The implementation of the change must be monitored to identify and remove obstacles as they arise.
- **Motivational skills.** Change requires the members of the organization to leave the comfort and security of the familiar. Managers should look for opportunities to recognize and reward progress, and they should be ready with encouragement and reminders about an initiative's ultimate goal when progress is difficult.

Change agents

Major or minor—regardless of the nature of change—there should be one individual who leads and manages the change effort. Without someone to take charge, the likelihood that nothing will happen or that the change initiative will falter increases. A change agent fulfills this role.

A change agent is an individual who facilitates change within the organization. A change agent may or may not be the initiator of the change effort and may be from within or outside the organization.

In *The Change Agents' Handbook*, David W. Hutton describes the role of a change agent in terms of the following categories:

- Educate and work with upper management to initiate and sustain the transformation.
- Support and advise other colleagues.
- Manage specific projects.
- Develop and manage a support network.

In some consultative engagements, an internal auditor may serve as a change agent. This is feasible only if the auditor has no conflict of interest or management responsibility for the areas under consideration.

With assurance engagements, internal auditors should be aware of any ongoing or anticipated changes. If there is a major change initiative, the auditor may want to evaluate the change management process. The process should specifically address risk and control considerations. An ineffective process may lead to a variety of control weaknesses.

Topic 2: Build and Maintain Networking with Other Organization Executives and the Audit Committee (Level P)

A report by PriceWaterhouseCoopers on creating a strategically focused internal audit function begins with the need for the CAE to understand stakeholder expectations—how the board and senior management each define the value of internal auditing. Exhibit I-1 lists the most common internal auditing value drivers.

Exhibit I-1: Key Drivers for Internal Audit Value to Organization

- Risk management and control assurance
- Assessment of internal control effectiveness and efficiency
- Regulatory and corporate compliance assurance
- Relevant regulatory readiness assessment and ongoing testing
- Ability to respond to urgent events
- Return of value from internal audit investment
- Fostering awareness of risk and control across organization
- Consultative business partnering to address complex issues
- Source of management talent and development
- Effective management of audit fees through coordination with external auditing firm

CAEs must understand, however, that boards and senior management may prioritize these values differently. While the board values assurance of controls and risk management, senior management and executives are looking for information and changes that can help them achieve their business objectives.

Delivering these values to these different stakeholders requires a variety of organizational conditions and internal auditing capabilities:

- **Independence of internal auditing and flexibility in deploying resources.** The function needs to be able to deliver critical assessments of performance without fear of organizational repercussions. It needs to be able to adjust audit budgets if issues emerge.

- **Business understanding.** The CAE and auditing staff must be familiar with the organization's business: its strategy and objectives, the processes of the functions being audited, the competitive pressures on the business, and practical limitations on the audit client's ability to implement internal auditing's recommendations. The audit plan should be aligned with the organization's strategy and objectives. Recommendations should target root causes and propose cost-effective controls. Understanding the organization's business also includes seeing the organization as an enterprise, comprising multiple and interdependent functions and processes. Internal auditing must be able to monitor risks across the enterprise.

- **More expanded role for internal auditing.** The CAE must promote a new orientation within the function, in which the staff goes beyond assessing to playing an active role in initiating change.

- **Expertise in IT tools for data collection and analysis.** This will allow internal auditing to supplement an area of knowledge that may be weak in the board and senior management. It will also help the function go beyond simple reporting to making insightful connections between observations. IT tools can also support benchmarking for more consistent performance management in global organizations.

- **Monitoring, reporting, and demonstrating value.** Both the board and senior management expect to see if the organization's investment in internal auditing (and/or external auditing services) has been merited. The CAE needs to set performance measurements, monitor accomplishments, and report specific results, such as increases in productivity, increases in quality, lower purchasing costs, or decreases in waste or losses.

The path to understanding stakeholder expectations is also the path to building a stronger network of relationships within the organization. As the CAE becomes more engaged with the organization's stakeholders—in formal meetings as well as informal, private meetings—the internal auditing function has the opportunity to become more familiar with perspectives and emerging concerns and to establish its credibility, expertise, and business understanding. By facilitating ERM workshops, internal auditing delivers value and establishes relationships.

The CAE should also focus on instilling this awareness of stakeholder expectations in staff. Opportunities should be found to deepen the staff's understanding of the functions and processes they audit. Staff development and performance appraisals should emphasize the strategic importance of internal customer service and communication skills.

Topic 3: Organize and Lead a Team in Mapping, Analysis, and Business Process Improvement/Operational Auditing (Level P)

In a strategically managed organization, internal auditing may be involved in assuring the operational efficiency and effectiveness of specific processes or functions. CAEs should be familiar with the discipline of business process improvement and the methodologies and tools used to describe, analyze, and improve the efficiency, effectiveness, and quality outcome of processes.

Business process improvement, or operational auditing, benefits both the organization and internal auditing. For organizations, business process improvement provides a clear picture or map of the steps in a process and the time, labor/staff, technology and tools, and material resources needed at each step. Further, the process map should indicate interdependencies (e.g., the need for another function or a supplier to deliver certain components before the process can continue). This facilitates the identification of process vulnerabilities and the creation of risk management or business continuity strategies. Maps can also be used to identify inefficiencies, such as time lost while waiting for materials to be conveyed from a warehouse to the manufacturing floor, or to locate where in the process and why quality issues are arising. The process map can be a benchmark and monitoring tool for successful processes or a diagnostic tool for problematic ones. In addition, process mapping can support employee development and staffing by more accurately identifying the numbers of workers needed, specific responsibilities for each position, and the skills each position requires.

For internal auditing, operational auditing provides an opportunity to deliver and demonstrate value to the board and senior management by assessing and reporting on the organization's key performance indicators and assuring ERM by identifying risks embedded in complex, often cross-functional processes. It also provides an opportunity for auditing staff to learn the organization's business processes in greater depth. Operational audits also provide opportunities for building relationships between internal auditing and functions involved in processes.

Auditing business processes

Operational audits may be assurance or consulting engagements. An assurance audit may start with an analysis of an existing process map and proceed to a comparison of the map with actual performance and an analysis of the process from the perspective of efficiency and effectiveness.

A consulting engagement may be used to create a process map, or it may begin when an organization detects a problem. For example, costs of operation may have increased, customer reports of quality defects or late deliveries may have risen, or increased competition may be driving the organization to increase efficiency to support a lower price or a profit margin.

Integrated auditing

Until the middle of the 20th century, the structure of the traditional corporation, along with its reward systems, management objectives, incentives, and evaluations, surrounded each department with both visible and invisible walls. Marketing was separate from design, which was separate from production, which was separate from procurement, and so on. In a process-oriented organization, each process might have its own audit executive with a staff of process-oriented auditors.

With the post–World War II rise of total quality, continuous improvement, Six Sigma, and similar organizational innovations, those walls began to crumble. New organizational models with names like collaborative planning, forecasting, and replenishment (CPFR) emphasized processes that cut across departmental (and geographic) boundary lines, bringing together work teams comprising, for example, marketing representatives, product designers, production engineers, transportation specialists, and field sales representatives, all focused on creating products and services that incorporated the expertise and met the needs of each area—as well as the end customer.

Reorganization to emphasize cross-disciplinary processes presents a challenge to traditional audit practice, which had of necessity focused on distinct products, organizations, accounts, locations, etc.—and may, in fact, continue to do so when audits target a single risk. The business process audit often requires integrated auditing to respond to the challenge of measuring the efficiency and effectiveness of cross-functional processes. The risks present in a complex, cross-functional process—such as developing a new product or service—may include not only operational risks but also marketing, financial, environmental, safety, fraud, IT, and compliance risks. An integrated audit considers all relevant risks.

Integrated auditing places certain requirements on the internal auditing function:

- The audit will probably require the use of multiple auditing techniques, which will affect the audit's budget and staffing. The audit leader will have to coordinate the participation of experts from other areas of the organization or from outside the organization.
- The CAE will have to weigh available budget and resources against the organization's risk model and prioritize integrated auditing engagements in the annual plan.

Topic 4: Assess and Foster the Ethical Climate of the Board and Management (Level P)

Companies come to terms with values and ethics in different ways. History has shown that a strategy of simply hoping that people will behave ethically and relying on periodic admonitions to "always act ethically" does not typically produce great success. But a carefully planned approach that starts at the top and cascades throughout the organization can create a culture in which people are committed to core organizational values and ethics.

Visible and vocal commitment from the board and management is a prerequisite for organizational ethics compliance. The board and management must model this commitment in their actions, in the values they espouse, and in the decisions they make for the organization.

Internal audit's role in governance and ethics

In the International Professional Practices Framework (IPPF) definition of the "control environment," the first element of control is integrity and ethical values. Performance Standard 2100, "The Nature of Work," notes the role of ethics and values in the governance process and underscores the inextricable relationship between governance, risk management, and control processes.

The level and nature of risks related to an organization's ethical climate will vary by type of business, internal and external pressures, and culture (both organizational and societal). An organization's culture may determine the extent to which ethical values and policies are followed, ignored, or modified for the purpose of convenience.

It is the responsibility of internal auditing to develop a clear picture of the current ethical climate and propose controls designed to sustain or improve it.

Related *Standards*

The *Standards* related to the internal audit activity's role in governance are listed in Exhibit I-2.

Exhibit I-2: Internal Audit Governance Related Standards

Standard
Performance Standard 2110, "Governance" The internal audit activity must assess and make appropriate recommendations for improving the governance process in its accomplishment of the following objectives: • Promoting appropriate ethics and values within the organization; • Ensuring effective organizational performance management and accountability; • Communicating risk and control information to appropriate areas of the organization; and • Coordinating the activities of and communicating information among the board, external and internal auditors, and management.
Implementation Standard 2110.A1 (Assurance Engagements) The internal audit activity must evaluate the design, implementation, and effectiveness of the organization's ethics-related objectives, programs, and activities.
Implementation Standard 2110.A2 (Assurance Engagements) The internal audit activity must assess whether the information technology governance of the organization supports the organization's strategies and objectives.

Evaluating ethics

The internal audit activity should periodically assess the state of the ethical climate of the organization and the effectiveness of its strategies, tactics, communications, and other processes in achieving the desired level of legal and ethical compliance.

Information about the adequacy of ethical controls must be gathered, often through auditing techniques not used in traditional engagements. This information must be analyzed to determine the root causes for risks related to the ethical environment and the scope of the problem. Recommended new controls or changes to existing controls should be practical and aligned with local practices. The CAE must gain the support and buy-in of the board and senior management to ensure required access and the receptivity of the board and senior management to findings. The CAE must also communicate results of the engagement with sensitivity and awareness of the need for confidentiality.

Internal auditors can assess the ethical climate of an organization through several actions, including:

- Evaluating the completeness of ethics policies and codes—whether the organization's policies and codes include appropriate subjects and guidance.
- Reviewing the adequacy of positive personnel practices in supporting an ethical climate.
- Determining whether appropriate communications are occurring and if employees and other stakeholders understand the information.
- Evaluating how well employees truly embrace the message.
- Determining if there are explicit strategies to support and enhance the ethical culture (e.g., regular programs to update and renew the organization's commitment to an ethical culture).
- Evaluating the effectiveness of the processes established to enable employees to communicate concerns regarding inappropriate behavior to management or the board (e.g., a whistleblower process).
- Determining if the appropriate process exists to ensure that allegations of misconduct are investigated and resolved, findings are properly reported, and corrective action is taken to improve controls.
- Evaluating board oversight responsibilities and board monitoring activities.

The list is not all-inclusive. The internal auditor's involvement in ethics will vary. In some organizations, internal auditors may even be at the level of serving as the primary driver behind all the ethics-related initiatives.

Nontraditional assessment tools may be required to evaluate the ethical environment. These tools can include:

- Employee surveys and compliance forms (e.g., annual reports of financial dealings that might constitute conflict of interest). Internal auditing can perhaps work with human resources to include questions related to ethics and governance in annual employee surveys.
- Informal and continual networking of the CAE and staff throughout the organization, which allows observation of behaviors and attitudes.

The use of surveys is discussed further below.

Use of surveys

Internal auditors can use surveys to assess the effectiveness of the communication process and the ethical climate of the organization. Any survey will generate data. But to improve the reliability and validity of the data, an auditor should:

- Have the support of top management and position the survey as a feedback tool.
- Design the questions carefully to ensure ease of response, by using, for example, yes/no responses or Likert agreement/disagreement or satisfied/dissatisfied rating scales. (An example of the Likert scale is shown in Exhibit I-3.)
- Include space for comments and invite people to explain why they chose a rating, especially when the rating points to a weakness.
- Keep the survey at a reasonable length.
- Field-test the survey.
- If feasible, have surveys returned to an independent market research firm and the statistical analysis and typed comments returned to internal audit.

Exhibit I-3: Examples of Likert-Type Response Formats

Strongly Disagree	Disagree	Neither Agree nor Disagree	Agree	Strongly Agree

Very Dissatisfied	Dissatisfied	Neither Satisfied nor Dissatisfied	Satisfied	Very Satisfied

If survey participants have any fear of retribution, survey results will be jeopardized. Ensuring confidentiality lowers this fear. On the other hand, the ability to follow up can be powerful and may warrant consideration. Another key point is that survey participants need to feel that management considers the survey as meaningful and is committed to acting on the results. Participants will need to see that their input led to positive changes.

Identifying root causes

Additional sources of ethics violations are organizational factors that directly or indirectly promote dishonest or unethical acts. Consider a few examples:

- Emphasis on results, especially short-term
- Focus on the bottom line (such as sales revenues and profit goals)
- High-pressure sales tactics
- Ruthless negotiations
- Rewards that are tied to reported financial and nonfinancial information

Internal auditor's role in assessing codes of conduct

Organizational codes of conduct that govern acceptable employee behavior are another important consideration for the internal audit activity. These codes are intended to clearly communicate the kind of conduct that the organization expects in various situations. Codes reinforce the need to promote ethics in business decisions. Specific codes of conduct vary across organizations, but most include sections addressing:

- Conflicts of interest.
- Confidentiality.
- Fair dealing.
- Proper use of organizational assets.
- Gifts and gratuities.
- Compliance with laws, rules, and regulations.
- Reporting of illegal or unethical behavior.

For example, a written statement about conflicts of interest should:

- Generally define conflicts of interest.
- Address the expected behavior for employees, other corporate agents, and suppliers.
- Include provisions for activities, investments, or other interests that reflect on the entity's integrity or reputation.

Codes of conduct are intended to provide a proactive statement on the organization's position on ethics and compliance issues. They are not intended to have the force of law.

Investigation and disposition of ethics violations

Just as management is responsible for the governance process, it is also responsible for investigating alleged violations of ethics, compliance, or business conduct practices and making recommendations for resolution of misconduct, including disciplinary action.

Many corporate ethics programs have a chief ethics officer. An ethics officer is the logical management representative to lead an investigation. When violations are found, they should be investigated no matter what the rank in the organization of the perpetrator.

Actions taken in response to ethics violations should be handled in a consistent manner. No one is immune from penalties. That means if a senior manager and a mailroom clerk both commit the same illegal act, their penalties should be consistent.

The disposition of an ethics violation will depend on the specific nature and seriousness of the act. Possible disposition scenarios include:

- An internal progressive disciplinary process that may start with verbal counseling or probation for a first offense and potential termination for repeated offenses or for serious first-time violations.
- Reporting to the appropriate regulatory agencies any violations of rules.
- Reporting to legal authorities any illegal acts such as theft or workplace violence.

Violations should be appropriately documented and records retained as required. Of course, the overall goal is to have processes and policies in place that encourage all employees to behave in an ethical manner.

Fostering a healthy ethical climate

There are many things an organization can do to promote ethical behavior. Best practices include:

- Setting the "tone at the top" for honesty and integrity and reinforcing that every manager, director, and employee needs to maintain these values.
- Developing a written code of ethics and ensuring that it reflects current business conditions.
- Delivering the ethics message via multiple communication media (e.g., e-mail, fax, bulletin board postings, company communications, and in person).
- Conducting employee ethics interviews.
- Designing and administering employee and stakeholder ethics attitude surveys.
- Designing and delivering ethics training.
- Supporting open communications.
- Promoting employee involvement.
- Valuing diversity and institutional fairness.
- Providing whistleblower hotlines for reporting incidents.
- Promoting a compliance-supporting culture.

In today's hypercompetitive global environment, organizations need ways to stimulate employee creativity and commitment. Values, ethics, and codes of conduct can be the essential glue that holds an organization together. But they need to be bedrock beliefs that everyone in the organization actually feels deep down to their toes, not mere platitudes. Values, ethics policies, and codes of conduct must be clearly communicated, understood, and accepted by all employees. Because after all, successful organizations are much more than plush buildings, strategic plans, and bottom lines. Successful organizations are still human institutions.

Internal auditor's role in assessing the ethical climate of the board

The board is the focal point for an organization's governance practices. Although the board does not have any direct management responsibility, it does set the big-picture perspective for the organization by establishing the "tone at the top" and overseeing all governance activities. Ultimately, the board has the accountability for all organizational affairs and performance.

An organization's ethics and core values are the foundation for all governance practices. Ethics and values define the moral boundaries that the organization believes it should work within.

Stakeholders trust that the board will practice honest and ethical conduct. Effective governance is diminished if stakeholders have any distrust of the board or if any board violations to codes of conduct and ethics occur.

The internal audit activity can play an important role in supporting the ethical aspects of the board's governance by assessing the areas identified in Exhibit I-4 on the next page and—as warranted—assisting in and/or making recommendations for improvements.

A few caveats apply here.

- **Board structure, objectives, and dynamics.** A board may want to consider whether internal audit involvement would be beneficial and acceptable with appropriate safeguards to preserve internal auditor objectivity and independence.

- **Awareness of governance obligations and practices.** Internal auditors could also take a proactive role in assisting the board with current governance obligations and practices. This could be accomplished by developing networks and processes to maintain awareness of governance requirements and working with business round tables, professional trade associations, internal and external subject matter experts, and internal compliance or risk assessment committees. Auditors would then be prepared to assess:
  - Whether the organization is in compliance.
  - The ramifications of noncompliance.
  - The adequacy of the disclosures relating to the organization's governance system in its annual report.

- **Board education and training.** Internal auditors can assist the board in these efforts by developing and delivering training and providing related administrative support.

Exhibit I-4: Assessing the Board's Ethical Climate

Area	To Assess . . .
Board structure, objectives, and dynamics	Whether the board and its committees are appropriately structured and chartered to operate effectively to ensure: • Healthy board and management interaction. • Adequate board meeting time devoted to open discussion. • A full range of issues considered at board meetings. • Appropriate board composition (e.g., number of board members, absence of conflicts of interest, and capabilities of board members). • Sufficient frequency and duration of meetings. • Board self-assessment of performance. • Meetings in private executive sessions.
Board committee functions	• Board meeting schedules, establishment of agendas, dissemination of advance information, and adherence to the committee charters. • Whether the board committees maintain a calendar of responsibilities and regularly monitor performance in regard to published responsibilities. • Evaluation of CEO performance, including ethical culture metrics. • Care in development of incentive programs to ensure that improper behavior is not rewarded. • Board member compliance with laws and code of conduct.
Board policy manual	• The process of developing and maintaining the board governance policy or policy manual. • Compliance procedures.
Processes for maintaining awareness of governance requirements	The organization's processes for maintaining external awareness of relevant governance codes and compliance requirements.
Board education and training	• Provisions for ongoing education on the significant issues facing the organization, changing technology, and emerging risk areas. • Provisions to train and educate new board members to prepare them properly for their new responsibilities. • The adequacy of the education provided to board members compared to best practices from other organizations.

Source: *Organizational Governance: Guidance for Internal Auditors,* The Institute of Internal Auditors, 2006. (As of February 2010, this publication is suppressed.)

Further information

More information on organizational governance is available through the following resources.

The Institute of Internal Auditors

- *Corporate Governance and the Board—What Works Best.* Altamonte Springs, Florida: The Institute of Internal Auditors, 2000.
- *Audit Committee Effectiveness—What Works Best,* third edition. Altamonte Springs, Florida: The Institute of Internal Auditors, 2005.

Government and stock exchange guidance/regulations

- "Revised Guidance for Directors on the Combined Code." Financial Reporting Council, www.ecgi.org/codes/documents/frc_ic.pdf.
- "Corporate Governance Principles and Recommendations with 2010 Amendments." ASX Corporate Governance Council, www.asxgroup.com.au/media/PDFs/cg_principles_recommendations_with_2010_amendments.pdf.
- "The Laws That Govern the Securities Industry—Sarbanes-Oxley Act of 2002." Securities and Exchange Commission, www.sec.gov/about/laws.shtml.
- "Corporate Governance: A Practical Guide." London Stock Exchange, www.ecgi.org/codes/documents/rsmi_lse_guide2004.pdf.

Topic 5: Educate Senior Management and the Board on Best Practices in Governance, Risk Management, Control, and Compliance (Level P)

The obligation of the CAE to educate the board and senior management on best practices in governance, control, and compliance may be seen as part of the way in which internal auditing "adds value to the organization" (Performance Standard 2000, "Managing the Internal Audit Activity").

In an organization committed to governance and ERM, the board and senior management's ability to provide oversight and to make sound decisions may be limited by various factors. Board members, for example, may not have sufficient expertise and experience in the organization's business and regulatory environments. Senior management may be driven by business imperatives and the need to meet objectives and may "de-prioritize" governance issues. Both the board and senior management may not be familiar with the principles of risk management and how that should be affecting both oversight and business decisions.

The CAE can educate the board and senior management by:

- Reviewing the role of the board, senior management, operations, and internal auditing in the risk management process. This may be offered as a tutorial or workshop during an annual meeting. It can also be required training for new board members and senior managers. ISO 31000:2009, "Risk Management," can provide a basis for this training. The IPPF Practice Guide "Assessing the Adequacy of Risk Management Using ISO 31000" notes, "Management is responsible for setting the organizational attitude regarding risk and the board is responsible for determining whether the risk attitude is aligned with the best interests of shareholders."

  To fulfill these responsibilities, the board and management must understand the processes for identifying and assessing risk, defining a risk attitude, developing risk management strategies, and continually monitoring and improving the organization's risk management. The CAE can illustrate this process—or the urgent need for ERM—by organizing field visits to locations or operations that pose specific risks to the organization's health and continued existence.

- Reviewing key, amended, and new laws, regulations, legal decisions, and standards that affect the organization's governance and operations. Periodically the CAE can include this review as an agenda item in the board meeting. This might include, for example, changes in financial reporting requirements and executive compensation guidelines or legal decisions about failure to monitor risks that increase the board's and management's criminal and/or financial liability. It may be necessary for the CAE to "connect the dots"—to clarify and illustrate the implications of these laws and regulations.

- Facilitating workshops designed to identify emerging risks associated with the organization's business environment.

- Presenting at board meeting on best practices in governance and risk management as practiced in peer organizations.

Further information

More information on this topic can be found in the following resources.

The Institute of Internal Auditors

- "Assessing the Adequacy of Risk Management Using ISO 31000." IPPF Practice Guide, December 2010.
- "Interaction with the Board." IPPF Practice Guide, August 2011.
- "Auditing Governance Processes" by Norman Marks. *Internal Auditor (Ia),* February 2012.

Other sources

- "Enhancing Board Oversight." COSO, March 2012, www.coso.org/documents/COSO-EnhancingBoardOversight_r8_Web-ready%20(2).pdf.
- "Risk Assessment in Practice." COSO, October 2012, www.coso.org/documents/COSOAnncsOnlineSurvy2GainInpt4Updt2IntrnlCntrlIntgratdFrmwrk%20-%20for%20merge_files/COSO-ERM%20Risk%20Assessment%20inPractice%20Thought%20Paper%20OCtober%202012.pdf.

Topic 6: Communicate Internal Audit Key Performance Indicators to Senior Management and the Board on a Regular Basis (Level P)

In order to perform its role in assuring governance, risk management, and operational effectiveness and efficiency, the internal audit activity must assure its own efficiency and effectiveness and report its performance to senior management and the board at agreed intervals.

As specified in Performance Standard 2060, "Reporting to Senior Management and the Board," "The chief audit executive must report periodically to senior management and the board on the internal audit activity's purpose, authority, responsibility, and performance relative to its plan. Reporting must also include significant risk exposures and control issues, including fraud risks, governance issues, and other matters needed or requested by senior management and the board."

Interpretation expands on this concept: *"The frequency and content of reporting are determined in discussion with senior management and the board and depend on the importance of the information to be communicated and the urgency of the related actions to be taken by senior management or the board."*

Additional guidance about reporting to the board and senior management is found in Practice Advisory 2060-1, "Reporting to Senior Management and the Board," which tells us: "The chief audit executive (CAE) should agree with the board about the frequency and nature of reporting on the internal audit activity's charter (e.g., purpose, authority, responsibility) and performance. Performance reporting should be relative to the most recently approved plan to inform senior management and the board of significant deviations from the approved audit plan, staffing plans, and financial budgets; reasons for the deviations; and action needed or taken."

Because the board is the focal point for key organizational activities, effective communications with the board are critical. There must be mechanisms in place for senior management, operating management, and internal and external auditors to report to the board on internal controls. The internal audit activity should assess whether management's system for reporting information to the board is adequate and effective. Relevant considerations include:

- Is the board getting all the information it needs from management?
- Is the information accurate?
- Are the information sources reliable?

As noted above, the obligation to communicate internal audit key performance indicators to senior management and the board also holds true for communication and reporting from external service providers. According to Performance Standard 2070, "External Service Provider and Organizational Responsibility for Internal Auditing," "When an external service provider serves as the internal audit activity, the provider must make the organization aware that the organization has the responsibility for maintaining an effective internal audit activity."

Quality assurance and improvement program

Interpretation states that the reporting responsibility is demonstrated through the quality assurance and improvement program (QAIP), which assesses conformance with the International Professional Practices Framework's Definition of Internal Auditing, Code of Ethics, and *Standards.*

Attribute Standard 1300, "Quality Assurance and Improvement Program," requires the CAE to "develop and maintain a quality assurance and improvement program that covers all aspects of the internal audit activity." As the interpretation of this standard explains, the QAIP enables evaluation of the activity in terms of its compliance with the IPPF, assesses the activity's efficiency and effectiveness, and identifies opportunities for improvement.

Practice Advisory 1310-1 defines the QAIP as an:

> Ongoing and periodic assessment of the entire spectrum of audit and consulting work performed by the internal audit activity. QAIPs include evaluations of:
> - Conformance with the Definition of Internal Auditing, the Code of Ethics, and the *Standards*.
> - Adequacy of the internal audit activity's charter, goals, objectives, policies, and procedures.
> - Contribution to the organization's governance, risk management, and control processes.
> - Compliance with applicable laws, regulations, and government or industry standards.
> - Effectiveness of continuous improvement activities and adoption of best practices.
> - The extent to which the internal audit activity adds value and improves the organization's operations.

According to Attribute Standard 1311, "Internal Assessments," internal assessments must include:

- Ongoing monitoring of the performance of the internal audit activity; and
- Periodic self-assessments or assessments by other persons within the organization with sufficient knowledge of internal audit practices.

Interpretation of Standard 1311, "Internal Assessments," tells us:

> *Ongoing monitoring is an integral part of the day-to-day supervision, review, and measurement of the internal audit activity. Ongoing monitoring is incorporated into the routine policies and practices used to manage the internal audit activity and uses processes, tools, and information considered necessary to evaluate conformance with the Definition of Internal Auditing, the Code of Ethics, and the* Standards.
>
> *Periodic assessments are conducted to evaluate conformance with the Definition of Internal Auditing, the Code of Ethics, and the Standards.*
>
> *Sufficient knowledge of internal audit practices requires at least an understanding of all elements of the International Professional Practices Framework.*

External assessments of QAIPs must also be conducted. Attribute Standard 1312, "External Assessments," states that:

> External assessments must be conducted at least once every five years by a qualified, independent assessor or assessment team from outside the organization. The chief audit executive must discuss with the board:
> - The form and frequency of external assessment; and
> - The qualifications and independence of the external assessor or assessment team, including any potential conflict of interest.

QAIPs are discussed further in Topic 7 of Chapter B in this section.

Key performance indicators

Care must be taken to identify appropriate performance measures—measures that are aligned to the organization's objectives and the internal audit charter and that target performance necessary to meet activity objectives. The IPPF Practice Guide "Measuring Internal Audit Effectiveness and Efficiency" describes a four-step process in establishing an effective performance measurement process.

1: Define internal audit effectiveness.

This definition will be based on the Definition of Internal Auditing, the Code of Ethics, the *Standards*, existing charters, agreed internal audit deliverables, and internal consensus on what constitutes an efficient and effective internal audit activity.

2: Identify key internal and external stakeholders.

Internal stakeholders may include the board or audit committee, senior management, operations and support management, and internal auditors. External stakeholders may include regulators and standard-setting bodies, external auditors, third-party vendors, and customers. In-depth interviews and surveys can be conducted to develop a clearer understanding of the needs and expectations of each of these stakeholders.

3: Develop measures, or key performance indicators, of internal audit effectiveness and efficiency.

Key performance indicators (KPIs) focus on accomplishments or behaviors that are valued by the organization. They are valid indicators of performance (i.e., they measure the right target) and are understandable to the internal audit staff who use them to guide and improve their performance.

KPIs are valuable to the internal audit activity because they allow the CAE to detect shortcomings in the activity and plan remedial action. They also allow the CAE to demonstrate the value of internal auditing to customers, and they can be used to support requests for resources needed to support the desired level of performance. Because of the close relationship between the internal auditing activity's KPIs and the expectations of the board and senior management, the CAE should establish KPIs in a group with these stakeholders. In this way the CAE can ensure that the activity's KPIs focus on meaningful performance that is aligned with the organization's strategic goals.

Whether internal auditors are evaluating KPIs during an audit project or looking at organization-wide KPIs, they need to answer two questions.

- Are these the right measures? (Do they cover all the objectives? Do they reflect changes in actual performance? Can users understand them? Are they timely?)
- Are they operating effectively? (Are the numbers accurate? Are the information sources reliable?)

Usually, KPIs measure outcomes (e.g., sales, production). Sometimes they measure process characteristics (e.g., timeliness, accuracy). KPIs may be quantitative (e.g., the percentage of planned audits that have been completed) or qualitative (e.g., internal customer satisfaction with audit performance).

Sometimes they measure risk and are referred to as key risk indicators or KRIs (e.g., delinquency rates, the trend in error rates). KRIs are often used as leading indicators of risk. That is, if the KRI trends dangerously upward or crosses a predefined threshold, management can identify and correct the root cause before actual damage occurs.

A new kind of KPI is rapidly emerging as organizations are focusing on what is usually called sustainability or corporate social responsibility. The basic concept is that organizations are not responsible just for short-term financial results; they are also responsible to the communities in which they operate and to the environment that sustains all humankind. As organizations implement formal sustainability programs and practices, they are developing related performance measures. Increasingly, organizations are reporting their corporate social responsibility performance measures to external stakeholders. Internal auditors are starting to play a role in auditing sustainability programs and the design and reliability of the measures.

A balanced scorecard approach can be used to develop specific KPIs. A balanced scorecard examines performance from four different perspectives: financial needs, customer satisfaction, business processes required to accomplish the activity's mission, and learning and growth to ensure continuous improvement. Exhibit I-5 lists sample KPIs from these different perspectives.

Exhibit I-5: Stakeholders/KPIs Alignment

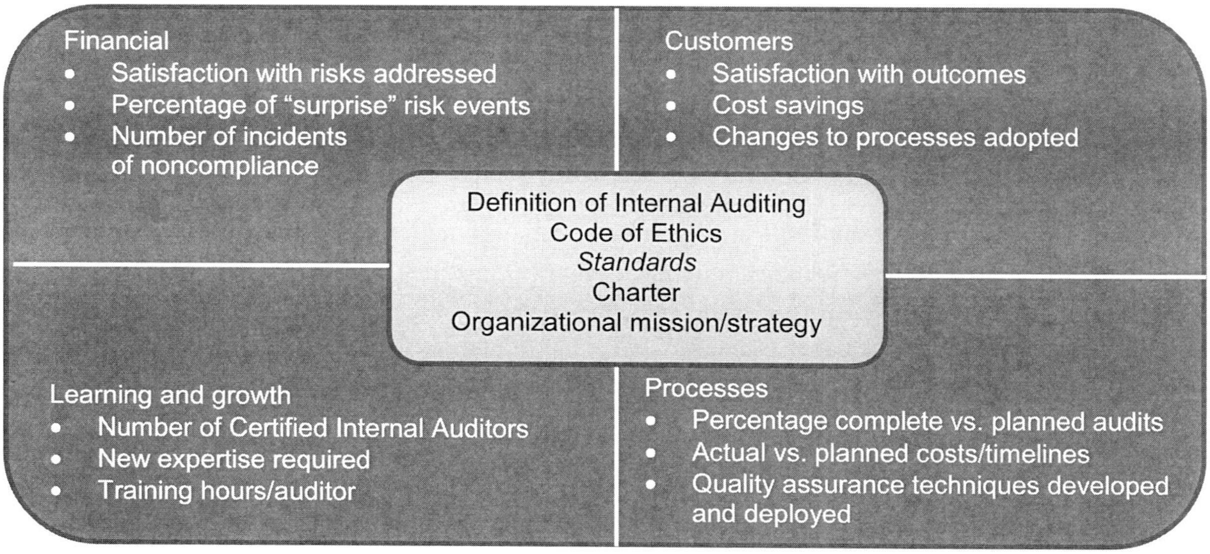

4: Monitor and report results.

The CAE must ensure that performance against agreed KPIs is monitored, considered as the basis for quality improvement, and reported at a frequency agreed with the board and senior management—for example, quarterly—and in the manner desired by stakeholders (e.g., presentations, automated dashboard, e-mails).

Practice Advisory 1311-1 recommends the following ongoing assessment processes and tools:

- Engagement supervision
- Checklists and written procedures (e.g., auditing manual)
- Feedback from audit customers and other stakeholders
- Selective peer reviews of work papers by staff not involved in the affected audits
- Project budgets, time records, audit schedules, projected cost recoveries

Occasionally, in-depth interviews and surveys should be conducted with stakeholders. The CAE should also consider periodically benchmarking the activity's KPIs against those of similar peer organizations.

Topic 7: Coordinate Internal Auditing Efforts with External Auditor, Regulatory Oversight Bodies, and Other Internal Assurance Functions (Level P)

Internal audit activity's role in response to agency comments/ external audits

The internal auditing activity may be involved in coordinating with and supporting both internal and external groups engaged in assuring compliance with laws and regulations or with organizational policies. These groups could include other functions within the organization, such as quality assurance or regulatory affairs, or external groups, such as regulatory agencies and external auditors.

The goal for the CAE is to support a level of accuracy, transparency, and integrity consistent with good governance. In addition, internal auditing should seek ways to make its own work more efficient through coordination with these other groups.

This topic will focus primarily on coordination of internal audit with regulatory oversight bodies, internal assurance functions, and external auditors.

Relevant *Standards* and Practice Advisories

Performance Standard 2050, "Coordination," states "the chief audit executive should share information and coordinate activities with other internal and external providers of assurance and consulting services to ensure proper coverage and minimize duplication of efforts."

Practice Advisory 2050-1, "Coordination," states: "Oversight of the work of external auditors, including coordination with the internal audit activity, is the responsibility of the board. Coordination of internal and external audit work is the responsibility of the chief audit executive (CAE). The CAE obtains the support of the board to coordinate audit work effectively."

Practice Advisory 2050-2, "Assurance Maps," states: "With responsibility for assurance activities traditionally being shared among management, internal audit, risk management, and compliance, it is important that assurance activities be coordinated to ensure resources are used in the most efficient and effective way. Many organizations operate with traditional (and separate) internal audit, risk, and compliance activities. It is common for organizations to have a number of separate groups performing different risk management, compliance, and assurance functions independently of one another. Without effective coordination and reporting, work can be duplicated or key risks may be missed or misjudged."

Practice Advisory 2050-3, "Relying on the Work of Other Assurance Providers," states: "The internal auditor may rely on or use the work of other internal or external assurance providers in providing governance, risk management, and control assurance to the board."

Coordinating with regulatory body reviews

Compliance with legal or regulatory requirements has become a commonplace activity in conducting business worldwide. Organizations must ensure that they meet the compliance requirements imposed by stock exchanges (the NASDAQ, NYSE, London Stock Exchange, and others), industry regulators (e.g., banks, insurance companies), legislative bodies (e.g., the US Congress with the Sarbanes-Oxley Act of 2002), and myriad other agencies. Most organizations have responded by implementing certain structures and processes to ensure compliance.

Internal audit activities should coordinate with regulatory bodies having relevant oversight responsibilities. Different industries have different oversight bodies and different requirements, so it is not realistic to examine specifics here. But the primary goal is to exchange information that could minimize duplicate efforts and/or focus engagement activities on the most significant areas. Internal auditors, for example, can supply external auditors with internal audit documentation and reports as evidence of regulatory compliance and reduce the work of the external auditors.

Practical examples demonstrating coordination between internal audit activities and external regulatory auditors include:

- Internal auditors reviewing copies of regulatory reports in planning related internal engagements.
- Regulatory auditors sharing their perspective with the internal audit activity regarding organizational conformance to the regulations as well as organizational risk management, control, and governance.

Coordinating with internal assurance functions

Coordination with other internal assurance functions can further reduce redundancies and optimize the effectiveness and efficiency of the internal audit activity. Internal assurance functions will vary from enterprise to enterprise, depending on size, industry, and other variables. Common examples found in many organizations include security, safety, enterprise risk management, quality control, and compliance functions.

Security

Potential coordination with security could be achieved by holding periodic meetings with security personnel to keep them apprised of ongoing audit projects. These meetings can also provide a forum to gather security input on potential risks, ongoing security investigations that may be related to control breakdowns, and any areas where past improprieties have occurred.

Safety

Potential coordination with safety should establish mechanisms so that dangers are immediately reported for investigation and necessary corrective actions can be evaluated.

Enterprise risk management

The annual identification and evaluation of risks by the organization helps identify the most important areas for management to focus on in order to achieve the organization's objectives. The utilization of this information by internal audit helps to establish appropriate priorities for the audit activity and background information in performing internal audit evaluations.

Quality control

A quality control function often conducts a variety of audits such as product quality audits, process quality audits, and quality system audits. The internal audit activity and the quality control department should exchange audit schedules and reports.

Compliance

A compliance function conducts audits to ensure adherence to laws and regulations related to an organization's scope of operations. Issues such as protection of personal information (e.g., medical, financial, personal preferences), governance structure and activities, public reporting of an organization's financial and nonfinancial information, environmental and animal protection, and consumer protection are receiving significant attention in many organizations. The compliance focus can be specific by industry. For example, banks will ensure compliance with money-laundering laws and regulations. Internal audit needs to be aware of relevant laws and regulations when conducting a review of an area that may be affected by them.

The compliance function will be involved in communication and training programs as well as assurance reviews and special investigations, if required. The compliance officer will typically be a senior-level executive reporting to the chief executive officer or chief legal counsel. A committee of the board of directors will usually provide oversight for the activities of the compliance function. This could be part of the audit committee's charter or that of a separate compliance committee.

Coordinating with external auditors

Practice Advisory 2050-3 includes as examples of external assurance providers "external auditors, joint venture partners, specialist reviews, or third-party audit firms." Let's review the basic differences between internal and external auditors:

- They have different objectives and accountability.
- They may possess different qualifications.
- They engage in different auditing activities.

These basic differences are summarized in Exhibit I-6.

Exhibit I-6: Scope for Internal and External Auditors

	Scope	Defined by . . .
Internal auditors	• Apply a systematic, disciplined approach to evaluate and improve the effectiveness of organizational risk management, control, and governance processes. • Concerned with all aspects of the organization (e.g., financial and nonfinancial and with the prevention of fraud in any form). • Focus on future events as a result of their continuous review and evaluation of controls and processes.	Section 2100 of the *Standards*.
External auditors	• Ordinary examination is designed to obtain sufficient evidential matter to support an opinion on the overall fairness of the annual financial statements. • Approach is historical in nature.	Their professional standards; they are responsible for judging the adequacy of procedures performed and evidence obtained for purposes of expressing their opinion on the annual financial statements.

Acknowledging these differences, Practice Advisory 2050-1, "Coordination," includes the following endorsed and strongly recommended guidance about coordinating internal audit activity efforts with those of external auditors.

> Oversight of the work of external auditors, including coordination with the internal audit activity, is the responsibility of the board. Coordination of internal and external audit work is the responsibility of the chief audit executive (CAE). The CAE obtains the support of the board to coordinate audit work effectively.
>
> Organizations may use the work of external auditors to provide assurance related to activities within the scope of internal auditing. In these cases, the CAE takes the steps necessary to understand the work performed by the external auditors, including:
>
> - The nature, extent, and timing of work planned by external auditors, to be satisfied that the external auditors' planned work, in conjunction with the internal auditors' planned work, satisfies the requirements of Standard 2100.
> - The external auditor's assessment of risk and materiality.
> - The external auditors' techniques, methods, and terminology to enable the CAE to (1) coordinate internal and external auditing work; (2) evaluate, for purposes of reliance, the external auditors' work; and (3) communicate effectively with external auditors.
> - Access to the external auditors' programs and working papers, to be satisfied that the external auditors' work can be relied upon for internal audit purposes. Internal auditors are responsible for respecting the confidentiality of those programs and working papers.
>
> The external auditor may rely on the work of the internal audit activity in performing their work. In this case, the CAE needs to provide sufficient information to enable external auditors to understand the internal auditors' techniques, methods, and terminology to facilitate reliance by external auditors on work performed. Access to the internal auditors' programs and working papers is provided to external auditors in order for external auditors to be satisfied as to the acceptability for external audit purposes of relying on the internal auditors' work.
>
> The CAE is responsible for regular evaluations of the coordination between internal and external auditors. Such evaluations may also include assessments of the overall efficiency and effectiveness of internal and external audit activities, including aggregate audit cost. The CAE communicates the results of these evaluations to senior management and the board, including relevant comments about the performance of external auditors.

Practice Advisory 2050-3 notes the importance of ensuring that the internal audit activity will have access to the work of external auditors, that engagement expectations are clearly defined in a work agreement or contract, and that the external auditor's work is performed with attention to "independence, objectivity, competencies, elements of practice, adequacy of execution of audit work, and sufficiency of audit evidence to support the given level of assurance."

Practical examples demonstrating the coordination of internal audit activity efforts with external auditors include:

- Comparing annual internal and external audit plans to eliminate duplication and encourage cooperation in performance of an audit activity where appropriate.
- Enterprise-wide agreement, so that results of activities (e.g., final reports) are shared to help the organization achieve objectives and eliminate risks.
- Communication/sharing of the external audit perspective on risk management, control, and governance processes with the internal audit activity to help with internal audit planning.

Benefits of coordination and cooperation to auditors

The two parties—internal and external—have mutual interests that make coordination of their efforts important. Cooperation becomes a key factor in the process. Without compromising either group's independence or objectivity, coordination and cooperation between internal and external auditors is prudent because of the potential to increase the economy, efficiency, and effectiveness of the total audit activity for the organization.

- **Economy.** Basic costs associated with performing both internal and external audits (time, materials, and resources) rise with inflation. Financial reporting standards necessitate increased financial audits and increased fees. Simply put, coordination between internal and external auditors can help combat rising costs for both types of engagements.

- **Efficiency.** The efficiency of the total audit effort is increased if internal and external auditors share audit results with each other as needed and in a timely manner. The enterprise benefits when both parties accept each other's work. Such cooperation can provide board members and senior management with further assurance that financial and operational reports and statements are proper, controls are adequate and effective, and any weaknesses will be promptly identified.

  If the two types of audits are not coordinated, overlaps and duplication of efforts during engagements are inevitable, which, in turn, unnecessarily increases auditing costs and confuses responsibilities. On the other hand, coordination and information sharing can increase efficiency and minimize redundancies in audit activities. Testing is a good example. If the external audit has performed detailed tests and results are shared, the extent and need for the internal audit activity to repeat such tests can be greatly lessened.

- **Effectiveness.** Internal and external auditors each have special expertise they bring to their activities. Coordination and information sharing allows each party to accumulate useful information and knowledge they otherwise might not have, and new areas of risk or concern might be identified.

  The type of audits to be performed by either internal or external auditors relates to the training, experience, and organizational knowledge to make certain that the right audits and audit activities are being performed. The knowledge of the auditors, the amount of time, and the depth of the testing will all help in having a positive effect on the process being audited. Using the right audit organization and the right auditors helps to provide the most meaningful results to the management of the organization being audited.

Studies have demonstrated that the benefits of coordination and cooperation extend beyond the total audit activity. Collaboration can improve internal and external auditors' competency in other ways. Both parties generally benefit from the interchange of new/different auditing techniques, procedures, ideas, and information. External auditors gain better insights into client operations, control systems, and so on, typically much more quickly than when left to independent discovery. Collaboration also allows both parties to focus on more significant issues during their respective engagements.

Certainly much of the work the internal audit activity performs is not relevant to the efforts of external auditors. For example, internal audit engagement objectives intended to assess compliance, efficiency, and effectiveness of operations have little application to external audits focused on the fairness of presentation of financial statements. But when synergies are possible (such as in the case of understanding controls, risk management techniques, and testing in financial reporting areas), everyone stands to gain from coordination and cooperation. Proper planning provides the foundation for the success.

Responses to external audits

Transparency requires full disclosure of relevant financial and operational information and the internal processes management has put into place for oversight and control. The Sarbanes-Oxley Act of 2002, the SEC, and international stock exchanges impose many additional requirements in these areas for companies.

The internal audit committee and external auditors both have key roles related to transparency and disclosure.

For the internal audit committee, the primary concerns are financial accuracy, including the completeness of financial disclosures, significant business and accounting policy changes, correct and truthful reporting, and interim reviews of financial statements. The internal audit committee must have the financial acumen to assess the significance of complex or unusual transactions, financial statement presentations, changes in the organization's selection or application of accounting principles, and the effect of regulatory and accounting initiatives, as well as off-balance-sheet structures.

External auditors primarily assess the effectiveness of internal controls over financial reporting. External auditors are independent of the organization. To preserve this independence, the audit committee should own the relationship with the external auditors and have oversight responsibilities. General ownership and oversight responsibilities are listed in Exhibit I-7.

Exhibit I-7: Audit Committee Ownership and Oversight Responsibilities for External Auditors

Ownership Responsibilities	Oversight Responsibilities
• Direct reporting • Ongoing open communication • Frequent meetings • Robust discussions about audit scope and results	• Compensation • Engagement scope • Selection criteria • Independence • Rotation • Monitoring • Performance assessment

External auditors issue a formal written report at the conclusion of the engagement, including their observations and opinions. If ongoing communications have been adequate, there should be no surprises in the final report.

The audit committee should have a clear understanding of all information reported by the external auditors, including:

- The external auditors' judgments about the quality of accounting policies.
- The external auditors' conclusions regarding the reasonableness of management accounting estimates.
- Significant adjustments arising from the audit that could have a significant effect on financial statements.
- Reported disagreements with management that could have a significant effect on financial statements and whether or not they were satisfactorily resolved.
- Difficulties encountered with management in performing the audit.
- Significant deficiencies or material weaknesses in internal control.
- Fraud or illegal acts.

Management has the primary responsibility for acting on the external audit findings. To support management's follow-up, the audit committees should:

- Discuss the issues with the external auditors to ensure a full understanding of concerns and acceptable corrective actions.
- Discuss any identified issues with management to ensure a full understanding of the implications.
- Determine whether additional resources should be consulted.
- Establish a reasonable time line to address the issues.
- Develop a checklist and other necessary tools for monitoring the resolution of issues.
- Discuss the resolution of issues with management and external auditors.

Exhibit I-8 on the next page presents an excerpt from a sample audit committee charter outlining an audit committee's responsibilities related to external auditing.

Topic 8: Assess Adequacy of the Performance Measurement System and Achievement of Organizational Objectives (Level A)

Internal auditors should assess the organization's performance measurement system and whether the central corporate objectives are being achieved. The basic considerations in assessing performance are:

- Identifying related standards for performance.
- Comparing the performance to the identified standard.
- Evaluating performance gaps (deviations or variances from the standard).

Exhibit I-8: Sample Audit Committee Responsibilities for External Auditing

- Review the external auditors' proposed audit scope and approach, including coordination of audit effort with internal auditing.
- Review the performance of the external auditors and exercise final approval on the appointment or discharge of the auditors. In performing this review, the committee will:
  - At least annually, obtain and review a report by the independent auditor describing the firm's internal quality control procedures; any material issues raised by the most recent internal quality control review, or peer review, of the firm, or by any inquiry or investigation by governmental or professional authorities, within the preceding five years, respecting one or more independent audits carried out by the firm, and any steps taken to deal with any such issues; and (to assess the auditor's independence) all relationships between the independent auditor and the company.
  - Take into account the opinions of management and internal auditing.
  - Review and evaluate the lead partner of the independent auditor.
  - Present its conclusions with respect to the external auditor to the board.
- Ensure the rotation of the lead audit partner every five years and other audit partners every seven years, and consider whether there should be regular rotation of the audit firm itself.
- Present its conclusions with respect to the independent auditor to the full board.
- Set clear hiring policies for employees or former employees of the independent auditors.
- On a regular basis, meet separately with the external auditors to discuss any matters that the committee or auditors believe should be discussed privately.

Source: "The Audit Committee: Purpose, Process, Professionalism," www.theiia.org/download.cfm?file=6676.

Required corrective actions should be specified and completed in a timely manner. Ultimately, an effective performance management system is one that supports the achievement of organizational goals as well as individual and personal goals.

The most common weaknesses in performance measurement systems involves using the wrong key performance indicators. The chief audit executive should review the activity performance measurement system regularly to ensure that internal audit KPIs are still aligned with the organization's strategic objectives and most recent risk assessment. For example, if a manufacturer sets a strategy to distinguish itself in its market through innovative products built on resource-intensive research and development programs, the CAE may expand or shift the activity's focus area from auditing controls on operational efficiency to auditing controls on security of proprietary information.

The CAE should also consider whether the organization is meeting its goals, possible reasons for performance gaps, and the role internal auditing could play in addressing these gaps. For example, if a credit card company has not been able to lower users' default rates, the CAE might include in the internal auditing activity's KPIs performance objectives related to identifying lapses in procedures for approving credit.

Chapter B: Operational Role of Internal Audit

Chapter Introduction

From the strategic level described in Chapter A—the role internal audit plays in the organization as a whole—we move to the operational level, how the chief audit executive ensures that the activity can fulfill its role and responsibilities.

The CAE's operational tasks include:

- Formulating policies and procedures that support the activity's independence, objectivity, proficiency, and due professional care (Topic 1).
- Defining and communicating the activity's role in risk management (Topic 2).
- Directing administrative functions that allow the activity to operate efficiently and effectively (Topic 3).
- Ensuring the availability of competent staff through interviewing job applicants (Topic 4).
- Reporting on the activity's work in evaluating the organization's risk management processes and framework (Topics 5 and 6).
- Ensuring that the activity incorporates processes that result in quality audit work and continuous improvement in auditing practices and capacity (Topic 7).

Topic 1: Formulate Policies and Procedures for the Planning, Organizing, Directing, and Monitoring of Internal Audit Operations (Level P)

Relevant Standards

The role of the CAE in formulating policies and procedures is defined in Standard 2040, "Policies and Procedures": "The chief audit executive must establish policies and procedures to guide the internal audit activity."

The interpretation of this standard stipulates that: "*The form and content of policies and procedures are dependent upon the size and structure of the internal audit activity and the complexity of its work.*"

Practice Advisory 2040-1 explains that in small internal audit activities close and daily supervision may take the place of formal administrative and technical manuals. However, in large internal audit activities, more formal and comprehensive policies and procedures may be "essential to guide the internal audit staff in the execution of the internal audit plan."

Audit manual

The audit manual provides a guide to existing and new members of the internal auditing activity about the activity's objectives and the way these objectives will be accomplished. The CAE is responsible for ensuring that an audit manual is created and maintained, that it is distributed throughout the internal auditing activity, and that the policies and procedures contained in the audit manual are consistently and continually enforced.

The purpose of the audit manual is, in general, to:

- Provide guidance to activity members that will support adherence to the profession's Code of Ethics and professional standards.
- Define a high level of performance expectations for staff that will enable the activity to fulfill its role in supporting the organization's governance and risk management and to fulfill the activity's own strategic objectives.
- Focus activity members on key objectives and values. For example, an activity may focus on assuring controls or adding value to the organization by identifying opportunities for greater efficiency and quality—or it may balance both roles.
- Coordinate roles and responsibilities within the activity and in relation to other internal and external bodies.
- Codify critical processes, such as the steps involved in performing different types of engagements, and policies, such as protection of confidential information and communication and monitoring of engagement results.
- Provide the basis on which to evaluate the internal auditing activity's performance.

As suggested in Practice Advisory 2040-1, audit manuals can vary in content and format. Exhibit I-9 lists possible topic headings for audit manuals.

Exhibit I-9: Sample Audit Manual Content (continued on next page)

Topic	Description
Internal audit charter	Mandate for the activity, scope of authority, responsibilities of internal audit executive and activity, professional standards and responsibilities, ethics/code of conduct
Internal audit organization	Reporting structures, services provided by internal audit
Internal audit strategic plan	Process and schedule for developing strategic goals and objectives
Annual audit plan	Process for developing and modifying the annual audit plan, from identifying audit universe through risk analysis and allocation of resources, including risk management tools to be used

Exhibit I-9: Sample Audit Manual Content (concluded)

Topic	Description
Personnel	Roles and responsibilities, training and career development, performance management system
Communication	Guidelines for communicating with internal clients and external bodies; handling of confidential information
Audit engagement process	Procedures to be followed, from planning through reporting; requirements regarding work papers; report template
Administration	Policies regarding tracking of time, documentation and document retention, transition process

Topic 2: Review the Role of the Internal Audit Function within the Risk Management Framework (Level P)

The internal audit activity's role in enterprise risk management

Internal auditors are expected to identify and evaluate significant risk exposures in the normal course of their duties. The internal audit activity's role in the risk management process of an organization can change over time and may be found at some point along a continuum that ranges from:

- No role, to
- Auditing the risk management process as part of the internal audit plan, to
- Providing insight and historical data on risk events identified by internal audit findings, to
- Active, continuous support and involvement in the risk management process such as participation on oversight committees, monitoring activities, and status reporting, to
- Managing and coordinating the risk management process.

Senior management and the board determine the role the internal audit activity will play in the organizational risk management process. In most organizations, internal auditors have a key role in evaluating the effectiveness of enterprise risk management and for recommending improvements. They contribute to ERM through assurance and consulting activities.

As a function within the organization, the internal audit activity must comply with the organization's policies and procedures, including risk management processes, and must use risk management methodologies in the design and implementation of internal auditing practices.

Practice Advisory 2120-2, "Managing the Risk of the Internal Audit Activity," reminds us: "The internal audit activity is not immune to risks. It needs to take the necessary steps to ensure that it is managing its own risks.

Risks to internal audit activities fall into three broad categories: audit failure, false assurance, and reputation risks."

The IIA Position Paper "The Role of Internal Auditing in Enterprise-Wide Risk Management" identifies the following roles the internal audit function should not undertake:

- Setting the risk appetite
- Imposing risk management processes
- Management assurance on risks
- Taking decisions on risk responses
- Implementing risk responses on management's behalf
- Accountability for risk management

Assurance roles

An organization's board needs to have assurance that risk management processes are functioning as expected and key risks are being managed to an acceptable level. In most organizations, this assurance comes from different sources and at different levels. For example, operational areas in an organization having assigned functional risk management responsibilities report to the board on their performance levels. These functional reports are augmented by the objective assurance of external audits, specialist reviews, and internal audits.

Providing assurance is the core contribution of the internal audit activity to risk management. The internal auditor typically provides assurance on:

- Risk management processes, including their design and how well they are working.
- Management of key risks, including the effectiveness of the controls and other activities.
- Reliable and appropriate assessment of risks and reporting of risk and control status.

Providing assurance requires the internal auditor to formulate an opinion on whether the organization's risk management methodology is understood by key groups or individuals involved in corporate governance, including the board and the audit committee. The internal auditor must also ascertain if risk management processes are sufficient to protect the assets, reputation, and ongoing operations of the organization.

Performance Standard 2120, "Risk Management," states, "The internal audit activity must evaluate the effectiveness and contribute to the improvement of risk management processes."

Interpretation tells us:

> *Determining whether risk management processes are effective is a judgment resulting from the internal auditor's assessment that:*
>
> - *Organizational objectives support and align with the organization's mission;*
> - *Significant risks are identified and assessed;*
> - *Appropriate risk responses are selected that align risks with the organization's risk appetite; and*
> - *Relevant risk information is captured and communicated in a timely manner across the organization, enabling staff, management, and the board to carry out their responsibilities.*
>
> *Risk management processes are monitored through ongoing management activities, separate evaluations, or both.*

Practice Advisory 2120-1 guidance indicates:

> The techniques used by various organizations for their risk management practices can vary significantly. Depending on the size and complexity of the organization's business activities, risk management processes can be:
>
> - Formal or informal.
> - Quantitative or subjective.
> - Embedded in the business units or centralized at a corporate level.
>
> The organization designs processes based on its culture, management style, and business objectives . . . . The internal auditor determines that the methodology chosen is sufficiently comprehensive and appropriate for the nature of the organization's activities.

When assessing the adequacy and effectiveness of any system, including risk management, internal control, and governance, there are distinctions between the terms that an internal auditor should understand.

Adequacy of risk management, control, and governance processes:

> Is present if management has planned and organized (designed) in a manner that provides reasonable assurance that the organization's risks have been managed effectively and that the organization's goals and objectives will be achieved efficiently and economically. Efficient performance accomplishes objectives and goals in an accurate, timely, and economical fashion. Economical performance accomplishes objectives and goals with minimal use of resources (i.e., cost) commensurate with the risk exposure. Reasonable assurance is provided if the most cost-effective measures are taken in the design and implementation stages to reduce risks and restrict expected deviations to a tolerable level. Thus, the design process begins with the establishment of objectives and goals. This is followed by connecting or interrelating concepts, parts, activities, and people in such a manner as to operate together to achieve the established objectives and goals.

Effectiveness of risk management, control, and governance processes:

> Is present if management directs processes in such a manner as to provide reasonable assurance that the organization's objectives and goals will be achieved. In addition to accomplishing the objectives and planned activities, management directs by authorizing activities and transactions, monitoring resulting performance, and verifying that the organization's processes are operating as designed.

Consulting roles

The internal audit may also provide consulting services that improve organizational risk management and control processes. "The Role of Internal Auditing in Enterprise-Wide Risk Management" mentions the following topics as possibilities for consulting engagements:

- Educating management about the risk and control tools and techniques used by the internal audit activity and sharing those tools
- Being a champion for introducing ERM into the organization and sharing the internal audit activity's expertise
- Providing advice, facilitating workshops, and coaching the organization on risk and control
- Acting as the central point for coordinating, monitoring, and reporting on risks
- Supporting managers as they work to identify the best way to mitigate a risk

The extent to which the internal audit activity actually provides risk management consulting services is a function of various factors:

- Resource availability—the internal and external resources available to the board
- The risk maturity of the organization—the maturity level of organizational risk management processes and structure and the organizational role and qualifications of the internal auditors
- The objectivity of the internal auditor—whether the internal auditor is assuming a role in managing the risk

When the internal audit activity extends its services to include consulting engagements, safeguards should be in place to preserve its independence and objectivity.

As we have seen, the internal audit activity can be a valuable contributor in ensuring success through assurance and consulting activities and supporting management and board responsibilities. But it must be clear that management remains responsible for risk management.

To preserve the integrity of the internal audit function within the organization's risk management framework, the IIA Position Paper recommends that:

- Internal auditors should provide advice and challenge or support management's decisions on risk, as opposed to making risk management decisions.
- The nature of internal auditing's responsibilities should be documented in the audit charter and approved by the audit committee.

Topic 3: Direct Administrative Activities of the Internal Audit Department (Level P)

Traditionally, management—and this includes the chief audit executive—includes four basic functions:

- **Planning.** This is a strategic-level activity. It includes activities such as developing a risk-based audit plan and reviewing staff competency needs and planning for hiring and development. The audit plan is discussed in the next chapter.

- **Organizing.** This is an operational activity that involves designing structures and processes aimed at achieving activity objectives and overall goals of efficiency and effectiveness. This may include:
  - Assigning auditors to specific engagements. Auditors can be selected based on their experience with similar engagements.
  - Allocating time for separate engagement activities, including planning, developing and implementing the audit program, conducting fieldwork, and writing reports. The time allocated will depend on the staff's level of experience and the complexity of the audit.

  As directed by Performance Standard 2040, "Policies and Procedures," CAEs and designees may develop processes to support engagement work, such as engagement initiation/transition meetings and report review processes, processes for qualifying and contracting with external service providers, structures for communicating different types of activity information, monitoring processes aimed at maintaining quality and budget adherence, and channels for gathering this data (e.g., time sheets).

- **Directing.** This includes the many tasks involved in leading the internal audit activity. Communication must be maintained within the organization and with external bodies. External audit service providers must be selected. New staff members must be interviewed and hired. Performance management systems must be implemented, including appraisals at the end of engagements and annually. Motivation can be sustained by being mindful of staff stress levels and offering both rewards and career development opportunities.

- **Controlling.** The CAE is ultimately responsible for ensuring that policies and procedures are followed; that budgets are monitored and assessed; that the audit committee, senior management and engagement clients are satisfied; and that the activity is meeting its strategic objectives, including the requirements of the audit plan.

Topic 4: Interview Candidates for Internal Audit Positions (Level P)

Attribute Standard 1200, "Proficiency and Due Care," focuses on the human resource ingredients required to perform auditing engagements:

- Standard 1210 notes that internal auditors "must possess the knowledge, skills, and other competencies needed to perform their individual responsibilities." As a whole entity, the internal audit activity must "possess or obtain" necessary knowledge, skills, and competencies. The explanation for the standard points to professional certifications as a demonstration of proficiency.

- Standards 1210.A2 and A3 require that internal auditors have sufficient knowledge to evaluate the risk of fraud and the effectiveness of fraud management and to have sufficient knowledge—but not expertise—in key information technology risks, controls, and audit techniques.

- Standards 1210.A1 and C.1 charge the chief audit executive with obtaining competent advice and assistance when the internal auditing activity does not possess skills and knowledge needed to perform engagements and with declining consulting engagements if the activity does not have the needed expertise.

For these reasons, it is imperative that the chief audit executive accurately assess knowledge and skills extant in the internal audit activity, align those strengths with the annual audit plan, and develop a plan to ensure the ability to perform engagement with proficiency and due care. This may be accomplished through hiring qualified staff, providing training and career development opportunities, and contracting for competent external services.

This topic focuses on the first tactic just mentioned: finding, interviewing, and hiring the right applicants for internal audit.

Selection process

The selection process begins with an accurate position description. It then proceeds to recruiting and screening applicants with the desired skills, knowledge, and characteristics; interviewing applicants to confirm that they possess the necessary qualifications; and selecting and hiring those applicants who can succeed in the job and the organization. In large organizations, the chief audit executive or designee may work with the human resources department. HR can offer experience in the selection process as well as awareness of local hiring laws and organizational hiring policies. In smaller organizations, the CAE or designee may benefit from using external service providers.

Defining job requirements

Before recruiting applicants, the CAE or designee should review existing job descriptions for the position being filled. The description should accurately and specifically reflect the requirements for the position but should also be in alignment with the organization's and the internal audit activity's strategic objectives. For example, an IT auditor may be expected to know specific platforms and applications, but, as an organization begins to expand its online presence, the IT auditor may also need an understanding of distributed or Web-based computing and associated security tools.

Interviewing applicants

Applicants may be interviewed first in brief (e.g., 10- to 20-minute) telephone conversations aimed at confirming what has been said on the application and what the applicant understands about the job's requirements and conditions. Screening calls may be first with HR and later with the CAE or designee.

Applicants are then selected for in-depth and longer interviews (e.g., two to four hours), which are usually conducted on site. Interviewers must prepare for the meeting by carefully reviewing the application against the job description and identifying critical areas that must be confirmed or explained. If multiple interviewers will be involved, their questions should be coordinated.

There are different approaches for interviewing applicants, which can be combined in a single interview:

- Structured interviews follow an interview guide that has been developed to focus on necessary skills, knowledge, experience, and attitudes. The guide helps ensure consistency and completeness in the interviewing process and also supports legal compliance. Applicants are asked the same questions, with follow-up questions as needed.
- Behavioral interviews focus on obtaining evidence of past behavior, considered a predictor of future job performance. Applicants may be asked how they handled a specific situation in a previous position, such as

coordinating with an engagement client to ensure access and efficient practices.

- Situational interviews are similar to behavioral interviews in that they try to obtain more concrete information about possible job performance, but in this case the applicants are asked about hypothetical situations rather than real, past experiences. For example, applicants might be asked how they would handle a client who would not accept audit findings and recommendations.

Interviewing skills

The interview should be a conversation that allows both the CAE or designee and the applicant to get to know one another and to determine if this working relationship will meet the needs of both the internal audit activity and the applicant. There are work dimensions to these needs, but also social dimensions. For example, those involved in interviewing applicants should consider whether an individual will thrive in the organization's culture. An applicant that tends toward abrupt, abrasive behavior may not work well in an organization that values positive relationships among employees.

For this reason, effective interviewing includes skills beyond asking the right questions. Effective interviewing skills include:

- Establishing a relaxed and open atmosphere that is more likely to produce honest and complete answers.
- Listening actively—asking follow-up questions that encourage the applicant to talk openly or that confirm the interviewer's understanding.
- Observing nonverbal behaviors and identifying red flags as one would in an engagement interview—physical signs that indicate an applicant may not be telling the truth or the whole story.
- Taking notes. Note taking should not interfere with the discussion, but notes will be invaluable later in remembering key points and supporting hiring decisions.

Topic 5: Report on the Effectiveness of Organizational Risk Management Processes to Senior Management and the Board (Level P)

Related *Standards*

Earlier we learned that the chief audit executive's responsibility to report to the board and senior management on the effectiveness of the organization's risk management processes is included in Performance Standard 2060, "Reporting to Senior Management and the Board": "The chief audit executive must report periodically to senior management and the board . . . . Reporting must . . . include significant risk exposures and control issues, including fraud risks, governance issues, and other matters needed or requested by senior management and the board."

The interpretation of this standard allows for the chief audit executive to work with senior management and the board to determine the frequency of reports. In some cases, the CAE may submit an annual report; in other organizations, with more volatile risks, it may be appropriate to hold more frequent and briefer discussions on the risk picture and the organization's assurance coverage.

Performance Standard 2100, "Nature of Work," states that "the internal audit activity must evaluate and contribute to the improvement of governance, risk management, and control processes using a systematic and disciplined approach."

The interpretation of Performance Standard 2120, "Risk Management," notes the criteria for effective risk management processes:

- Organizational objectives support and align with the organization's mission;
- Significant risks are identified and assessed;
- Appropriate risk responses are selected that align risks with the organization's risk appetite; and
- Relevant risk information is captured and communicated in a timely manner across the organization, enabling staff, management, and the board to carry out their responsibilities.

Role of internal audit in risk management processes

Practice Advisory 2120-1, "Assessing the Adequacy of Risk Management Processes," notes that the responsibility for managing organizational risk lies with senior management and board. Internal audit may be called upon to support senior management and the board in fulfilling this responsibility by "examining, evaluating, reporting, and/or recommending improvements to the adequacy and effectiveness of management's risk processes." The chief audit executive discusses the role of internal audit with senior management and the board, and the role is codified in the audit charter.

Through planned engagements, internal audit may provide assurance on a macro level, by assessing the organization's design and implementation of the risk management process, and on a micro level, by assessing management assertions about the effectiveness of risk identification and treatment in separate areas of the organization.

In some cases—for example, in smaller organizations without dedicated risk management functions—internal audit may also consult with individual areas to support risk identification and treatment. However, internal audit may not assess the effectiveness of risk management processes that it has helped design.

Providing assurance for risk management processes

Internal audit provides assurance for the entire risk management process by examining:

- Risk management's role in the organization. Does it have adequate management support? Have adequate resources been budgeted for the process? Is risk management part of the decision-making process, especially at higher levels within the organization?
- The risk management framework and the criteria used to assess risks. Are the framework and criteria appropriate for the organization's structure and external environment?
- Ability to implement the risk management processes. Have objectives and criteria for evaluating risks been clearly communicated? Are employees trained for their roles? Are employees held accountable for their parts in the process?
- Communication. Does the process allow feedback about the outcomes of risk management throughout the organization? Does the process include its risk management practices when communicating with external stakeholders? Does the process support compliance with external reporting requirements?
- Monitoring and reporting. Are risk identification and treatment activities monitored and reported regularly to senior management and the board? Can the process itself be measured against key performance indicators so that it can be improved continually?
- Consistency of implementation. Are definitions, criteria, and activities consistently applied across the organization?
- Responsiveness to change. Does the process recognize the need for reevaluating the organization's risk environment? Are risks reevaluated with a frequency appropriate to the organization's business and environment?

Coordinating with other assurance providers

The Practice Guide "Coordinating Risk Management and Assurance" notes that internal audit may be only one part of the organization's assurance provider framework, which may also include, in some organizations, external audit, governance, risk management, and other internal assurance providers, such as quality assurance or compliance. Given the fact that multiple assurance providers may be involved in identifying organizational risks and evaluating the effectiveness of the organization's risk management processes, it is critical that these different groups coordinate their reporting responsibilities. Internal audit provides a valuable service by coordinating assessment of the effectiveness of the risk management process by these various groups.

The chief audit executive can help the board and senior management understand the different roles in the organization's assurance framework and any gaps in assurance coverage that have been identified. To this end, the CAE may develop an annual report on the state of the organization's risk management processes or may "coordinate the development and distribution of this report through the organization's governance or risk management function."

Practice Advisory 2050-2, "Assurance Maps," notes the usefulness of assurance mapping exercises in communicating this information to the board and senior management—especially in organizations in which the CAE must deliver an overall opinion of risk management processes. An assurance map would include, for each business unit in an organization:

- Significant risk category.
- Risk owner (management responsible for coordinating assurance activities for that risk) and controls in place to manage the risk.
- Inherent risk rating (risk level before mitigation/control).
- Residual risk rating (risk level after mitigation/control).
- External audit coverage.
- Internal audit coverage.

Internal audit can identify the steps it is taking to mitigate the risk—for example, through the annual audit plan. It can also point out "significant risks with inadequate assurance coverage, or areas of duplicated assurance coverage."

Evaluating the risk management process

The Practice Guide "Assessing the Adequacy of Risk Management Using ISO 31000" cites the following characteristics of an effective risk management process:

- The risk management process is applied appropriately, and each element in the process is suitable and sufficient. The elements in the ISO 31000 risk management standard, which is a simple and concise framework that can be used by any size or type of organization, are listed in Exhibit I-10 on the next page.
- The process is aligned with the strategic needs and objectives of the organization.

- All significant risks are identified and treated.
- Controls are designed in keeping with objectives.
- Critical controls are adequate and effective.
- Line management reviews controls to maintain and continuously improve their effectiveness.
- The process's value improves with time, as the organization becomes more effective in applying it.

Exhibit I-10: ISO 31000 Risk Management Process Elements

Approaches to auditing risk management processes

"Assessing the Adequacy of Risk Management Using ISO 31000" describes three approaches to auditing the risk management process. An approach should be selected based on an organization's needs, but approaches can also be combined.

In a process element approach, internal audit considers each of the seven steps listed above in Exhibit I-10.

In a key principles approach, the organization's risk management process is assessed according to how well it incorporates 11 principles of risk management:

1. Risk management creates and protects value.
2. It is an integral part of the organization's processes.
3. It is part of decision making.

4. It explicitly addresses uncertainty.
5. It is systematic, structured, and timely.
6. It is based on the best available information.
7. It is tailored to the operations of the organization.
8. It takes human and cultural factors into account.
9. It is transparent and inclusive of all stakeholders.
10. It is dynamic, iterative, and responsive to change.
11. It facilitates continual improvement and enhancement of the organization.

A maturity model approach emphasizes the value that the risk management process delivers to the organization and the gradual evolution of the process from one focused primarily on compliance to one focused on effective treatment of risks. This approach measures growth against defined and evolving objectives.

Gathering evidence

Practice Advisory 2120-1 notes that internal auditors must obtain "sufficient and appropriate evidence" to support the soundness of risk management processes and their ability to meet risk management objectives. The advisory recommends the following audit procedures:

- Research internal and external events and trends that may affect the organization's risk picture. This might include the emergence of new competitors, changes in tax codes, or pending regulations.
- Gain understanding of the organization's business strategies and risk appetite by reviewing corporate policies and board minutes.
- Review previous risk evaluation reports from management, internal and external auditors, and other sources. The presence of unremediated risks may indicate a change in the organization's risk appetite.
- Interview line and senior management to understand business unit objectives, risks, and risk treatment.
- Evaluate the effectiveness of mitigation, monitoring, and communication related to risks and controls.
- Assess the appropriateness of reporting lines for risk-monitoring activities.
- Review the adequacy and timeliness of reporting on risk management results.
- Review the completeness of management's risk analysis and steps taken to respond to findings.
- Determine the effectiveness of management's self-assessment process through observation and direct tests.
- Discuss weaknesses in risk management processes and practices with senior management and the board.

Auditing tools can include observation, interviews, document review, analysis (e.g., risk model, control self-assessment, root cause, statistical, "near miss"), process mapping, and surveys.

Documentation

Although documentation of risk management processes may be lacking in some organizations, documentation of the evaluation of risk management processes is important—especially when an organization is reporting on the effectiveness of its ERM to external parties. "Assessing the Adequacy of Risk Management Using ISO 31000" recommends documentation of key characteristics of risk management processes, such as:

- An overall strategy for risk management.
- Risk communication structures.
- Allocation of resources.
- Analysis of cost-effectiveness of controls using technology.
- Performance of monitoring.
- Inclusion of risk management as a principle in decision making and performance management decisions.

Audit challenges

As noted previously, there may be multiple groups involved in evaluating risk management processes. In addition, while internal audits of risk management processes may occur at one time, they may also occur in phases. Coordinating these perspectives and aggregating data from separate audits can be a challenge, but it is critical to avoid missing important observations and patterns or trends. When possible, audits should be staffed by the same teams. These individuals can bring greater continuity to audit activities.

It is also important that chief audit executives consider the activity's risk management responsibility when managing human resources. Staff development should support understanding of risk management processes and its elements, but it should also support staff's ability to communicate risk management principles and process elements to their engagement clients.

Topic 6: Report on the Effectiveness of the Internal Control and Risk Management Frameworks (Level P)

The risk management process provides a framework within which the organization can apply risk management principles and develop a clear risk map of the organization, including objective-specific risks, an assessment of exposure, assignment of responsibilities for managing risks, and risk-specific control systems. "Assessing the Adequacy of Risk Management Using ISO 31000" describes the role of the risk management framework as providing an "end-to-end link between objectives, strategy, execution of strategy, risks, controls, and assurance across all levels of the organization."

The role of the internal audit activity is to provide assurance of and report on the effectiveness of the organization's internal control and risk management frameworks. This includes assurance that the organization is using an effective risk identification process, that the risks are being managed in a manner aligned with the level of risk that the organization is willing to accept, and that controls on risk are adequately designed, are working as intended, and are, in fact, effective and efficient in controlling the risk. Internal auditing is also responsible for recommending ways to improve the frameworks.

Frequency of evaluations on the control and risk management frameworks is decided between the chief audit executive, senior management, and the board.

Relevant *Standards*

Performance Standard 2100, "Nature of Work," states that: "The internal audit activity must evaluate and contribute to the improvement of governance, risk management, and control processes using a systematic and disciplined approach."

The interpretation of Performance Standard 2120, "Risk Management," notes the criteria for effective risk management processes:

- Organizational objectives support and align with the organization's mission.
- Significant risks are identified and assessed.
- Appropriate risk responses are selected that align risks with the organization's risk appetite.
- Relevant risk information is captured and communicated in a timely manner across the organization, enabling staff, management, and the board to carry out their responsibilities.

The internal audit activity must:

- Evaluate risk exposures relating to the organization's governance, operations, and information systems (Standard 2120.A1).
- Evaluate the potential for fraud and management of fraud risks (Standard 2120.A2).

- During consulting engagements, address risk according to engagement objectives, but be alert to the existence of other significant risks (Standard 2120.C1).
- Apply knowledge regarding risks from consulting engagements to assessing the organization's risk management processes (Standard 2120.C2).
- Refrain from assuming management's responsibility for managing risk. Although during consulting engagements, internal auditing may comment on and recommend improvements to risk management processes, the responsibility to manage organizational risk belongs to management alone (Standard 2120.C3).

Performance Standard 2130, "Control," states that: "The internal audit activity must assist the organization in maintaining effective controls by evaluating their effectiveness and efficiency and by promoting continuous improvement."

As with the responsibility for evaluating risk exposure, internal auditing must also apply knowledge concerning the adequacy of controls from consulting engagements to the evaluation of the effectiveness of the organization's control processes.

Topic 7: Maintain an Effective Quality Assurance and Improvement Program (Level P)

Organizations are continually changing. Operations undergo refinement, and internal processes change and evolve. As an organization changes, auditing services must keep pace. How can the internal auditor meet ever-changing management needs for auditing services and still ensure the highest-quality audit activity results? To ensure the consistent quality of internal audit activities, the internal audit function is required to have a quality assurance and improvement program (QAIP) in place.

Even an internal audit department that is fully out-sourced is required to have a QAIP, regardless of whether the out-source provider has completed one for its own overall activities. For example, PricewaterhouseCoopers completes a QAIP for its activities annually, but each of its clients (i.e., "XYZ Company") still needs one as well.

Standard 2070, "External Service Provider and Organizational Responsibility for Internal Auditing," states, "When an external service provider serves as the internal audit activity, the provider must make the organization aware that the organization has the responsibility for maintaining an effective internal audit activity." According to interpretation, "*This responsibility is demonstrated through the quality assurance and improvement program, which assesses conformance with the Definition of Internal Auditing, the Code of Ethics, and the* Standards."

Related *Standards* and Practice Advisories/ Guides

The *Standards,* Practice Advisories, and Practice Guides related to quality assurance and improvement of the internal audit activity are listed in Exhibit I-11.

Exhibit I-11: Quality Assurance and Improvement of the Internal Audit Activity *Standards* and Practice Advisories/Guides (continued on next page)

Standard	**Related Guidance**
Attribute Standard 1300, "Quality Assurance and Improvement Program" The chief audit executive must develop and maintain a quality assurance and improvement program that covers all aspects of the internal audit activity.	Practice Advisory 1300-1, "Quality Assurance and Improvement Program" Practice Guide, "QAIP to Help IA Functions Achieve and Maintain Quality"
Attribute Standard 1310, "Requirements of the Quality Assurance and Improvement Program" The quality assurance and improvement program must include both internal and external assessments.	Practice Advisory 1310-1, "Requirements of the Quality Assurance and Improvement Program"
Attribute Standard 1311, "Internal Assessments" Internal assessments must include: • Ongoing monitoring of the performance of the internal audit activity; and • Periodic self-assessments or assessments by other persons within the organization with sufficient knowledge of internal audit practices.	Practice Advisory 1311-1, "Internal Assessments"
Attribute Standard 1312, "External Assessments" External assessments must be conducted at least once every five years by a qualified, independent assessor or assessment team from outside the organization. The chief audit executive must discuss with the board: • The form and frequency of external assessment; and • The qualifications and independence of the external assessor or assessment team, including any potential conflict of interest.	Practice Advisory 1312-1, "External Assessments" Practice Advisory 1312-2, "External Assessments—Self-Assessment with Independent Validation"

Exhibit I-11: Quality Assurance and Improvement of the Internal Audit Activity *Standards* and Practice Advisories/Guides (concluded)

Standard	**Related Guidance**
Attribute Standard 1320, "Reporting on the Quality Assurance and Improvement Program" The chief audit executive must communicate the results of the quality assurance and improvement program to senior management and the board.	
Attribute Standard 1321, "Use of 'Conforms with the *International Standards for the Professional Practice of Internal Auditing*' " The chief audit executive may state that the internal audit activity conforms with the *International Standards for the Professional Practice of Internal Auditing* only if the results of the quality assurance and improvement program support this statement.	Practice Advisory 1321-1, "Use of 'Conforms with the *International Standards for the Professional Practice of Internal Auditing*' "
Attribute Standard 1322, "Disclosure of Nonconformance" When nonconformance with the Definition of Internal Auditing, the Code of Ethics, or the *Standards* impacts the overall scope or operation of the internal audit activity, the chief audit executive must disclose the nonconformance and the impact to senior management and the board.	

Establish and maintain a quality assurance and improvement program

Attribute Standard 1300 states that "the chief audit executive must develop and maintain a quality assurance and improvement program that covers all aspects of the internal audit activity." Interpretation tells us: *"A quality assurance and improvement program is designed to enable an evaluation of the internal audit activity's conformance with the Definition of Internal Auditing and the* Standards *and an evaluation of whether internal auditors apply the Code of Ethics. The program also assesses the efficiency and effectiveness of the internal audit activity and identifies opportunities for improvement."*

Practice Advisory 1300-1, "Quality Assurance and Improvement Program," states:

> The CAE is accountable for implementing processes designed to provide reasonable assurance to the various stakeholders that the internal audit activity:
>
> - Performs in accordance with the internal audit charter, which is consistent with the Definition of Internal Auditing, the Code of Ethics, and the *Standards*.
> - Operates in an effective and efficient manner.
> - Is perceived by those stakeholders as adding value and improving the organization's operations.
>
> These processes include appropriate supervision, periodic internal assessments and ongoing monitoring of quality assurance, and periodic external assessments.

Key elements of a QAIP

QAIP elements range from policy/procedure development to record-keeping functions for internal audit activity engagements.

Exhibit I-12 provides an overview of internal and external quality assessments.

Exhibit I-12: QAIP Internal and External Assessments

Description	Purpose	Performance	Timing
Internal quality assessment			
Ongoing internal evaluations of the internal audit activity coupled with periodic self-assessments and/or reviews.	Ongoing reviews of the performance of the internal audit activity. Periodic reviews performed through self-assessment or by other individuals within the organization with knowledge of internal auditing practices and the *Standards*.	Conducted by persons within the organization's internal audit activity. Supervised by the direction of the CAE. (Note: CAE involvement precludes total objectivity.)	Usually incorporated into the routine policies and practices used to manage the internal audit activity. May include ad hoc, special purpose reviews and compliance testing.
External quality assessment			
Evaluation of internal audit activity confor-mance to the Definition of Internal Auditing, the Code of Ethics, the *Standards*, the use of best practices, and internal audit activity efficiency and effectiveness.	Assess the effectiveness of an internal audit activity in providing assurance and consulting services to stakeholders. Assess conformance to the mandatory guidance and provide an opinion as to whether the internal auditing activity generally conforms to all of the *Standards*. Identify opportunities and offer recommendations to the CAE and staff for improving performance and services and promoting the image and credibility of the internal audit function.	Conducted by qualified independent reviewer or review team from outside the organization.	At least once every five years.

Internal auditors should consult the related *Standards* and Practice Advisories for these types of QAIP assessments. A synopsis of important elements follows.

Internal assessments

Ongoing internal assessments are practices put into place by the CAE to do routine evaluations of the practices and policies of performing individual audits. The type and amount of these assessments will vary depending on the nature of the organization. Specific processes and tools should be developed for each organization. Conclusions should be developed on an ongoing basis, and appropriate actions should be taken to improve the quality of the ongoing audit activities.

Periodic reviews are another important aspect of the internal assessment process. This is more of a scheduled self-assessment approach to determine if the right activities are being performed should changes be made to the internal audit practices and procedures in order to enhance the quality of the programs. This periodic self-assessment process is also used by many organizations to perform their own evaluation of conformance to the *Standards.* Many organizations use this type of review to perform their own evaluation before an external quality assessment is to be performed.

Scope of internal assessments

Such assessments should include:

- Routine and continuous supervision and testing of the performance of audit and consulting work.
- Ongoing measurements and analyses of performance metrics (e.g., audit plan accomplishment, cycle time, recommendations accepted, and customer satisfaction).
- Periodic validations of compliance with applicable laws, regulations, and government or industry standards.
- Periodic validations of compliance with the *Standards* and Code of Ethics, including timely corrective actions to remedy any significant instances of noncompliance.
- Evaluation of the adequacy of the internal audit activity's charter, goals, objectives, policies, and procedures.
- Assessment of contribution to the organization's governance, risk management, and control processes.
- Evaluation of the effectiveness of continuous improvement activities and adoption of best practices.
- Whether the auditing activity adds value, improves operations, and helps the organization achieve its objectives.

Quality measures

Practice Advisory 1311-1 provides extensive guidance in establishing performance measures for reviews of the internal audit activity. This guidance is recommended in conjunction with consideration of the *Standards* and other common measurement practices.

Although this advisory provides examples of several specific measurements considered to be critical, it is important to understand that there is no single set of measurements that is universally effective for all audit activities. Both quantitative metrics and qualitative assessments are important to demonstrate audit activity performance to key stakeholders.

Exhibit I-13 provides a point-in-time snapshot of performance measurements that were considered important to a limited number of CAEs.

Exhibit I-13: QAIP Internal Performance Measurements

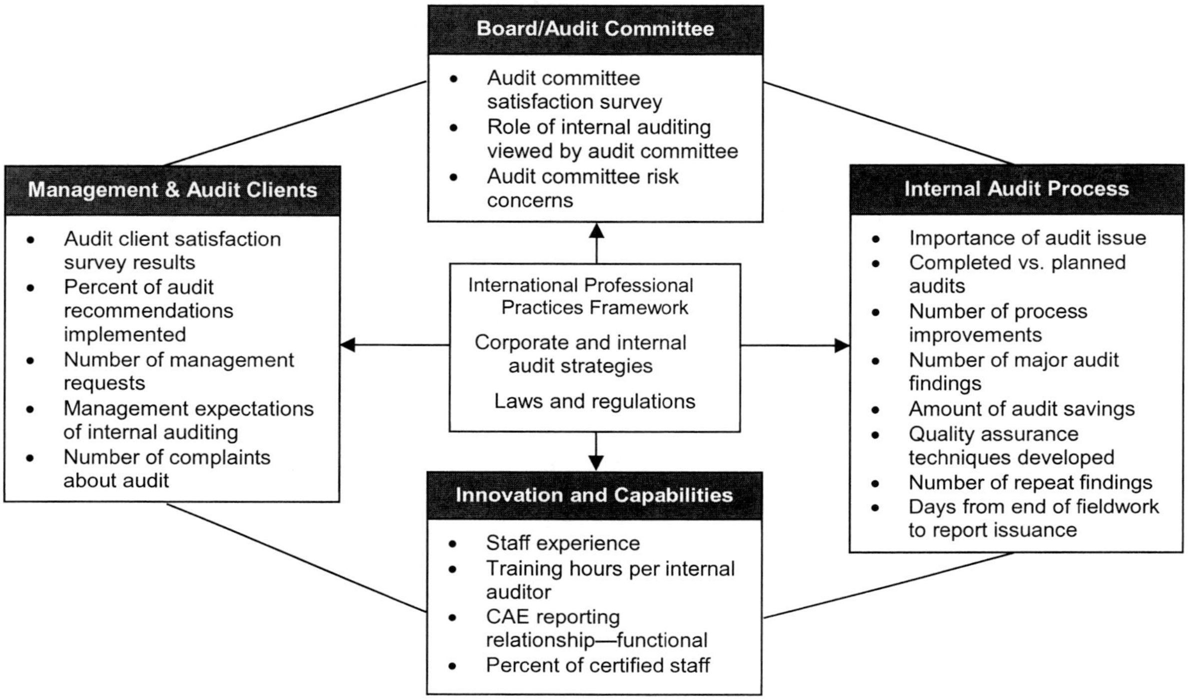

Source: Adapted from *A Balanced Scorecard Framework for Internal Auditing Departments* by Mark L. Frigo.

It is the CAE's responsibility to establish a structure for reporting results of periodic reviews that maintains appropriate credibility and objectivity. Typically, those individuals conducting ongoing and periodic reviews should report to the CAE while performing the reviews and should communicate their results directly to the CAE.

If internal assessment results determine that there are areas for improvement, the improvements should be implemented by the CAE through the QAIP.

For additional information about performing ongoing internal reviews, consult Practice Advisory 1311-1, "Internal Assessments."

External assessments

Interpretation of Standard 1312 tells us:

> *External assessments can be in the form of a full external assessment, or a self-assessment with independent external validation.*
>
> *A qualified assessor or assessment team demonstrates competence in two areas: the professional practice of internal auditing and the external assessment process. Competence can be demonstrated through a mixture of experience and theoretical learning. Experience gained in organizations of similar size, complexity, sector or industry, and technical issues is more valuable than less relevant experience. In the case of an assessment team, not all members of the team need to have all the competencies; it is the team as a whole that is qualified. The chief audit executive uses professional judgment when assessing whether an assessor or assessment team demonstrates sufficient competence to be qualified.*
>
> *An independent assessor or assessment team means not having either a real or an apparent conflict of interest and not being a part of, or under the control of, the organization to which the internal audit activity belongs.*

External quality assessment reviews may be performed by.

- A team that is totally independent of the organization that is being reviewed. (These teams are available from The IIA or consulting organizations that have knowledge of the requirements of the standards for audit performance.)
- Self-assessment with independent validation by an independent reviewer.
- A peer review team made of members from at least three different organizations.

The required qualifications are the same for all three of these types of assessment teams. An external review team should also include members with information technology expertise, relevant industry experience, and expertise in other specialized disciplines (such as accounting, taxation, or environmental affairs, as necessary).

Integrity and objectivity are critical considerations in the selection process. The CAE should involve senior management and the board in the selection process for an external reviewer and obtain their approval.

Scope of external assessments

Practice Advisory 1312-1 guidance recommends that external assessment consist of a broad scope of coverage that includes the following elements of the internal audit activity:

- Conformance with the Definition of Internal Auditing; the Code of Ethics; and the *Standards*; and the internal audit activity's charter, plans, policies, procedures, practices, and applicable legislative and regulatory requirements,
- Expectations of the internal audit activity expressed by the board, senior management, and operational managers,
- Integration of the internal audit activity into the organization's governance process, including the relationships between and among the key groups involved in the process,
- Tools and techniques employed by the internal audit activity,
- Mix of knowledge, experience, and disciplines within the staff, including staff focus on process improvement, and
- Determination as to whether or not the internal audit activity adds value and improves the organization's operations.

Additional information about external assessments is found in the *Quality Assessment Manual* and Practice Advisories 1312-1 and 1312-2.

Report the results of the quality assurance and improvement program

The *Standards* and various Practice Advisories identify specific reporting results of both internal and external assessments for stakeholders. For internal assessments, the CAE should share the results, necessary action plans, and their successful implementation with stakeholders such as senior management, the board, and external auditors. For external assessments, the preliminary results of the review should be discussed with the CAE during and at the conclusion of the assessment process. Final results should be communicated in a formal report to the CAE or other official who authorized the review for the organization, preferably with copies sent directly to appropriate members of senior management and the board.

The formal report for external assessments should:

- Contain an opinion on the internal audit activity's compliance with the Definition of Internal Auditing, the Code of Ethics, and the *Standards* based on a structured rating process.
- Assess and evaluate best practice usage, both that observed during the assessment and others potentially applicable to the activity.
- Provide appropriate recommendations for improvement.

The CAE should also communicate the specifics of planned remedial actions for significant issues and subsequent information as to the accomplishment of those planned actions.

Conformance to the *Standards*

Internal and external assessments of an internal audit activity should appraise and express an opinion as to the internal audit activity's conformance to the Definition of Internal Auditing, the Code of Ethics, and the *Standards*. Practice Advisory 1321-1 defines what the *Standards* mean by conformance and nonconformance:

- Conformance "means [that] the practices of the internal audit activity, taken as a whole, satisfy the requirements of the Definition of Internal Auditing, the Code of Ethics, and the *Standards.*"
- Nonconformance "means [that] the impact and severity of the deficiencies in the practices of the internal audit activity are so significant they impair the internal audit activity's ability to discharge its responsibilities."

The Practice Advisory also clarifies that the report on the independent assessment should express, if relevant to the overall opinion, the degree of partial conformance with the Definition of Internal Auditing, the Code of Ethics, and/or individual standards.

Interpretation of Standard 1321 tell us: *"The internal audit activity conforms with the* Standards *when it achieves the outcomes described in the Definition of Internal Auditing, Code of Ethics, and* Standards. *The results of the quality assurance and improvement program include the results of both internal and external assessments. All internal audit activities will have the results of internal assessments. Internal audit activities in existence for at least five years will also have the results of external assessments."*

As appropriate, the assessments should include recommendations for compliance improvement.

Use of the compliance phrase

The compliance phrase to be used in the formal report may be expressed in one of three ways.

- "In compliance with the *Standards*"
- "In conformity to the *Standards*"
- "In accordance with the *Standards*"

The use of any of these compliance phrases requires an external assessment at least once during each five-year period, along with ongoing and periodic internal assessments that have concluded that the internal audit activity is in compliance. Any instances of noncompliance that have been disclosed by a quality assessment that impair the internal audit activity's ability to discharge its responsibilities should be adequately remedied and remedial actions appropriately documented and reported to the relevant assessor(s), senior management, and the board.

Conduct quality assurance procedures/ recommend improvements to internal audit activity

The IIA *Quality Assessment Manual* provides specific guidelines for internal assessment reporting and follow-up, including the following recommendations:

- To reinforce the independence and objectivity of the assessment team, the team and the CAE should agree on the reporting medium and format at the beginning of the assessment.
- The CAE should document in writing a response/action plan and implementation timetable for each recommendation from the final written report.
- Copies of final reports sent outside the internal audit activity should include a copy of the internal audit activity's response and implementation plan.

Standard 1320 states that "the chief audit executive must communicate the results of the quality assurance and improvement program to senior management and the board."

Interpretation of Standard 1320 clarifies what is included in this communication: *"To demonstrate conformance with the Definition of Internal Auditing, the Code of Ethics, and the* Standards, *the results of external and periodic internal assessments are communicated upon completion of such assessments and the results of ongoing monitoring are communicated at least annually. The results include the assessor's or assessment team's evaluation with respect to the degree of conformance."*

According to The IIA *Quality Assessment Manual*, the most important aspect of the external assessment is the team's evaluation of the internal activity's conformance with the *Standards* and its charter along with the extent of its use of current best practices and its program of continuous improvement. These evaluations are also intended to disclose opportunities for improvement and recommendations to enhance conformance with the *Standards*, add value for clients, and generally be a catalyst for positive change in the organization.

The external assessment reporting process involves a systematic process of conferences, a report draft, and a final report. The board is required to receive a copy of the external quality assessment report. It is the CAE's responsibility to respond to the recommendations and provide an action plan for remediation.

In most organizations, the external assessment reporting process typically unfolds in the following manner:

- External assessments results are reported to senior management and the audit committee and documented in an external quality assessment report.
- The lead person from the external audit team may be requested to make presentations to organizational executive management and the audit committee to ensure an understanding of the identified opportunities for an enhanced internal audit program.
- The planned action of the CAE to provide improvements to the internal audit program is included in this report.
- The CAE reports to the audit committee on the progress in enhancing the internal audit program.

Chapter C: Establish a Risk-Based Internal Audit Plan

Chapter Introduction

Management is responsible for establishing and maintaining a system of internal controls within an organization. The *Standards* Glossary defines control as "any action taken by management, the board, and other parties to manage risk and increase the likelihood that established objectives and goals will be achieved. Management plans, organizes, and directs the performance of sufficient actions to provide reasonable assurance that objectives and goals will be achieved." Structures, activities, processes, and systems that help management effectively mitigate risk are all examples of internal controls. Internal controls are an integral component in risk management.

Because internal auditors are experts in understanding organizational risks and internal controls available to mitigate these risks, they are in a unique position to help management protect their organizations from risk exposures—present and future—ranging from minor disruptions to major catastrophes. The internal audit activity assists both management and the oversight body (the board or its audit committee) in enterprise risk management by:

- Helping management to understand internal controls and risk management processes.
- Developing and implementing a risk assessment framework for internal audit planning.

- Bringing a systematic, disciplined auditing approach to assessing the effectiveness of internal controls and risk management processes.
- Providing objective and independent assurance that the organization's risks have been appropriately mitigated.
- Making recommendations for improvements, as warranted.

No organization is immune from risk. Ideally, enterprise risk management is a robust process that identifies and mitigates threats and/or occurrences that can thwart organizational success. The internal auditing function's risk assessment role plays an important part in confirming management successes and identifying exceptions for management actions.

While helping an organization to embrace a framework of internal control and an ERM framework are critical for organizational governance and are integral to most controls, internal auditing itself needs to incorporate the same ERM techniques into its audit planning procedures. To be truly value-added to the organization, the annual audit plan and specific engagements must focus on significant risks, with significant being defined as those risks that are considered likely to have a real impact on the achievement of the organization's objectives or goals for that area.

For example, Standard 2201, "Planning Considerations," requires focus on significant risks:

> In planning the engagement, internal auditors must consider:
> - The objectives of the activity being reviewed and the means by which the activity controls its performance;
> - The significant risks to the activity, its objectives, resources, and operations and the means by which the potential impact of risk is kept to an acceptable level;
> - The adequacy and effectiveness of the activity's governance, risk management, and control processes compared to a relevant framework or model; and
> - The opportunities for making significant improvements to the activity's governance, risk management, and control processes.

In another example, Standard 2210.A1 states, "Internal auditors must conduct a preliminary assessment of the risks relevant to the activity under review. Engagement objectives must reflect the results of this assessment."

Auditing maturity level

When developing a risk-based internal audit plan, it is important for auditors to assess the internal audit activity's ERM maturity level. Consider the following maturity levels of annual audit planning and audit engagement objective setting:

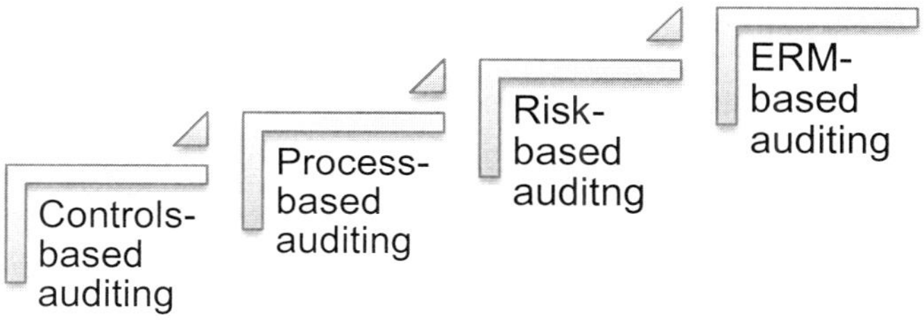

- **Controls-based auditing.** Prior to the 1980s, controls-based internal auditing was the standard method of auditing. This method is basically an extension of external audit procedures and consists primarily of providing assurance of the validity of various account balances and other financial details; audits of compliance with laws, regulations, policies, and procedures; and audits of specific transaction controls from initiation to reporting. The focus was to understand the laws, regulations, policies, and procedures in the area and then to identify and correct exceptions and errors.

- **Process-based auditing.** Process-based audits were developed in the 1980s to address some flaws with controls-based auditing such as its low value to decision makers. Process-based audits look at processes as a whole and evaluate their design, efficiency, and effectiveness. These audits began to stress achievement of business objectives as a key gap to measure between a current and an actual process, but the primary focus of an audit was often still controls-based.

- **Risk-based auditing.** Risk-based auditing was developed in the 1990s to demonstrate further added value, especially as more consulting firms entered into co-sourcing arrangements for internal auditing and had to justify their fees. The intent was to limit the audit engagement to significant risks starting by developing a thorough understanding of the organization and its risks. Relatively low-risk controls could be omitted from engagements to ensure a greater return on the investment in auditing. This auditing maturity level satisfies the mandates of the *Standards* to be risk-based in selecting engagements, audit objectives, and specific audit tests. It is a method that is intuitive for management to understand and endorse. However, organizations that have relatively mature ERM processes can also move to a higher auditing maturity level.

- **ERM-based auditing.** ERM-based auditing developed in the late 1990s as a counterpart to the organization-wide use of ERM for holistic risk-based assessment and decision making. In addition to setting project priorities based on perceived risk to key business objectives, it also focuses strongly on measuring risk based on relevant KPIs, accounting for risk appetite and risk tolerance levels, and planning responses based on what enterprise risk management capabilities already exist. Rather than focusing just on mitigating risks to an acceptable level, ERM-based auditing assesses how well ERM activities are supporting organizational objectives by managing risks to an acceptable level within a risk appetite/tolerance. Thus the focus is on the gaps in ERM effectiveness based not only on the auditor's objective assessment of what risks are significant but also on management's assessment of those risks.

  Advantages of maturing to an ERM-based auditing methodology include:

  - Creating a foundation for audit judgments based on organizational strategy and objectives, risk appetite, and governance maturity.
  - Developing an assurance framework for assessing the adequacy of ERM and governance activities.
  - Synchronizing the auditor's tolerance for risk with management's tolerance for risk rather than focusing solely on the former as in prior audit methods.
  - Emphasizing the critical need to base performance measurements on what will provide real incentives to accomplish organizational objectives.
  - Focusing on the organization's future capability to assess and manage risk rather than on just its historical risk response track record.

The remainder of this chapter refers to risk-based auditing, which should be taken as a generalization that could refer to either risk-based or ERM-based audits, with the goal of achieving the maturity level of an ERM-based audit.

The chapter starts by discussing the need to establish a framework for assessing risk. The second topic indicates the importance of understanding the organization and its industry and market when considering audit priorities. The third topic shows how to use an ERM framework to identify and interpret risks when proposing areas for engagements. The fourth topic discusses how to rank and validate risks by priority. The fifth topic discusses how CAEs must ensure that their audit team possesses sufficient knowledge, skills, and abilities to address significant risks. The sixth topic discusses how to communicate with the board to gain agreement and buy-in on what areas are truly the most significant risks and thus obtain approval for the annual audit plan based on those risks.

The seventh topic differentiates between assurance and consulting engagements in preparation for the final topics in the chapter, which provide detailed descriptions of various types of assurance and consulting engagements. Although all audit engagements have common elements and factors, such as developing an audit plan or putting together an audit team, each type of engagement also has individual and specialized components. It is critical that internal auditors can identify these differences and apply the correct methods of performing an audit engagement.

Topic 1: Establish a Framework for Assessing Risk (Level P)

Internal auditors cannot evaluate every possible risk facing an organization. The multiple sources of potential engagements coupled with the related scope of work require the efficient use of limited internal audit resources. A risk assessment framework provides a systematic way for the CAE and the internal audit function to assess internal and external risk factors and develop an annual audit plan. The risk assessment framework is a tool used to comply with Performance Standard 2010, "Planning," which tells us: "The chief audit executive must establish a risk-based plan to determine the priorities of the internal audit activity, consistent with the organization's goals."

Interpretation helps us understand how to develop the framework:

> *The chief audit executive is responsible for developing a risk-based plan. The chief audit executive takes into account the organization's risk management framework, including using risk appetite levels set by management for the different activities or parts of the organization. If a framework does not exist, the chief audit executive uses his/her own judgment of risks after consideration of input from senior management and the board. The chief audit executive must review and adjust the plan, as necessary, in response to changes in the organization's business, risks, operations, programs, systems, and controls.*

To some extent, frameworks for assessing and developing risk-based plans will vary from enterprise to enterprise. An organization's size, formality, management team dynamics, industry, regulatory requirements, and other demographics are just some of the potential influencing factors. But, in general, most risk-based frameworks for internal audit planning encompass the steps listed in Exhibit I-14.

Exhibit I-14: A Risk-Based Assessment Framework for Internal Auditing

Step	Description
Determine the audit universe.	• Identifies all organizational sources of potential engagements and all potential auditable activities; not limited to functions such as payroll or accounting but also considers specific activities within the function that pose potential risks. • Varies depending on the industry or nature of the organization, for example, locations, processes, products, or divisions may be considered. **Example:** A listing of all units and processes in the organization (which may well be hundreds of items).
Examine organizational risk factors.	• Assesses internal and external organizational risks viewed more from the perspective of their impact on organizational goals and objectives than on the extent of change within specific functions. • Considers potential engagement sources. • Involves discussing the audit universe with organizational senior managers to identify levels of risk, planned new activities, and/or process changes. • Incorporates ERM results—if the organization has an ERM process. • Considers other internal and external assurance activities. **Example:** Consideration of size of revenue or assets, visibility of areas, liquidity or cash flow, results of other reviews, and reported problems.
Prioritize audits.	• Evaluates proposed engagements. • Establishes criteria and ranks the risks based on their significance to organizational success and the organization's risk appetite (tolerance for risk). • Considers if the internal audit staff is sufficient to cover all the primary risks and whether some can be delayed and/or handled by external auditors. • Leads to the annual audit plan. **Example:** Identification of the most important areas to audit during the upcoming year based on high-level risk evaluations, planned process changes, and requests from management coupled with the internal audit resources available.

Standard 2010.A1, "Planning," further states: "The internal audit activity's plan of engagements must be based on a documented risk assessment, undertaken at least annually. The input of senior management and the board must be considered in this process."

Internal audit activities adopt their organization's ERM framework—if one exists—and apply it to the selection of audit engagements, engagement criteria, and audit tools.

There are numerous ERM models. They generally vary in their focus and complexity. We will first examine the ERM model of the Committee of Sponsoring Organizations of the Treadway Commission (COSO), including critical principles and components and how risks should be identified, assessed, responded to, and controlled to support an organization's objectives and goals. Following the COSO discussion, we will look at two other well-accepted risk management approaches—ISO 31000 and the Turnbull guidance.

COSO's ERM framework

COSO's *Enterprise Risk Management—Integrated Framework* is an example of a comprehensive framework that applies ERM in a strategic setting. The COSO framework is applicable to all industries and all types of risk. Starting at the top and supporting an organization's mission is what differentiates COSO from most other risk models. The model describes the connection between objectives (what the organization strives to achieve) and ERM components (what is needed to achieve the objectives).

COSO's ERM objectives

During the strategic planning process, an organization's management sets strategic objectives, selects appropriate strategies, and establishes supporting objectives that cascade throughout the organization. The COSO framework includes four categories of organizational objectives:

- **Strategic** (tied to high-level organizational goals and aligned to and supporting the organization's mission)
- **Operations** (related to the effective and efficient use of organizational resources)
- **Reporting** (related to the reliability of reporting)
- **Compliance** (related to organizational compliance with applicable laws and regulations)

The achievement of reporting and compliance objectives is generally within an organization's control. In other words, if related activities are performed efficiently and effectively, these objectives should be met. That is not always the case with strategic and operations objectives; mitigating circumstances can, and often do, prevent the fulfillment of these objectives. Large financial losses resulting from a bad capital budgeting decision or an unplanned flood at a key manufacturing facility that delays the launch of a new product are both examples of events that could thwart the achievement of strategic and operations goals. While implementation of the COSO framework cannot prevent such bad management judgments or unforeseen events, it does enhance the likelihood of management making better, more informed decisions.

COSO's ERM components

ERM components are derived from the way management runs an enterprise and are integrated with the management process. COSO's ERM components are shown in Exhibit I-15.

Exhibit I-15: COSO ERM Components

Component	Description
Internal environment	The internal environment encompasses the tone of an organization and sets the basis for how risk is viewed and addressed by an entity's people, including risk management philosophy and risk appetite, integrity and ethical values, and the environment in which they operate.
Objective setting	Objectives must exist before management can identify potential events affecting their achievement. Enterprise risk management ensures that management has a process in place to set objectives and that the chosen objectives support and align with the entity's mission and are consistent with its risk appetite.
Event identification	Internal and external events affecting achievement of an entity's objectives must be identified, distinguishing between risks and opportunities. Opportunities are channeled back to management's strategy or objective-setting processes.
Risk assessment	Risks are analyzed, considering likelihood and impact, as a basis for determining how they should be managed. Risks are assessed on an inherent and a residual basis.
Risk response	Management selects risk responses—avoiding, accepting, reducing, or sharing risk—developing a set of actions to align risks with the entity's risk tolerances and risk appetite.
Control activities	Policies and procedures are established and implemented to help ensure that the risk responses are effectively carried out.
Information and communication	Relevant information is identified, captured, and communicated in a form and time frame that enables people to carry out their responsibilities. Effective communication also occurs in a broader sense, flowing down, across, and up the entity.
Monitoring	The entirety of enterprise risk management is monitored and modifications are made as necessary. Monitoring is accomplished through ongoing management activities, separate evaluations, or both.

Source: *Enterprise Risk Management—Integrated Framework,* COSO.

COSO describes enterprise risk management as a dynamic, multidirectional process. It is not serial, where one component affects only the next in sequence. In the COSO model, any component can influence the others.

The relationship of objectives and components in the COSO framework

The COSO model establishes a direct relationship between organizational objectives and ERM components. The relationship is depicted as the cube-shaped three-dimensional matrix shown in Exhibit I-16.

Exhibit I-16: COSO ERM Matrix

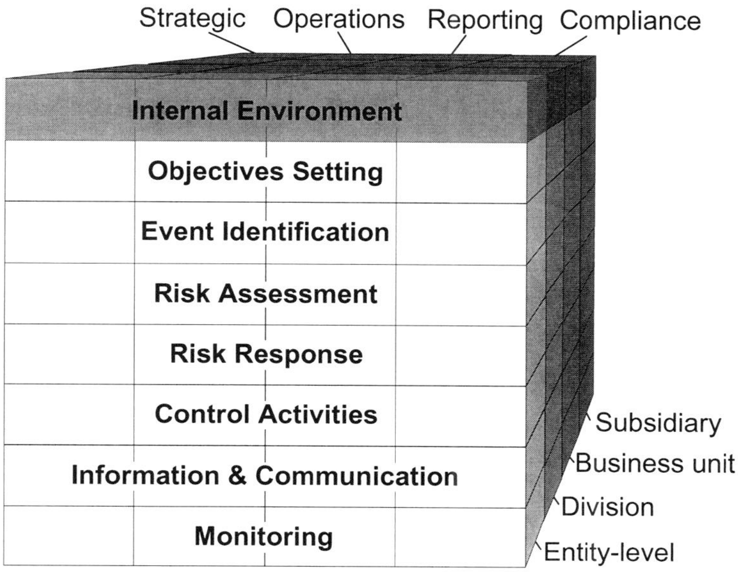

Source: *Enterprise Risk Management—Integrated Framework,* COSO.

Note the following characteristics about the COSO matrix:

- The vertical columns depict the four categories of objectives.
- The horizontal rows represent the eight components.
- The entity and its units (division, business unit, and subsidiary) are depicted by the third dimension.

The objectives and the components cut across each other. Ongoing monitoring activities, for example, would apply to all four objectives categories. Monitoring would help to ensure that strategies are on track, business operations are being managed effectively, reporting is reliable, and the organization is complying with all applicable laws.

Roles and responsibilities

The practice of managing risk includes a variety of activities that attempt to identify, assess, manage, and control risk across the entire spectrum of an organization, ranging from single events or projects to narrowly defined types of risk (e.g., market risk) to threats and opportunities facing the entire enterprise. Traditionally, risk management responsibilities were assigned to individual business units and/or parts of business units. In theory risk management was considered an organizational initiative. But in practice risk management activities rarely fanned across the organization.

Effective risk management requires everyone in the organization—at all levels—to participate in the process. Producing information used to identify risks, taking necessary actions to effect risk management, and supporting information and communication flows are implicit and explicit in everyone's job descriptions. However, COSO notes that the board, management, risk officers, financial executives, internal auditors, and certain external parties have special roles and responsibilities. We will examine these individuals and groups next (with the exception of the internal audit activity, which is covered in the remainder of this chapter).

The board

The board, or its equivalent, serves several functions. The board helps to set strategy and formulate high-level objectives. Often the board delegates the monitoring and assurance responsibilities to management, reserving authority for key decisions.

COSO describes the board's oversight of enterprise risk management as:

- Knowing the extent to which management has established effective enterprise risk management in the organization.
- Being aware of and concurring with the entity's risk appetite.
- Reviewing the entity's portfolio view of risk and considering it against the entity's risk appetite.
- Being appraised of the most significant risks and whether management is responding appropriately.

The board is part of the internal environment component in the COSO model. Through its actions, the board sets precedents for integrity and ethical values. The board may employ resources to conduct special investigations and use board committees to carry out certain duties. A compensation committee, for example, would assume the responsibilities for various aspects of the rewards system. Or the audit committee would oversee the reliability of external reporting. Ultimately, the board's makeup, commitment, focus, and activities largely influence whether risks are managed at an acceptable level.

Management

Management assumes the primary responsibility for identifying and managing risk and for implementing enterprise risk management in a structured, consistent, and coordinated approach. The specific responsibilities of managers at the different levels vary from organization to organization. But a fairly universal truth is that the chief executive officer (CEO) has ultimate ownership for the enterprise risk management process, setting the "tone at the top" and ensuring a positive internal control environment.

Management and the board work together during the strategy-setting process to determine an organization's risk appetite. COSO defines risk appetite as "the amount of risk, on a broad level, an entity is willing to accept in pursuit of value." Risk appetite is partially determined by an organization's operating environment. For example, pharmaceutical companies work in an operating environment that requires protecting the brand value and minimizing risks by investing in early research and testing. However, even such an organization can choose to follow a strategy that exposes it to more or less risk, such as a decision to enter a new market or to remain in more stable, mature markets. Internal auditors play a role in assuring that the organization has sufficient risk tolerance, or capacity to absorb variations from objectives, to account for the organization's resource allocations and strategic choices related to risk appetite.

COSO outlines the CEO's responsibilities as:

- Providing leadership and direction to senior managers.
- Meeting periodically with senior managers responsible for major functions (such as sales, marketing, finance, human resources, and so on) to understand risks inherent in operations, risk responses, required control improvements, and status of ongoing initiatives.
- Monitoring activities and risks in relation to the organization's risk appetite.

Senior managers convert the risk management strategies into operations. Managers in specific processes, functions, or departments provide the tactical, hands-on role in devising and executing specific risk management procedures. They also report on status and recommend improvements to upper-level managers.

Management authority and accountability are imperative in enterprise risk management. Each manager should be accountable to the next higher level, with the CEO being accountable to the board.

Risk officer

In some organizations, a risk officer (also referred to as a chief risk officer or risk manager) provides central coordination for enterprise risk management across the organization. Empowered by the CEO, a risk officer has the resources to work with other managers in establishing effective risk management practices, monitoring progress, and assisting those managers in reporting.

COSO lists a risk officer's specific enterprise risk management responsibilities as:

- Establishing relevant policies.
- Defining roles and responsibilities and helping to set implementation goals.
- Framing related authority and accountability in business units.
- Promoting competence throughout the entity.
- Guiding the integration with other business planning and management activities.
- Establishing a common risk management language and common measures.
- Facilitating reporting protocols.
- Reporting the status to the CEO, including recommended actions.

Some organizations appoint an individual to serve exclusively in the capacity of risk manager. Others assign the related enterprise risk management responsibilities to the chief financial officer, general counsel, or another senior officer.

Financial executives

Finance and controllership activities cut across all operating and business units. Budgeting and financial planning as well as tracking and analyzing performance and reporting are all in the domain of the chief financial officer, the chief accounting officer, the controller, or others in the financial function. These individuals and respective activities are central to how management executes risk management.

External parties

Several external parties contribute to an entity's objectives and enterprise risk management activities:

- **External auditors.** External auditors provide an independent and objective view that can contribute to an organization's achievement of external financial reporting objectives as well as other entity objectives. While most financial statement audits do not have a significant focus on enterprise risk management, COSO points out that the information provided can be helpful to management in carrying out its risk management responsibilities. Audit findings, analytical information, and recommended actions are pertinent to the achievement of established objectives. If an external audit uncovers any deficiencies in risk management and control, the auditor may also report those findings along with recommendations for improvement. Should the external audit be required by law or regulation (e.g., the Sarbanes-Oxley Act) to assess an entity's internal control over financial reporting, the audit scope in those areas will be more rigorous.

- **Legislators and regulators.** Many laws and regulations affect the enterprise risk management of particular entities. Legislators and regulators establish rules that require an entity's risk management and control systems to meet minimum statutory and regulatory requirements. When regulatory agencies examine an entity (such as federal and state bank examiners examining a bank's operations), the organization typically receives useful information in applying enterprise risk management and recommendations and/or directives regarding needed improvements.

- **Business associates.** Other parties who conduct business with an entity (customers, vendors, creditors, and the like) can be useful information channels for risk management activities. Items such as demands for new products and services, quality control issues, ethical concerns, and shipping or billing discrepancies can be valuable input toward the achievement of strategic, operations, reporting, or compliance objectives.

- **Out-sourcing providers.** Many organizations choose to out-source day-to-day activities (such as payroll, finance, or information technology) in order to concentrate activities and resources on core business competencies. Out-sourcing generally allows an organization to capitalize on the expertise of other firms that are more efficient, effective, or knowledgeable at specialized tasks that are peripheral to those core businesses. COSO makes the point that management cannot delegate associated risk management activities to these external providers. Programs must be devised and implemented to monitor those activities.

- **Financial analysts, bond rating agencies, and news media.** Financial analysts and bond rating agencies evaluate a variety of factors to formulate an opinion about the soundness of an organization and its worthiness as an investment. The financial media often undertake similar analyses. The observations and insights these groups garner may be helpful to management in improving risk management activities.

More information on COSO's *Enterprise Risk Management—Integrated Framework* can be found on the COSO Web site, at www.coso.org.

ISO 31000

ISO 31000:2009, "Risk Management—Principles and Guidelines," is an international standard framework for risk management that is simple and concise. ISO 31000 is a framework for the systematic development of enterprise risk management that can be used successfully by any size or type of organization because the organization can adapt the framework to the proper scope and environmental context. As the organization's risk management activities become more mature, the framework can likewise be augmented. The ISO has also published a complementary resource, ISO Guide 73:2009, "Risk Management Vocabulary," which helps organizations discuss risks using a common set of risk management terms.

ISO 31000 is gaining popularity, in part because it is an international standard and also because many organizations find it to be more intuitive and easier to explain to management and the board. This is especially true for non-US organizations and those organizations just adopting a risk management framework.

The purpose of ISO 31000 is to help organizations manage uncertainty. An organization that can manage uncertainty and adapt quickly to change will not only be better able to achieve its objectives but will be more attractive to investors. ISO 31000 also helps organizations benchmark their own risk management practices against those of other organizations adopting ISO 31000.

ISO 31000 principles

ISO 31000 is a brief, principles-based document that is intended to generate transparency and credibility within the risk management function. These principles state that risk management:

- Is a value-added activity.
- Is inseparable from the organization's decision-making processes and operations.
- Addresses uncertainty in a structured, orderly, unambiguous, and timely fashion.
- Makes use of the best information available.
- Is customized to the organization's operating environment, culture, and objectives.
- Is transparent, auditable, and inclusive of all stakeholders.
- Uses an iterative cycle to generate continual improvement, organizational learning, and the ability to quickly respond to changing environments.

ISO 31000 cycles

The ISO 31000 framework, at a high level, is a cyclical process that begins with top executives expressing a strong commitment toward risk management and mandating its adoption based upon the aforementioned principles. The framework is then designed and customized. Once implemented, it is monitored and reviewed to enable continual improvement and further customization.

The implementation phase has its own cycle, as shown in Exhibit I-17.

Exhibit I-17: ISO 31000 Implementation Phase Process Framework

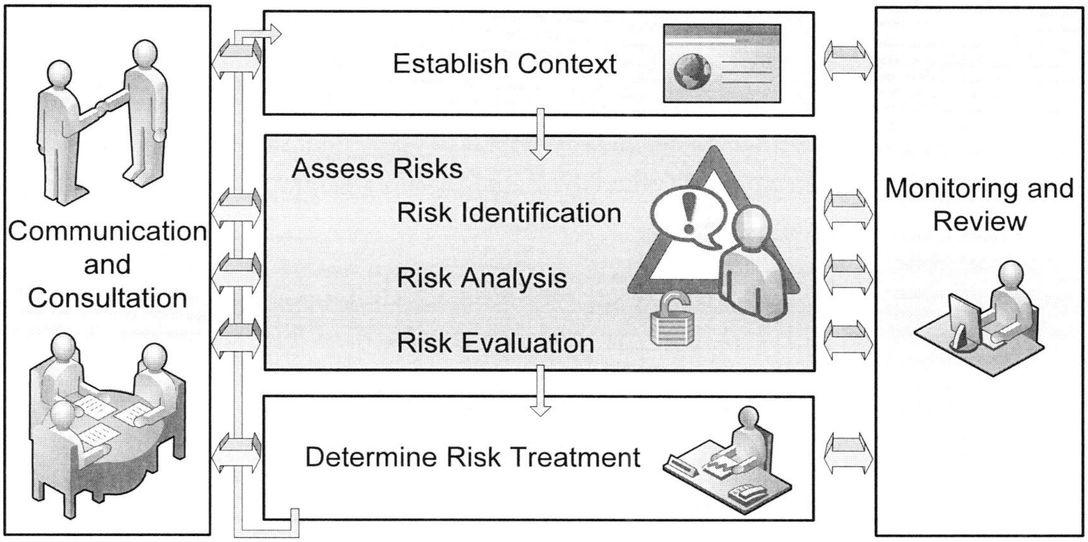

AS/NZS 4360:2004 superseded by AZ/NZS ISO 31000:2009

Note that ISO 31000 has been adopted by the joint Australian/New Zealand standards body as AS/NZS ISO 31000:2009 and that this standard supersedes its AS/NZS 4360:2004 standard for risk management. The rationale for this decision was that ISO 31000 expands upon and further develops the 2004 framework from AS/NZS 4360. It also has a clearer explanation of principles for managing risk. AS/NZS ISO 31000:2009 includes an informative annex that provides information on enhanced risk management attributes.

For more information on ISO 31000:2009, visit the ISO Web site at www.iso.org/iso/home/standards/iso31000.htm. The introduction to AS/NZS ISO 31000:2009 can be viewed at sherq.org/31000.pdf, and the entire standard can be purchased at infostore.saiglobal.com/store.

How the ISO 31000 and COSO ERM frameworks compare

The objectives of the ISO 31000 and COSO ERM frameworks are very similar. Both approaches:

- Attempt to help organizations achieve their business objectives through the effective management of internal and external risks.
- Recognize the importance of embedding a risk management mentality in the culture of the organization.

- Recognize the importance of the "tone at the top" in risk management.
- Are deliberately broad in focus.
- Recognize that risk management is a complex iterative process requiring multidisciplinary skills to implement and manage properly.

While the risk management processes are parallel in nature, there are some subtle differences. One difference is in terminology. ISO 31000:2009 uses "risk treatment," where COSO employs "risk response." Another difference is that the components of COSO ERM and ISO 31000 do not align precisely, as is shown in Exhibit I-18. (Note that some components are repeated to show where they apply to more than one component of the other process.)

Exhibit I-18: Differences Between COSO ERM and ISO 31000 Components

COSO ERM Components	ISO 31000 Components
Internal environment Objective setting	Mandate and commitment Design of framework for managing risk Implementing risk management Communication and consultation Establishing the context
Event identification	Risk identification
Risk assessment	Risk assessment Risk evaluation Risk analysis
Risk response	Risk treatment
Control activities	Monitoring and review of the framework
Information and communication	Communication and consultation
Monitoring	Monitoring and review Continual improvement of the framework

The Turnbull guidance

"Internal Control Guidance for Directors on the Combined Code" was originally published in 1999 in the United Kingdom. The names "Turnbull guidance" or "Turnbull" are more commonly used for it, after Nigel Turnbull, the chairman of the working party that developed the risk management guidance. It was revised in 2005 to reflect developments in the UK and the global arena and to incorporate the experience gained from implementations.

The Turnbull guidance discusses the adoption of a risk-based approach to internal control and the assessment of its effectiveness. It is linked to disclosure requirements of the London Stock Exchange. Turnbull calls for all companies listed on the London Stock Exchange to have implemented a risk management plan for their businesses. While specific implementation details are left to the discretion of a company, the guidance requires that a plan be put in place and actively managed. Similar to requirements imposed by the Sarbanes-Oxley Act of 2002, related US Securities and Exchange Commission (SEC) rules, and American stock exchange rules, noncompliance with Turnbull results in a disclosure in the annual report. In fact, the SEC has identified the Turnbull guidance as a suitable framework for complying with US requirements to report on internal controls over financial reporting as set out in Section 404 of Sarbanes-Oxley and related SEC rules.

However, the Turnbull guidance is not just for stock exchange compliance purposes. The principles to manage risk effectively and embed internal control in business processes make sound business sense for any entity. Organizations may selectively choose principles appropriate to their circumstances. Listed below are some of the key tenets of the Turnbull guidance:

- **A focus on significant risks.** If too many risks are identified, it becomes difficult to identify and manage the significant ones. Turnbull recommends that risk identification focus on those risks that have been identified by senior management as being potentially damaging to the achievement of the organization's objectives.

- **Emphasis on risk management.** Turnbull positions risk management as essential in reducing the probability that organizational objectives are jeopardized by unforeseen events. It promotes proactively managing risk exposures.

- **Ongoing, continuous monitoring of risk and control.** An organization's risk management and internal control strategies and policies must be continuously monitored and fine-tuned in response to changing exposures. A feedback process should be in place to learn from mistakes and to harness potential improvements and risk reductions.

- **Engaging all employees.** Turnbull maintains that all employees have some responsibility for internal control and accountability for achieving organizational objectives. Employees must have the necessary knowledge, skills, information, and authority to establish, operate, and monitor the system of internal control within their sphere of responsibility. They must understand organizational objectives and the industries and markets in which the entity operates as well as the risks it faces.

- **Streamlining risk management databases.** Control should be embedded in the organizational processes. Rather than developing separate risk reporting systems, Turnbull recommends building early warning mechanisms into existing management information systems.

It is apparent through this Turnbull guidance overview that there are many similarities among the risk management approaches presented. And similar to both the COSO ERM and ISO 31000 frameworks, an organization can realize many benefits from adopting the Turnbull risk-based approach. Some of the key ones include the improved ability to:

- Provide objective assurance to the board and management as to the adequacy and effectiveness of organizational risk management and internal control processes.
- Provide advice on effective risk management, especially those issues surrounding the design, implementation, and operation of internal control systems.
- Identify opportunities to save on costs of control and/or to avoid operational and similar losses.
- Reduce the possibility of unwelcome events occurring.

For additional information on the 2005 Turnbull guidance, visit www.ecgi.org/codes/documents/frc_ic.pdf.

Whichever ERM framework is selected by the organization, auditors can help ensure that it is a proactive approach that focuses on anticipating future events and preventing problems from occurring. A best practice is to adopt the same ERM framework for internal audit prioritization that the organization is using to manage risk. As we will see, using a risk-based assessment methodology for the internal audit function sets the stage for this paradigm shift from historical review to future readiness.

Topic 2: Use Market, Product, and Industry Knowledge to Identify New Internal Audit Engagement Opportunities (Level P)

The audit universe

In most organizations, the potential audit universe is vast and includes an organization's operating entities, such as those listed below:

- Accounts payable
- Accounts receivable
- Cash management
- Customer service
- Environmental
- Finance
- General services
- Health and safety
- Human resources
- Inventory management
- Legal
- Locations
- Manufacturing
- Marketing
- Payroll
- Production/operations
- Products and services
- Procurement/purchasing
- Research and development
- Sales and collections
- Security

The audit universe in a risk-based perspective is not defined solely by operating entities. It also encompasses the organization's strategic plan and the controls management has in place to mitigate risks, achieve organizational goals and objectives, and ensure that customer needs are being met. As noted earlier, change is constant and changing environments pose myriad organizational risks. The internal auditor looks to evaluate and report on the efficiency and effectiveness of management governance, ERM, and controls and their likelihood of achieving the established strategic organizational goals and objectives.

The organization's strategic plan

Practice Advisory 2010-1, "Linking the Audit Plan to Risk and Exposures," states: "The audit universe can include components from the organization's strategic plan." Strategic plans are based on some degree of environmental analysis (environmental scanning) that provides intelligence on what is and what will potentially be happening inside and outside the organization. To a degree, every organization is unique and shaped by the environment in which it operates. But organizations generally scan the following areas to understand potential sources of opportunities and threats:

- **Legal factors.** The laws, law-making activities, and litigation promulgated by legal entities (e.g., federal, state, county/provincial, or city laws) and enforced by punishment that can impact the success of an organization's products or services.

- **Regulatory factors.** The regulations, principles, and rules promulgated by agencies under legal entities as well as nongovernmental entities (such as self-regulating bodies and professional societies) designed to control or govern behavior and that can result in some form of punishment or disenfranchisement.

- **Market forces, industry trends, and the competition.** The environment in which the organization competes for employees, customers, goods and services, etc.

- **Stakeholder groups.** The wide array of people, departments, and other organizations that have an investment or interest in the success of or actions taken by the organization.

- **Technology trends and internal capabilities.** Key technologies critical to competitive advantage and base technologies that are necessary to compete as well as the organization's technical strengths, weaknesses, and priorities.

- **Customers.** Assessments of both internal and external customers to understand their needs, preferences, behaviors, expectations, etc.

- **Internal capability analysis.** An assessment of the current infrastructure, employee capabilities, and process capabilities that can support or impede organizational activities.

- **Strength, weakness, opportunity, threat (SWOT) analysis.** The framework to identify and classify the various elements that can help or hinder an organization in the environment in which it operates.

Internal audit consideration of environmental analysis data can surface many potential risks. Practice Advisory 2010-1 tells us: "By incorporating components of the organization's strategic plan, the audit universe will consider and reflect the overall business' objectives. Strategic plans also likely reflect the organization's attitude toward risk and the degree of difficulty to achieving planned objectives. The audit universe will normally be influenced by the results of the risk management process. The organization's strategic plan considers the environment in which the organization operates. These same environmental factors would likely impact the audit universe and assessment of relative risk."

Management and employees

Beyond functional entities and the strategic plan, the potential audit universe in risk-based auditing also includes organizational management and employees. The risk perspective of executives and key operational managers is important, as they are responsible for establishing plans, allocating the resources to achieve the plans, monitoring the activity to achieve the plans, and reviewing results. The employees' perspectives are also important, as they are closest to the business activities. Both parties can offer valuable insights on the risks the organization faces.

Information can be solicited from management and employees in different ways. Exhibit I-19 on the next page provides an overview of the most common methods.

Management requests

Management may have special projects that should be included in the audit universe. Standard 2010.C1, "Planning," states: "The chief audit executive should consider accepting proposed consulting engagements based on the engagement's potential to improve management of risks, add value, and improve the organization's operations. Accepted engagements must be included in the plan."

Special requests can come in many forms and cover tangible and intangible assets. For example, the director of information technology may request an internal audit of a newly installed mainframe computer. Risks could range from physical damage to the mainframe or theft of the hardware and the consequences of such damage or loss.

Regulatory mandates

While some regulations are voluntary, many have the force of law or may be part of the law. An organization may not be able to compete in an industry if it does not comply with regulatory mandates. Some regulatory mandates cut across a variety of industries (such as an environmental protection regulation restricting pollution or occupational safety and health regulations protecting workers). Industries may also have unique regulations (such as aviation, banking, or forestry). Any regulatory mandates that relate to an organization should be considered part of the audit universe.

External business relationships

Organizations may out-source business activities to other organizations, may contract with individuals who act in quasi-employee functions, or may be involved in joint venture partnerships or other relationships that present risks. While the organization may manage those risks through contracts (risk transfer), it retains responsibility and must monitor those risks. "Internal auditing plays a key role in assisting management and validating management's efforts," as noted in the Practice Guide "Auditing External Business Relationships."

Exhibit I-19: Management and Staff Information-Gathering Techniques

Technique	Description	Considerations
Interviews	• A structured discussion between two parties: one representing internal auditing and the other representing a potential engagement client or information source about business risks. • Intended to solicit an unbiased view from the individual being interviewed. • Typically a precursor to focus groups and surveys. **Examples:** • The CAE meets annually with the board chair, the audit committee chair, general counsel, and others who have identified organizational risks and mitigating controls. • Internal audit managers meet with division managers and other managers to gain their perspective on organizational objectives.	• Must be conducted in an objective manner without any preconceptions about the outcome. • Most effective when the interviewer builds rapport early, probes for additional information as necessary, and summarizes throughout to facilitate a substantive discussion. • Generates qualitative information that can be explored further in a focus group or quantified by a survey.
Focus groups	• Small groups of current managers or employees (normally six to 12 people) are invited to participate in a structured discussion facilitated by a representative of the internal audit function. • Usually lasts two to three hours. **Examples:** • The CAE or internal audit manager meets with business unit leaders and facilitates activities where participants compile, discuss, and prioritize risks based on the magnitude and probability of occurrence. Or the group may explore risks articulated in management interviews in greater depth. • A control self-assessment (CSA) meeting may be implemented to get a combined assessment on certain risks and an opportunity to get an organizational evaluation of the process.	• Requires effective planning, clearly defined objectives, and a skilled moderator to maximize the time. • Can include group brainstorming, decision making, and prioritization. • Can incur conformity ("groupthink") if individuals are easily influenced by what others say. • Provides a good foundation for and supplement to quantitative surveys.
Questionnaires/ surveys	A way to quantify management and employee attitudes and perceptions. **Example:** A "top ten" list of risks is compiled from interview and focus group data. Participants are surveyed about their perceptions of the efficiency and effectiveness of internal controls and actions for each risk.	• Typically provides an easy way to obtain information. • Can help to identify serious risks. • May not get honest and/or complete answers; information received may be too general and, therefore, not very useful if people don't take the time to provide thoughtful responses and write out details to any open-ended questions.

Information technology (IT)

IT risks and controls are an important consideration for most organizations and for the CAE to include when identifying the audit universe and developing the annual plan. Results from several IIA external quality assessment reviews reveal that the IT audit plan is one of the weakest links in internal audit activities. Many times, internal auditors simply review what they know or out-source IT auditing to other companies, letting them decide what to audit. GTAG-11, "Developing the IT Audit Plan," can help the CAE and auditors define and understand the IT environment, identify the role of risk assessments in determining the IT audit universe, and formalize the annual IT audit plan.

Other sources

In some organizations, internal assurance functions (e.g., security, quality, health) or external assurance activities (e.g., external auditors, regulators, partners) may be sources of potential engagements. Internal audit may review areas of weakness identified by these assurance functions and may also evaluate the quality of the assurance functions as part of the audit universe.

As we have seen here, the sources for the audit universe are many and varied. The point of this step in risk assessment is to identify a comprehensive list of all potential engagements for further consideration and prioritization.

The importance of gathering qualitative and quantitative data

Gathering comprehensive information from a variety of sources is of paramount importance during risk assessment. The internal auditor should use techniques that solicit both qualitative and quantitative data, as described in Exhibit I-20.

Exhibit I-20: Qualitative and Quantitative Data

Description	Examples	Considerations
Qualitative data		
Subjective, or soft, measures focusing on perceptions and attitudes	• Interviews/walk-throughs • Focus groups • Observations • Meetings	• Allows individuals the opportunity to provide information using their own words • Can identify critical risks and provide insights about organizational priorities • May be open to interpretation
Quantitative data		
Measures derived from concrete, objective criteria	• Studies (e.g., quality and productivity measurement) • Reports (e.g., market share and market share growth, revenue, and profit) • Surveys (e.g., statistical data)	• Provides scorecards, trend data, data that can be benchmarked, or other useful numbers that can be readily averaged • May indicate symptoms rather than causes

Why are both types of data important? Objective criteria are not always applicable when assessing certain risks such as board concerns. Combined, soft and hard data facilitate a more comprehensive understanding of risks facing the organization. This knowledge, in turn, enhances the firm's opportunity to make better business decisions.

Topic 3: Use a Risk Framework to Identify Sources of Potential Engagements (Level P)

Risk frameworks can help an organization filter the audit universe down to selected targets based on the areas of significant risk. Internal auditors can use the risk framework to identify sources of potential engagements. The purpose is to identify new audit areas based on key risks.

The nomenclature for risk categories may vary. But in most models CAEs follow a process that includes risk identification, risk measurement, and risk prioritization. Under COSO ERM, these are the "event identification" and "risk assessment" components. Under ISO 31000, these are the "risk identification," "risk analysis," and "risk evaluation" components.

Risk identification

Risk identification takes a systematic look at the nature of risks and opportunities facing the organization. Risks and opportunities are often grouped as strategic, project/program/process, or operations, as shown in Exhibit I-21.

Exhibit I-21: Types of Organizational Risks (continued on next page)

Description	Sources	Outcomes
Strategic risks		
Reflect elements of the strategic plan	Review of organizational documents such as mission, vision, values, and strategic plan in order to establish a clear understanding of organizational goals and objectives	• Development of matrices that classify strategic risks according to their time horizon so that short-term issues are distinguishable from medium- and long-term issues • Use of creative tools (e.g., brainstorming, multi-voting, what-if scenario analysis) to identify the most significant strategic risks • Determination of which risks are likely to have the greatest impact (e.g., financial impact, asset liquidity, reputation) on the achievement of organizational goals and objectives

Exhibit I-21: Types of Organizational Risks (concluded)

Description	Sources	Outcomes
Project/program/process risks		
Examine specific projects, programs, and processes	Derived from functional areas as well as external customers	Establishment of risk factor criteria (e.g., financial impact, management competence, quality of internal controls, complexity, client/customer satisfaction)
Operations risks		
Day-to-day operational risks to the organization and its stakeholders	• Health • Safety • Physical (environmental) • Security and system functions	Determination of risks to employees, visitors to the organization, and physical assets (e.g., equipment and buildings)

Risk measurement

This step evaluates the potential impact of the risks based on the likelihood and impact of risk occurrence, where likelihood is "the probability that a given event will occur" and impact is "the result, effect, or consequences of an event." The combination of these elements is an assessment of the severity of the risk, or the degree to which the risk will result in a consequence that could materially impact the organization's ability to achieve goals and objectives.

Approaches include:

- Probability estimates (e.g., expected loss or annual loss).
- Risk factor measures (e.g., statistical or subjective).
- Weighted matrices.

Risk measurement scores are then used in risk prioritization.

Risk prioritization

Risk prioritization uses various methods to rank risks and establish the relative strength of each risk and the potential consequences of each. Methods include:

- **Absolute ranking.** Ranks risk management scores and places them in order of magnitude.
- **Relative ranking.** Groups risk measurement scores into natural clusters and assigns relative values such as low, medium, or high.
- **Matrices ranking.** Further analyzes the matrices used to measure risks and consequences and places them in quadrants of low, medium, or high.

Topic 4: Rank and Validate Risk Priorities to Prioritize Engagements in the Audit Plan (Level P)

Solicit potential engagement topics from various sources

Three standards apply when determining potential audit engagement topics.

- Implementation Standard 2010.A1 (Assurance Engagements): The internal audit activity's plan of engagements must be based on a documented risk assessment, undertaken at least annually. The input of senior management and the board must be considered in this process.
- Implementation Standard 2010.A2 (Assurance Engagements): The chief audit executive must identify and consider the expectations of senior management, the board, and other stakeholders for internal audit opinions and other conclusions.
- Implementation Standard 2010.C1 (Consulting Engagements): The chief audit executive should consider accepting proposed consulting engagements based on the engagement's potential to improve management of risks, add value, and improve the organization's operations. Accepted engagements must be included in the plan.

As these standards state, management and board requests should be considered. Regulatory mandates are also applicable.

Current industry or economic situations could be valid sources for potential engagements. For example, in 2007, the subprime mortgage crisis that caused the Great Recession in the United States led to internal audits of organizational mortgage-backed securities and collateralized debt obligations.

Analyze risks

To reduce risk and improve efficiency, the CAE must take a closer look at the risk assessment data. Practice Advisory 2010-1 recommends steps to help ensure that proposed engagements are aligned to organizational objectives: "The CAE prepares the internal audit activity's audit plan based on the audit universe, input from senior management and the board, and an assessment of risk and exposures affecting the organization. Key audit objectives are usually to provide senior management and the board with assurance and information to help them accomplish the organization's objectives, including an assessment of the effectiveness of management's risk management activities."

Analyzing risks involves taking a closer look at the key risks an organization is facing, whether identified by the ERM process, by the board or management, or during consulting engagements. The intent is to better understand the sources and drivers of these risks and to design metrics that will help show when the risk may be occurring or about to occur. Spending more time measuring key risks can also provide additional information on the likelihood or impact of the key risk. Note that analyzing risks is a distinct stage in ISO 31000 but is still part of "risk assessment" in COSO's ERM framework.

Risk source analysis

A root cause analysis for risk starts with analyzing the source of the risk. In other words, where does source of the risk occur? A basic categorization is internal versus external sources.

For risks that relate to internal sources, it is important to identify the specific department, business unit, function, process, or job role that is the true source of the risk. This allows the organization to deploy targeted resources in the correct area. The true source of an internal risk may not be obvious. For example, if an organization is having trouble matching the low price of competitors due to high cost of goods sold, the source may be poor transfer pricing agreements with subsidiaries, a poor cost allocation model that loads too many costs on the key product, or a bottleneck in the production process. Designating the risk source as a sales or marketing problem would be a poor way to address this price risk.

For risks that relate to external sources, the organization can use this information to direct energies in different ways, since the risk cannot necessarily be directly managed and any focus that treats this as an internal risk will likely be ineffective. Instead, the organization can focus on monitoring the external risk, such as a competitor's actions, diligently. Some external actions may also be possible, such as lobbying to change regulations or laws.

Risk driver analysis

Another key step in a root cause analysis is to determine the drivers of the risk. Risk drivers are the forces that address why a risk is occurring, such as a market bubble, an internal control weakness, or poor worker morale. Risk drivers can be broadly categorized as either events that can be specifically identified or as pervasive risks.

Events that can be specifically identified can be tracked and may have a window in which they could occur. This could be a monsoon or hurricane season, a workplace accident or equipment failure, or a market downturn. Pervasive risks are usually one large control deficiency or a number of small control deficiencies that collectively increase the likelihood or impact of a failure. Pervasive problems may also involve a control environment weakness such as a "tone at the top" permissive of ethical violations in pursuit of profits or an inconsistent maintenance schedule for equipment.

Understanding the type of driver can provide important benefits. First, it helps organizations prepare for the risk by illustrating how it will likely develop. Knowing the drivers can help infer what effect the driver is likely to produce so this can be planned for as well. Second, the drivers themselves can be prioritized based on just those drivers most likely to trigger a key risk event or be leading indicators. For example, loss of Internet connectivity will lead to the loss of connection to the accounting department's cloud-based accounting system. This loss can be tolerated for a certain window of time before it creates problems for customers. A specific response can then be designed and tested in advance.

Re-measure key risks and develop metrics

While a broad brush may have been used to measure risks while ranking and prioritizing them, those risks identified as significant can be further measured in terms of impact and likelihood. Organizations may perform sensitivity analyses, create simulations or models, and use other analytical techniques to better understand a risk, for example, in terms of base-case, best-case, and worst-case scenarios. Often organizations use historical data to test these models. The results may lead to identification of key performance indicators, leading economic indicators, or other metrics that can be used to monitor the risk. The results may also be helpful in determining the best risk response and often can show where certain risks can be aggregated or bundled so they can be dealt with using the same response. Other risks will not lend themselves to quantitative analysis, and these can be further analyzed to develop a consensus of opinion regarding their significance, how to measure them, and the appropriate response.

Strategic risk responses

Organizations can choose to manage identified and prioritized risks in a number of different ways, including:

- **Avoidance.** Identifying ways to prevent risk exposure.
- **Reduction** or **control.** Establishing internal controls for reducing the potential negative impact of risk and uncertainty or training employees in how to recognize potential risks and respond to prevent damage and reduce the effects.
- **Sharing** or **transfer.** Sharing or transferring the risk to insurance or to other parties (though a contractual arrangement).
- **Acceptance.** Accepting the risk because a response would not be cost-effective or identifying alternate ways to manage the risk such as establishing contingency plans.

Terminology may vary among organizations. For example, some use the terms "terminate," "treat," "transfer," and "tolerate" to describe the above activities.

CAE assessment of risk responses

Once the organization has selected strategic responses to significant risks, the CAE should balance the quantified risk priorities with the organization's risk response strategy. The CAE makes two main assessments at this point:

- What is the organization's ERM maturity level related to its response?
- What is the residual risk after the risk response is taken into account relative to the organization's risk appetite or tolerance to absorb the risk?

Assess organization's ERM maturity

The maturity level of an organization's ERM processes affects how much weight the CAE should give to a selected risk response. An organization may have the intent—but not the ability—to effectively address a risk. The enabling processes to address risks include people, processes, and technology.

- **People.** People include the leaders of the organization and whether they are developing and communicating strategies and risk appetite clearly and effectively. They also include all persons directly responsible for managing and owning specific risks. The organization must have the proper accountability structures in place, diligent hiring procedures, and training.

- **Processes.** Processes include policies, procedures, and tasks that must be performed as intended as well as audited to ensure that the intended process is executed, efficient, and effective.

- **Technology.** Technology includes information timeliness, availability, completeness, and relevance as well as the security and level of integration of the technology itself. This includes not only information systems but also production line technology and so on.

The organization's relative maturity level in each of these areas for its ERM capabilities will result in an overall organizational maturity level for ERM, as shown in Exhibit I-22 on the next page. (Different sources may use different names for stages.)

Lack of organizational maturity for the ERM function may result in making ERM processes one of the areas to audit in the upcoming audit cycle. The organization's relative level of ERM maturity should be taken into account when assessing the likelihood that a risk response will be adequate. More precisely, CAEs assess the degree of residual risk that they consider to be remaining for each significant risk given the organization's ERM maturity in this area. Residual risk is discussed next.

Exhibit I-22: Assessing the Organization's ERM Maturity Level

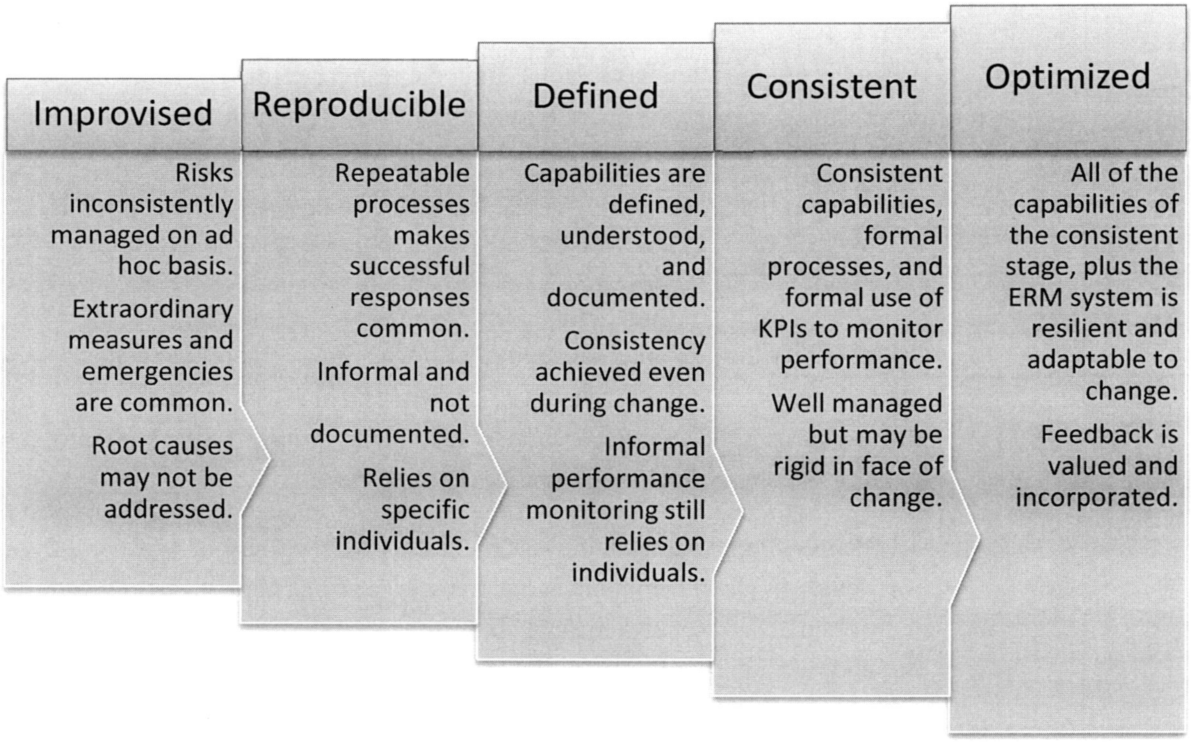

Assess residual risk versus risk appetite

Residual risk is the risk remaining after management takes action to reduce the impact and likelihood of an adverse event, including control activities in responding to a risk. It is contrasted with inherent risk, or the risk derived from the environment without the mitigating effects of internal controls.

ERM professionals may calculate or estimate residual risk, and the CAE can start with the results of this assessment and then make his or her own independent assessment of significant residual risks depending on the organization's ERM maturity level and the CAE's assessment of the strength of relevant controls in the area. If the organization's ERM maturity level is very low or there have been control weaknesses in a given area in the past, the auditor may decide to audit an area based on its inherent risks rather than assuming that the response will perform as expected. When ERM maturity is high and controls appear adequate, it may be sufficient to test the sufficiency and reliability of the risk monitoring techniques. Audit frequency may also be adjusted based on such considerations.

Significant residual and/or inherent risks must also be measured against the organization's risk appetite. A risk response that leaves significant residual risk relative to risk appetite levels will be a higher priority than a risk that has been reduced to below the risk appetite level in a reliable manner, such as the use of insurance from a solvent and reputable insurer. In other words, the CAE should measure the type of risk response and its reliability against the risk appetite and tolerance levels when determining the contents of the annual audit plan. For example, the organization may have chosen a risk acceptance strategy for the possibility of poor returns on a new investment because it has sufficient cash reserves to absorb the loss, but the CAE may determine that more substantive audit techniques are needed to prove that the actual risk impact and likelihood remain within the actual risk tolerance ability and risk appetite policies and procedures.

CAE validation of risk priorities

The CAE needs to make decisions for applying audit function resources based on the significance of risk and exposure related to achievement of organizational strategy and objectives. In validating the risk priorities, in addition to the analysis of risks and responses discussed above, other factors to establish the priority of engagements include financial impact, asset liquidity, management competence, quality of internal controls, degree of change or stability, time of last audit engagement, complexity, employee and government relations, etc.

In conducting audit engagements, methods and techniques for testing and validating exposures should also be reflective of the risk impact and likelihood of occurrence.

For additional information on coordinated approaches applied to leverage synergies between the organization's risk management and internal audit processes, consult Practice Advisory 2010-2, "Using the Risk Management Process in Internal Audit Planning."

Topic 5: Identify Internal Audit Resource Requirements for the Annual Internal Audit Plan (Level P)

As stated in Performance Standard 2030, "Resource Management," "The chief audit executive must ensure that internal audit resources are appropriate, sufficient, and effectively deployed to achieve the approved plan." Interpretation tells us: *"Appropriate refers to the mix of knowledge, skills, and other competencies needed to perform the plan. Sufficient refers to the quantity of resources needed to accomplish the plan. Resources are effectively deployed when they are used in a way that optimizes the achievement of the approved plan."*

Resource management involves consideration of:

- Staffing plans.
- Financial budgets.
- The knowledge, skills, and other competencies of internal audit staff.
- The knowledge, skills, and other competencies required to perform the engagements.
- The number and quality of auditors required.

It is the CAE's responsibility to communicate to senior management and the board what resources are available as well as any resource limitations that could potentially affect the scope of proposed engagements or execution of the engagement work schedule.

Certainly the least desirable course of action if resources are limited would be to eliminate proposed engagements. The CAE should consider alternatives such as co-sourcing to acquire temporary expertise, reassessing how information technology could be employed, or rescheduling engagements to coordinate them with regulatory bodies. The merits of these and other plausible options should be discussed with senior management and the board.

Topic 6: Communicate Areas of Significant Risk and Obtain Approval from the Board for the Annual Engagement Plan (Level P)

Performance Standard 2060, "Reporting to Senior Management and the Board," states, "The chief audit executive must report periodically to senior management and the board on the internal audit activity's purpose, authority, responsibility, and performance relative to its plan. Reporting must also include significant risk exposures and control issues, including fraud risks, governance issues, and other matters needed or requested by senior management and the board."

Getting all stakeholders on the same page with regard to what risks should be considered significant could be contentious, but once agreement has been reached in this area, it will naturally lead to easier acceptance of an audit plan based on those same risk exposures and control issues.

Participate in the engagement selection process

The introduction to this chapter explained how the internal audit activity assists both management and the oversight body (the board or its audit committee) and helps protect an organization from risk exposures. As the discussion of risk-based prioritization has shown, a thorough risk assessment executed in a timely manner should:

- Produce credible results about engagements.
- Establish buy-in through its participatory processes.
- Help management and the oversight body focus on top risks.

One way to ensure that the board and management have a clear understanding of the connection between significant risks and the achievement of business objectives is to link risks to specific processes. These can be processes that could be interrupted by a risk event or a process used to manage and control a risk. Tracing the links between key processes and related risks can help illustrate why the risk is significant and why a specific related process should be audited. A matrix showing significant risks in the columns and processes in the rows (or vice versa) can be used to assess the strength of the correlation and can show where more than one risk could be addressed by one process audit engagement. Strongly correlated risks and processes can be targeted.

A credible assessment should build respect for internal audit recommendations and legitimize the internal audit activity's involvement in the engagement selection process.

Select engagements

Aligning internal audit activities with strategic and operational goals and objectives through an internal audit risk assessment helps to ensure efficient use of internal audit resources while providing management with valuable insights on risk management activities. While risk analysis and assessment are not foolproof, the processes are better than relying on intuition. Educated decisions can be made about the selection of internal audit engagements.

A general rule of thumb for engagement selection is to recommend auditing just the risk management activities for those risks that are rated as high impact but low likelihood, under the assumption that they are low likelihood as a result of these risk management actions. For high to medium impact and high to medium likelihood risks, audit engagement objectives should be to identify the root cause(s) of the increased impact/likelihood if not already known and to produce actionable recommendations for positively influencing the root cause(s) once known.

Communicate and obtain approval of the engagement plan from the board

According to Performance Standard 2020, "Communication and Approval," "The chief audit executive must communicate the internal audit activity's plans and resource requirements, including significant interim changes, to senior management and the board for review and approval. The chief audit executive must also communicate the impact of resource limitations."

Once a risk-based audit plan is developed, the CAE should communicate the plan and resource requirements to senior management and to the appropriate governing body for review and approval. Showing how the plan was developed and the reasons for its development can help to win approval. Key points to address include:

- Why the area should be audited at this time instead of later.
- What the audit objectives are and how this relates to the audit scope.
- How the process is currently being monitored for performance/control.
- Relevant results or ongoing concerns from past audits.
- Relevant current events.
- Proposed, ongoing, or completed changes related to the process or risks.
- What significant new or ongoing risks or root causes the audit is designed to address.
- What resource limitations exist and what out-sourcing or co-sourcing arrangements may be necessary to accommodate them.

Ultimately, the engagement plan should address and support the most effective use of internal audit resources.

A risk assessment process should be conducted annually. But the resulting engagement plan cannot be static. Changes in management direction, objectives, emphasis, and focus as well as other evolving factors such as emerging trends should be reflected by changes to the audit universe and the related annual engagement plan. Frequent (quarterly) updating may be required, and any significant changes should be submitted to the oversight entities for review and approval.

Topic 7: Differentiate between Assurance and Consulting Engagements (Level P)

A further decision point for annual audit planning is whether to treat a particular engagement as an assurance engagement or a consulting engagement. Any given area that can be audited as an assurance engagement could alternately be audited as a consulting engagement or vice versa. It all depends on how it is agreed to be audited during engagement planning. Therefore, most of the types of assurance and consulting engagements listed in the next topics could be adapted for use as the other type if acceptable to the CAE. Decisions on what to audit as an assurance engagement relate to the internal audit function's requirement to provide independence and objectivity. It is a matter of deciding what areas can involve board or management participation on scope and subject matter and what areas must have more segregation of duties to provide the necessary level of independence and objectivity.

Exhibit I-23 defines and compares assurance services and consulting services.

Exhibit I-23: Assurance Services and Consulting Services

Type	Assurance Services	Consulting Services
Definition	An objective examination of evidence for the purpose of providing an independent assessment on governance, risk management, and control processes for the organization; examples may include financial, performance, compliance, system security, and due diligence engagements (*Standards* Glossary).	Advisory and related client service activities, the nature and scope of which are agreed to by the client and which are intended to add value and improve an organization's governance, risk management, and control processes without the internal auditor assuming management responsibility; examples include counsel, advice, facilitation, and training (*Standards* Glossary).
Parties involved	The internal auditor determines the nature and scope of the assurance engagement. Typically, three parties are involved in assurance services: • The person or group directly involved with the process, system, or other subject matter (the process owner) • The person or group making the assessment (the internal auditor) • The person or group using the assessment (the user)	Consulting services generally involve two parties: • The person or group offering the advice (the internal auditor) • The person or group seeking and receiving the advice (the engagement client)
Scope of activities	The internal auditor determines the nature and scope.	The client determines the nature and scope with agreement from the auditor.
Deliverable	Communicate an assessment, opinion, or conclusion of the assurance engagement result.	Advise, counsel, and add value to an organization's governance, risk management, and control processes.

Typical areas for assurance engagements include:

- **Financial assurance.** Providing assurance related to the achievement of one or more financial assertions (existence or occurrence, completeness, valuation and allocation, rights and obligations, presentation, disclosure).

- **Controls assurance.** Providing assurance related to the design and operation of key control activities; controls may be operational, financial, or compliance-related.

- **Information technology (IT).** Providing assurance related to the design and operation of general IT control activities or specific application control activities.

- **Compliance.** Providing assurance related to the design and operation of control activities and procedures in place to assure compliance with laws, regulations, policies, etc.

- **Operations.** Providing assurance related to the effectiveness and efficiency of an organization's operations, including performance and profitability goals and safeguarding resources against loss.

- **Integrated.** Providing assurance related to any combination of the others, for example, a full-scope audit may include assurances on all of the above types of engagements.

An example of a consulting engagement is a management request to immediately review problems at an offshore call center and to report back with recommendations for short- and long-term corrective actions regarding the high volume of customer service complaints. Another consulting engagement example is a due diligence assignment to review the existing control activities of a potential acquisition and report on the efforts required to raise the control activities to the level of the existing organization.

Relationship of assurance and consulting engagements

The view of internal auditing that is incorporated in both the IIA and COSO frameworks is broad enough to encompass internal consulting as well as assurance engagements. Standard 1000.C1 notes, "The nature of consulting services must be defined in the audit charter."

As long as the roles and responsibilities are defined in the audit charter, the internal auditor can perform any number of actions.

Many consulting engagements are special requests from audit clients to help review existing processes that need to be enhanced due to organizational changes, new technology, etc. Many other requests are because of the implementation of new products or services in the organization; internal auditors can give objective consideration of planned activities and procedures.

The auditor engaged in consulting may gain increased knowledge of the organization's processes while not impairing the attribute of objectivity. The internal auditor does not encroach on management's territory. He or she makes suggestions, not decisions.

Internal auditors may, like external auditors, enter into formal engagements with the organization. Formal engagements tend to last a significant amount of time.

Assurance and consulting do not exclude one another, nor do they exclude other kinds of appropriate services that draw upon the discipline of internal auditors. Consulting engagements often derive from assurance engagements. (For example, a performance assurance audit could evolve into a consulting engagement to devise improved performance measures.) The reverse is also true.

In all situations, a consulting engagement should not be conducted in an attempt to circumvent assurance engagement requirements such as the need to provide an opinion at the end of an engagement. This is consistent with the IIA's Code of Ethics. On the flip side—if deemed appropriate—services once conducted as an assurance engagement may be performed as a consulting engagement. However, such consulting activities should be coordinated with other internal audit assurance activities as well as external audit activities to minimize redundancy as per Standard 2050, "Coordination."

Topic 8: Conduct Assurance Engagements (Level P)

An assurance engagement has three parts:

- **Planning.** During this phase, the engagement objectives and scope are established. The auditing team seeks to understand more fully the process being audited. This includes the function's business objectives, its assertions (the accomplishments it reports), the risks that are unique to the process, and the controls that have been designed to manage these risks.

Based on this information and an assessment of the adequacy of the controls, the team develops a plan for testing the controls and a work program that lists specific audit procedures. The team identifies resources and expertise required to implement the auditing plan; this may include external resources. Work is assigned to team members, and a schedule is prepared.

- **Performance.** During this phase, the auditing team gathers evidence, evaluates data, and develops observations (or findings) and recommendations (or corrective actions).

- **Communication.** If necessary, the auditing team will bring certain critical issues to management's attention immediately, so that prompt corrective actions can be taken. The team reviews a draft report with management to clarify conclusions and recommendations. Final reports are then distributed to the designated parties.

Assurance engagements can be conducted for a variety of purposes. Some focus on assessing major areas of controls (governance, operations, financial reporting). Some focus on the efficiency, effectiveness, and compliance of certain business processes.

This topic discusses the following types of assurance audits in greater detail. (Note again that any of these could be alternately designed as a consulting engagement.)

- Control self-assessment
- External business relationships
- Quality
- Due diligence
- Security
- Privacy
- Performance
- Operational
- Financial
- Compliance

For each type of audit, the following aspects are discussed:

- Objectives
- Stakeholders
- Audit team composition
- Risks
- Audit methods
- Controls
- Evidence (or data to be gathered and analyzed)

Control self-assessment (CSA)

In 1987, the internal audit team for Gulf Canada Resources Ltd. developed a new approach to auditing called control self-assessment (CSA), now also referred to as control/risk self-assessment, or CRSA. This experiment revealed that a broader approach, based upon employee self-assessment workshops that were facilitated by senior internal auditors, resulted in more honest disclosures concerning significant factors affecting the success or failure of the organization. Further, the workshops created a sense of commitment to improving performance.

Sawyer's Internal Auditing defines CSA as: "A process whereby employee teams and management, at local and at executive levels, continuously maintain awareness of all material factors affecting the likelihood of achieving the organization's objectives, thereby enabling them to make appropriate adjustments. To promote independence, objectivity, and quality within the process, as well as effective governance, it is desirable that internal auditors are involved in the process and that they independently report results to senior management and board committees."

CSA is a useful and efficient approach for managers and internal auditors to collaborate in assessing and evaluating control procedures. In its purest form, CSA integrates business objectives and risks with control processes.

Objectives

Although CSA practitioners use a number of differing techniques and formats, most implemented programs share some key features and objectives. An organization that uses self-assessment will have a formal, documented process that allows management and work teams who are directly involved in a business unit, function, or process to participate in a structured manner for the purpose of:

- Identifying risks and exposures.
- Assessing the control processes that mitigate or manage those risks.

- Developing action plans to reduce risks to acceptable levels.
- Determining the likelihood of achieving the business objectives.

Stakeholders

Stakeholders to a CSA include the board and senior management in their monitoring and oversight roles; internal auditors in oversight, analysis, and interpretation roles; and the managers and work teams directly involved in a business unit, function, or process to be audited using CSA. These latter stakeholders participate directly in the CSA process. Other stakeholders may include persons or functions that provide inputs to the process, those affected by the process, or those affected by or who use its outputs, which could include other internal users or external customers, regulators, and society.

Audit team composition

The internal auditor's role in CSA varies widely between two extremes:

- Intense involvement, with internal audit undertaking to sponsor, design, implement, and effectively own the process; conduct training; supply facilitators, scribes, and reporters; and orchestrate participation of management and work teams
- Minimal involvement, with internal audit serving as an interested party, consultant, and verifier of the team's evaluations

Depending on the level of involvement, auditors should be alert to anything that will affect their objectivity. Standard 1120 notes, "Internal auditors must have an impartial, unbiased attitude and avoid any conflict of interest."

In most programs, internal audit's investment in the organization's CSA efforts is somewhere between the two extremes described above. As the level of internal audit's involvement in the CSA program and individual workshop deliberations increases, the chief audit executive should monitor the objectivity of the internal audit staff, take steps to manage that objectivity (if necessary), and augment internal audit testing to ensure that bias or partiality do not affect the final judgments of the staff.

Using a CSA in addition to traditional audit methods and practices does not change the responsibilities themselves. Rather, it shifts some of the responsibilities to other personnel such as client work teams.

Exhibit I-24 illustrates some of the differences associated with CSA audit team composition.

Exhibit I-24: Roles and Responsibilities

Responsibilities	Traditional Approach	CSA Approach
Setting business objectives	Management	Management
Assessing risks	Management	Management
Adequacy of internal controls	Management	Management
Evaluating risks and controls	Auditors	Work teams
Reporting	Auditors	Work teams
Validating evaluation of risks and controls	Auditors	Auditors
Objectives used	Audit's	Management's

Source: *Control Self-Assessment: A Practical Guide* by Larry Hubbard.

Risks

Risks related to CSA start with the risk that the process is being conducted in a manner unlikely to reveal significant risks. This can occur because participants either fail to contribute in a meaningful way, such as by failing to fill out open answer fields, or because participants could include some form of bias such as describing how a process or control is supposed to be done rather than how it is actually being done. Therefore the CSA process may itself be the subject of an audit, and a distinction should be made between an audit of the CSA process and the use of CSA as an audit tool within an engagement. For example, an audit of the CSA process could reveal ways to structure questionnaires so that they reduce the risks of low information or bias on the part of respondents. An audit that uses CSA as a tool may include the risk that this is not the most efficient or effective tool that could be included in the mix of tools used. For example, perhaps a walk-through would be a better use of resources.

Audit methods

Several principles seem to underlie valid approaches to control self-assessment:

- "Control" is a broad framework that integrates all the factors that bear upon achievement of an organization's objectives, with the people in an organization being the most significant factor. This perception parallels the findings of the Treadway Commission and the philosophical underpinnings of COSO.
- The auditor cannot adequately assess such broad-based controls alone. CSA is unique among audit approaches in presuming that an adequate

assessment of controls requires contributions from all who perform the relevant tasks. This is a major departure from traditional practice.

- Measurement is a necessary but not sufficient basis for control assessment. In the end, judgment has the final say in assessment, not statistical precision.

Although there are many approaches to control self-assessment, organizations often use COSO or CoCo (Criteria of Control) models to provide a control framework for CSA training sessions and workshops.

There are three major methods that are especially significant:

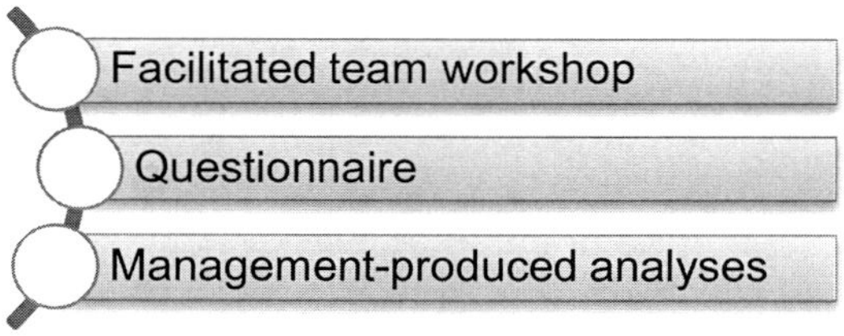

Facilitated team workshop approach
Facilitated team workshops gather information from work teams representing different levels of the business unit or function. Facilitation may be provided either by the client or by internal audit staff.

Categories of workshops include the following:

- **Objective-based** workshops focus on the best way to accomplish a business objective. Teams identify controls currently being used and then identify any remaining risks. The goal is to determine if the controls are working effectively.

- **Risk-based** workshops focus on identifying the risks of achieving an objective. Teams identify the risks or roadblocks to success and then determine if the controls are adequate for mitigating these risks.

- **Control-based** workshops focus on how well current controls are working. In this approach, the facilitator identifies the controls and key risks, not the participants. The goal is to determine if the controls are working the way management intended them to.

- **Process-based** workshops focus on selected activities that are elements of a process, usually a series of related activities with a beginning and an end, such as the various steps in purchasing or product development. The goal is to analyze, revise, or verify the effectiveness of a particular process.

Questionnaire approach

The survey form of CSA utilizes a questionnaire that tends to ask mostly simple yes/no or have/have not questions that are carefully written to be understood by the target recipients. Surveys are often used if the desired respondents are too numerous or widely dispersed to participate in a workshop. They are also preferred if the culture in the organization may hinder open, candid discussions in workshop settings or if management desires to minimize the time spent and costs incurred in gathering the information.

Control Self-Assessment: A Practical Guide by Larry Hubbard lists some factors to consider when creating a questionnaire:

- Use the recipient's language.
- Use one topic per question.
- Use words with clear meaning to the recipients.
- Ask easy-to-answer questions first.
- Keep the questionnaire short and simple.
- Address the questionnaire in a personal manner.
- Personally distribute and collect the survey.
- Use the questionnaire as a conversation tool in an interview.

Management-produced analyses approach

This form of self-assessment covers most other approaches by management groups to produce information about selected business processes, risk management activities, and control procedures. The analysis is often intended to reach an informed and timely judgment about specific characteristics of control procedures and is commonly prepared by a team in a staff or support role. The internal auditor may synthesize this analysis with other information to enhance the understanding about controls and to share the knowledge with managers in business or functional units as part of the organization's CSA program.

Hubbard provides some examples of management-produced analyses:

- A questionnaire developed and administered by management to support an opinion about internal controls required by a law or regulation such as the FDIC Improvement Act
- A discussion among senior financial management to support the annual representation letter required by external accountants
- An investigation into the reasons why a particular control breakdown or fraud occurred
- A review of the internal control implications of a new system being developed or the combination of business units/organizations

Management-produced analyses are not used as often as workshops or questionnaires in the CSA framework.

Controls

CSA can result in the following types of improvements to controls:

- People in business units become trained and experienced in assessing risks and associating control processes with managing those risks and improving the chances of achieving business objectives.
- Informal, "soft" controls are more easily identified and evaluated.
- People are motivated to take ownership of the control processes in their units, and corrective actions taken by the work teams are often more effective and timely.
- The entire objectives-risks-controls infrastructure of an organization is subject to greater monitoring and continuous improvement.
- Internal auditors become involved in and knowledgeable about the self-assessment process by serving as facilitators, scribes, and reporters for the work teams and as trainers of risk and control concepts supporting the CSA program.
- The internal audit activity acquires more information about the control processes within the organization and can leverage that additional information in allocating their scarce resources so as to spend a greater effort in investigating and performing tests of business units or functions that have significant control weaknesses or high residual risks.
- Management's responsibility for the risk management and control processes of the organization is reinforced, and managers will be less tempted to abdicate those activities to specialists such as auditors.
- The primary role of the internal audit activity will continue to include the validation of the evaluation process by performing tests and the expression of its professional judgment on the adequacy and effectiveness of the whole risk management and control system.

Evidence

The evidence that may be derived from self-assessment methodologies will vary depending on the objectives and methods of assessment. However, CSA audit evidence will typically be qualitative and subjective. Therefore, analysis should highlight areas of sufficient consensus among a sufficient number of respondents to remove the effects of low-information responses or bias from the evidence. Statistical methods can be used to determine when certain responses have statistical significance.

Audits of external business relationships

The IIA Practice Guide "Auditing External Business Relationships" explains that "'external business partners,' 'extended relationships,' and 'contractual relationships' are among the numerous names by which today's organizations define their external business relationships." This group includes joint venture partners, out-sourced service providers, agents, contract workers, vendors, franchisees, etc.

When contemplating the internal audit activity's external business relationship (EBR) responsibilities, consider the following:

- Organizations have multiple EBRs that satisfy a number of business requirements.
- Each relationship generates risks.
- It is management's responsibility to manage these risks and achieve the benefits of the relationship.
- Internal auditing plays an important role in helping management and validating their efforts.

Audits of EBRs often take the form of contract assurance. A contract is an agreement between parties, with terms and conditions that describe the agreement and constitute a legal obligation.

Objectives

The Practice Guide on EBRs states:

> Internal auditors need to understand all the elements associated with EBRs, from initiating a relationship, contracting and defining a relationship, procurement, managing and monitoring the continued relationship (including control environment considerations of objectivity and independence of those responsible for managing and monitoring), and finally discontinuing the relationship. After understanding the expectations of both parties, along with the appropriate processes to manage and monitor the relationship, the internal auditor develops an appropriate internal audit program with relevant audit objectives for internal audits of external relationships. In addition, internal audit procedures may include elements of evaluating adherence to (and compliance with) contractual terms to determine whether monetary and non-monetary obligations are met.

Conversely, third parties and independent parties may audit the organization for the same purposes.

Stakeholders

Stakeholders to audits of third parties include the organization and the third party, but specific individuals responsible for approving and signing contracts as well as for managing the relationship and monitoring and enforcing contract compliance need to be specified in each organization. Other stakeholders include internal auditors, legal counsel, and individuals responsible for providing inputs to or receiving outputs from the third party under contract. Courts of law may be considered another stakeholder, since this is the ultimate forum for interpreting contract language and compliance.

Audit team composition

Internal audits of EBRs may take the form of an audit of just that relationship or of an overall process that includes some organizational processes and EBR processes. It is important that the audit team possess some understanding of the organization to be audited, including its operating environment, business model, organizational structure, strategic goals, risks, and key controls. On-site audit staff may be needed to achieve this understanding. The CAE can decide to rely on the work of the EBR's internal auditors if he or she determines that this work is independent, objective, competent, and on topic.

The audit team should be composed of individuals who have some experience with auditing contracts, but as this is an increasingly common requirement for internal auditing, it is likely that the requisite experience level is available on staff. Including a team member with extensive legal experience may not be necessary if the team has access to or includes a lawyer to provide examples of standardized contract language, perform legal reviews, and provide advice as needed.

Risks

General EBR risks

Risks for external business relationships include all of the risks of the business process that is being out-sourced, since the end result is still the organization's responsibility and the organization will be held responsible for the actions of its partners and perhaps even the partners of those partners. Contracts can help transfer some of this risk, but other risks such as reputation risk cannot be transferred.

From a supplier's perspective, there is a risk that the buyer could attempt to create an unfair business relationship in contracts, which is more likely when working with large organizations with strong purchasing power. Unfair treatment of vendors may provide only a short-term gain for the buyer because that supplier may not be able to sustain operations if it is unprofitable. This can create supply instability.

Organizations monitor and manage EBR risks, and failure to do so properly is another risk. Other risks revolve around the process of finding the most appropriate partners, establishing controls over partners and contract management, contract compliance auditing, and customer and supplier relationship management. These are the risks of having ineffective, inefficient, or negative business relationships. For example, an EBR could violate laws or regulations or misrepresent organizational values. Internal auditors can perform due diligence audits at the start of a relationship to determine the risks of the EBR misrepresenting the organization's values.

Another risk is that not all EBRs are formally arranged and documented. For example, a procurement professional could have a relationship with an unofficial supplier that weakens the official purchasing contract relationships. Poor partner accounting or reporting are other risks, which could impact the organization's required accounting (e.g., uncollected revenues) and reporting (e.g., unable to verify if a certain toxic substance is found in supplier subcomponents).

Internal auditors also have a role to play in verifying that the EBR has sufficient and effective insurance to address insurable risks. This may include workers' compensation, liability to the public or of professionals, and vehicle insurance. When partnerships are formed, there is a risk that not all partners will be included in the insurance or that it may not be in effect in certain countries. Another risk is that the actions of one partner could void the insurance of another partner. Also, insurance could expire after contracts are signed, so there may be an ongoing need to receive insurance certificates as evidence.

EBRs may have conflicts of interest such as also working with a competitor. A control for this risk is to ensure that the EBR reports any actual, potential, or perceived conflicts of interest. Requiring such disclosures can allow some relationships to continue if it is within the organization's risk tolerance level.

Intellectual property (IP) is also at risk in any EBR relationship in which the organization must share confidential information. Clear contracts can reduce the risks of theft of IP or the associated revenue streams, but the contracts may not be enforceable in some countries. Contracts can be designed to share the risk of poor IP control with the EBR, such as a mutual loss of revenue.

Contract-specific EBR risks

A major risk of contracts is the risk of lawsuits related to perceived contract breach on the part of one party or the other. Major misunderstandings occur when contracts are worded in a way that allows product or service requirements to be interpreted differently by different parties. Lawsuits are expensive and even a successful outcome may be more costly than the benefit gained. They can also result in significant delays or damage to reputation.

Contracts are classified in a variety of ways, and each of the following classifications can also be used to describe some inherent risks:

- **Express and implied.** An express contract is one in which the terms are expressed verbally, either orally or in writing. Implied contracts are not expressed in words. An informal verbal agreement can be as binding and legally valid as a written contract. The risk is that an organization can be found to have unwittingly entered into an express or implied contract.

- **Bilateral and unilateral.** A bilateral contract is most common and is one in which both parties make a promise. In unilateral contracts, one party makes a promise (such as an insurance or reward contract). Risks involve being liable for the performance of promised work that is more costly than the agreed-upon payment or that cannot be supplied, such as in the case of a disaster; receiving products or services of unacceptable quality; or the other party defaulting on or delaying delivery or payment. Other risks specific to particular contract types are discussed later in this topic.

- **Void, voidable, and unenforceable.** Void contracts are contracts that are considered never to have come into existence (such as being based on an illegal purpose). A voidable contract is one in which one of the parties has the option to terminate the contract (such as a contract with a minor). An unenforceable contract is one in which neither party may enforce the other's obligations (if it violates the statute of frauds, for example). The risks here involve developing a contract that is void or unenforceable. One control for this risk involves including contract language to the effect that if one element is found to be unenforceable, the rest of the contract remains in force. (Legal wording will differ.) Voidable contracts should be entered into knowingly and willingly rather than being a loophole.

Audit methods

Audit methods include audits of certification to standards and audits of contracts with third parties.

Audits of certification to standards

Audits of certification to standards can be performed to ensure that partners have the proper quality controls, corporate social responsibility policies, or other standards. Certification requires testing by an accredited third-party testing organization. Internal auditors can provide assurance but not certification.

Statement on Standards for Attestation Engagements (SSAE) No. 16 is an example of an independent audit for certification to standards. Developed by the American Institute of Certified Public Accountants (AICPA), SSAE 16 is widely recognized as authoritative guidance that allows service organizations to disclose their control activities and processes to their customers and their customers' auditors in a uniform reporting format. In other words, the organization contracts with an independent accounting and auditing firm to perform an audit in accordance with SSAE 16 and is able to produce the certification document for multiple parties that want assurance rather than being audited by all of them.

Another type of independent audit is for certification to standards developed by organizations such as the International Standards Organization. These audits are performed by registered auditors whose task is to ensure that the organization conforms to the relevant standards, such as ISO 9000 or ISO 14000.

Audits of contracts

Organizations use contracts for a variety of products and services, including capital construction projects and out-sourcing of non-core-competency service or product requirements such as human resources, maintenance services, or IT equipment repair. Evaluating the soundness of these contracts is an increasingly important aspect of an internal auditor's job. Appropriate contracts will help ensure that an organization successfully meets its strategic objectives and avoid the risks associated with excessive costs, project delays, and quality issues.

A valid contract typically requires the following elements:

- Mutual agreement—There must be an express or implied agreement. There must be evidence that the parties understand and agree to the essential details, rights, and obligations of the contract.
- Consideration—Something of value must be exchanged by both parties, such as cash, goods, or a promise to do something.
- Competent parties—The parties must have the capacity to understand the terms of the contract. Minors and mentally disabled people do not have the capacity to form a contract.
- Proper subject matter—The contract must have a lawful purpose.
- Mutual right to remedy—Both parties must have an equal right to remedy a breach of terms by the other party.

While a contract does not need to explicitly state these elements to be enforceable (e.g., a verbal contract), internal auditors can ensure that these elements do exist to reduce the risk of a contract being successfully contested.

Rather than auditing every page of a contract (much of which will be a waste of time, as the legal language can get quite lengthy), a best practice is to begin by determining audit objectives and then to search the contract for expected clauses and details related to those objectives. Although each type of contract has its own set of risks and advantages, the common factor is that the auditor is typically looking for instances of poor control over costs for people, material, equipment, and supplies. Control over results is always important. Control over processes and methods may also be warranted in some cases, such as a contract designed to enforce corporate social responsibility policies.

Contracts fall into general categories. The following types are discussed next.

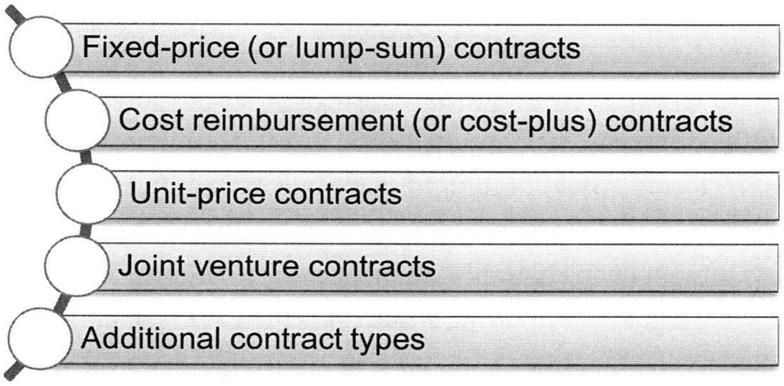

Fixed-price (lump-sum) contracts

A fixed-price contract (also called a lump-sum contract) requires a contractor to successfully perform the contract and deliver supplies or services for a price agreed to up front. A firm fixed-price contract is appropriate for supplies and services that can be described in sufficient detail to ensure that both parties completely understand the contract requirements and the inherent risks associated with performing the contract as written.

Fixed-price contracts often include:

- Economic price adjustment factors to allow for industries where costs fluctuate frequently either up or down.
- Various incentives that can be used to reward good performance or to impose provisions to deduct for poor performance.

- Re-pricing provisions that permit issuing an order on a fixed-price basis and allow for revisiting the reasonableness of that pricing later during the contract performance.
- A specified level of effort.

Clauses such as these can be used to reduce the risks of entering into an unfair contract or a contract that becomes unfair over time as economic conditions change. These contracts work well and are commonly used if the work required is uncomplicated and is completed as agreed upon. In these cases, there is little reason for an audit of the contract.

Sometimes these contracts are very complex. In these cases, which most often involve a change of scope and additional expenses, the contracts may be modified while the work is occurring. If there is a change, the additional cost may be borne by the hiring organization, but who this risk is transferred to (or shared with) must be specified in the contract.

The major risk of using fixed-price contracts is of receiving inferior-quality goods or services. If the contract is not reasonably explicit regarding expectations of quality, the contractor could substitute materials of lower quality. Detailed acceptance criteria, possibly specifying specific materials to be used, are often necessary to allow later enforcement of contract rights. Some of the other areas of risks that an internal auditor may be asked to review in a fixed-price contract include:

- Inadequate competition.
- Inadequate insurance and bond coverage.
- Certification of completion before work has actually been completed.
- Charges for equipment not received or activities not completed.
- Escalation clauses (provision for increasing charges to reflect specified conditions—inflation, for instance).
- Authorization for extras and revisions.
- Overhead expenses charged separately.
- Change orders.
- Inadequate inspection relative to specifications.

Cost reimbursement (cost-plus) contracts

In a project where there are numerous unknown factors, the most economical way of handling the difficulties of pricing the project is a cost reimbursement contract. In a cost reimbursement contract, also called a cost-plus contract, the contractor is reimbursed for any additional costs above what was specified. These additional costs are usually based on the initial costs plus a fixed fee or a fee based on a percentage of costs. If the contract calls for a fee based on a percentage, there is usually an incentive for the contractor to escalate costs, which is, obviously, a risk for an organization.

This type of contract places the least cost and performance risk on the contractor and requires the contractor only to use his or her "best efforts" to complete the contract. It is appropriate when the uncertainties of performance will not permit a fixed price to be estimated with sufficient accuracy to ensure that a fair and reasonable price is obtained.

The following are cost reimbursement contracts:

- Cost type—Involves payment of all incurred costs within a predetermined total estimated cost.
- Cost sharing—The organization and the contractor agree to split the cost of performance in a predetermined manner. No fee is given.
- Cost plus fixed fee—Allows for payment of all incurred costs within a predetermined amount plus an agreed-upon fee that will not change.
- Cost plus incentive fee—Provides for adjustment of the fee (either up or down) using a predetermined formula based on the total allowable costs in relation to total targeted costs.
- Cost plus award fee—Provides for negotiation of a base fee with an award fee that can be given based on an evaluation by the organization of the contractor's performance and cost control.

The last two cost reimbursement contract types require considerable monitoring and are usually reserved for the larger dollar value, more visible procurements or capital expenditures.

Significant risks of cost reimbursement contracts include being overcharged beyond the market value of the good or service received or being charged for goods that were not actually delivered. Common controls for these risks are to allow for payment of all incurred costs within a predetermined ceiling that can be allocated to the contract, are allowable within cost standards, and are reasonable. This cost ceiling is a key control that should be audited to ensure that such contracts cannot be used to overcharge or underdeliver to the organization.

The following are other risks for auditors to consider when auditing cost reimbursement contracts:

- Direct billing of overhead costs
- Inadequate cost controls on the contractor's part and no effort to obtain best prices

- Unreasonable charges for contractor-owned equipment
- Excessive hiring
- Excess billing over contractor costs
- Failure to pass along discounts, refunds, salvage, etc.
- Duplication of effort between headquarters and field offices
- Inadequate job site supervision, inspection, etc.
- Inadequate communication and follow-up from HQ
- Unreliable cost accounting and reporting
- Billing supervision as labor in violation of contract
- Idle rented equipment
- Poor work practices
- Poor quality
- Extravagant use or early arrival of material and supplies
- Excessively high standards for materials or equipment
- Poor physical protection of materials or equipment
- Lack of control over employees in regard to absences and overtime
- Negligence that raises costs

Unit-price contracts

In unit-price contracts, a price is agreed upon for each unit of work. These contracts work best for projects in which the contractor produces a large number of identical products or services. In these cases, the total cost can be calculated by multiplying the per-unit price by the number of units, such as yards of concrete poured or number of brochures printed.

The following risks are important for the auditor to consider:

- Excessive progress payments
- Improper reporting of units completed
- Prices unrelated to actual costs
- Improper changes to the original contract
- Unauthorized escalation adjustments
- Inaccurate field records
- Inaccurate extension of unit prices

Joint venture contracts

Joint venture contracts are often based on cost-, revenue-, or profit-sharing or profit-and-loss-sharing arrangements or combinations thereof. The engagement objective is often to evaluate compliance with agreement terms and conditions, which include financial and nonfinancial aspects.

Financial terms may include:

- Reliability of cost allocation and billing systems and data.
- Reliability of revenue management and distribution.

Nonfinancial terms may include:

- Safeguarding of assets, including information.
- Compliance with laws, regulations, and contractual obligations with third parties such as CSR policies and procedures.
- Reputation and/or brand management.
- Reliability of nonfinancial information.
- Reasonability of budgets and forecasts.
- Appropriate governance activities.

Additional contract types

Additional contract types include:

- Labor-hour/time and materials—Pay at fixed rates for services rendered and for materials at cost plus a handling fee.
- Letter contracts—A preliminary instrument that permits a contractor to begin work when all of the contract terms and conditions have not been agreed upon. This type of contract is used only in circumstances of unusual and compelling urgency.
- Indefinite delivery contracts—These contracts provide for delivery of goods or services upon the issuance of a delivery or task order as needs arise.

Controls

When reviewing contracts for risks, weaknesses, and control issues, it is important to keep the following items in mind:

- Price competition, price analysis, and cost analysis
- Type and complexity of contract requirements
- Urgency of the contract
- Contract period, payment terms, and delivery dates
- Cost-sharing arrangements
- Property rights
- Adequacy of contractor's technical capability and financial responsibility
- Performance measurement methodology, project reporting, and work acceptance
- Audit rights
- Dissolution procedures
- Change orders, cost accounting, billing, insurance coverage, and substantial completion terms

- Regulatory compliance
- Documentation requirements

Selecting the appropriate type of contract is important, and internal auditors should review the basis for selection and advise management regarding any inconsistencies with organizational goals, strategies, and objectives. However, contract provisions or clauses largely determine the success of a project or service.

A primary set of provisions is often called the scope of services or scope of work. These provisions spell out what the contractor is expected to deliver. Any detail left undefined could be exploited by a contractor to reduce its costs at the organization's expense. Another risk is that the contractor could add billable work that was not wanted or expected but fits within a vaguely worded contract such as "for consulting services." This amounts to unauthorized scope creep. Properly documenting invoices received from the EBR partner to show what requests are in and out of scope is one control. The scope should also be documented in terms of what will and will not be done along with acceptable minimum quality levels and maximum cost. The scope and quality should be defined and measured using acceptance criteria that both parties know in advance. Ensuring that these acceptance criteria are tested against final deliverables prior to official acceptance sign-off is a critical control. A specific individual should fulfill this responsibility.

There may also be a time frame associated with acceptance. Lack of a response prior to the deadline could indicate automatic acceptance, so it is important to know key deadlines and expectations for those deadlines. Warranties and guarantees may also expire, and product/service audits or other reviews should be conducted in time to ensure the ability to exercise such rights if needed. Ensuring that such dates exist in the organization's contracts with customers is necessary to limit liabilities related to rework, repair, return, and replacement.

Other critical contract provisions that should be looked for are a clear duty to report interim key performance indicators on a set schedule and a link between a specific compensation payment structure and specific deliverables. Contracts that authorize periodic payments without timely KPI reporting and hand-off of specific deliverables create risks of being overcharged or the other party missing deadlines with the organization having no legal recourse.

Auditing other contract clauses involves determining the existence of the proper clauses and the completeness of the legal language within each clause. The clauses to look for should be based on audit objectives. For example, if the contract with a business partner does not contain a right-to-audit clause, then internal auditors may not be allowed to audit this third party's documentation or relationship. A best practice is to word a right-to-audit clause in a way that allows internal auditors to address broader relationship risks as well as the right to audit books and records.

To audit for completeness, internal auditors compare the language of a contract clause against a representative source document that contains the official wording of the clause as reviewed and approved by legal counsel. Any variations from the standard wording should have had justification and legal review. The legal department may also directly review contracts as part of an audit team. These reviews may address compliance with laws and regulations, ethical standards, and organizational values.

Another control common to contracts is version control. Complex contracts go through multiple versions tracked by a contract date. The internal auditor needs to ensure that he or she is auditing the most current version and that relevant parties are using the latest contract. When dates are used for deadlines in contracts, including when the contract becomes and ceases to be in force, it is important that the internal auditor verify that all dates remain valid. For example, a delay in contract signing could result in unrealistic dates.

Finally, important contract clauses involve the right to terminate the contract. If the contract can be terminated only for poor performance, it may require that the organization remain in a contract that is not ideal or to determine a specific cause to cite, which could be contested. To avoid this possibility and the possible damages to a relationship that may need to be renewed in the future, organizations can specify a "right to terminate for convenience" or similar clause that allows either party to terminate the contract without cause, given sufficient notice. Internal auditors can include this as a recommendation for certain contracts, but only if the desire to be able to end the contract is greater than the business need for that contract to remain in force until it expires.

Evidence

Audit evidence from business relationship or contract analysis can help reveal unfair business practices, fraud, ineffective controls, ineffective monitoring, or noncompliance risks. Recommendations reflect constructive changes to increase fairness and controls and limit risks. Recommendations may apply to a contract currently in force, which may require renegotiation for changes, and/or to future contracts in general, which may involve changing standardized templates, policies, and procedures. In either case, getting legal review and approval of recommended changes is a critical control step.

Audit reports for EBR often have two formats:

- The audit engagement report to senior management and the board, following the guidance provided in the IPPF
- A report to the organization being audited (The CAE should develop appropriate reporting protocols for such reviews, in consultation with management, since management is responsible for handling the business relationship.)

Quality audit engagements

Auditors measure an organization's current operations against a set of standards or controls. Essentially, they assess the quality of the organization's controls and determine if controls are being updated and enhanced as organizational activities are changed, industrial practices are changed, and technology is enhanced through time.

Objectives

The objective of a quality audit engagement is to help organizations increase their quality and productivity by providing assurance that an organization's quality plans are such that, if followed, the desired quality will be attained. This may take the form of conformance to an organized quality system such as total quality management. The term "total quality management" (TQM) was first used by the US Naval Air Systems Command to describe the Japanese-style management approach to improving quality. The military was looking for a method that would provide them with the ability to improve their quality system and identify areas for corrective action.

A related objective is to provide assurance that the internal audit function is functioning at the desired quality level for the board and management. This type of assurance is discussed in Chapter B, Topic 7.

Stakeholders

As with TQM, all members of the organization must be involved for the organization to achieve long-term success, customer satisfaction, and positive benefits for its members and society at large. However, specific persons should be responsible and accountable for specific quality aspects. Management and the board are ultimately responsible for control and oversight.

Audit team composition

The audit team should include an internal auditor team member with formal training in the organization's quality control system, such as TQM or Six Sigma. Working closely with stakeholders directly responsible for the relevant quality controls is also necessary.

Risks

Risks of poor quality are often called the costs of quality. Costs of quality are the activities associated with the prevention, identification, repair, and rectification of poor quality. They also include the opportunity costs from lost production time and sales as a result of poor quality. Exhibit I-25 lists some of the most common costs of quality.

Exhibit I-25: Costs of Quality

Quality Cost Type	Quality Cost Components
Prevention costs (incurred to eliminate defective products before they are produced)	• Reengineering and design • Use of high-quality parts • Improved processes • Employee training
Appraisal costs (incurred to identify defective products before they are shipped)	• Inspecting and testing raw materials and work in progress
Internal failure costs (incurred when defects are discovered before sending products to customers)	• Handling and fixing products or disposing of them • Opportunity cost of not being able to sell disposed-of products
External failure costs (incurred when customer receives defective products)	• Cost of returns • Warranty work • Product liability claims • Opportunity cost of lost sales from damaged reputation

Audit methods

Effective quality systems consist of checks and tests that provide a way to identify needed corrective actions. One of the main items an internal auditor needs to focus on is an organization's procedures. These procedures must be defined, controlled, communicated to all relevant parties, and followed by all appropriate employees.

Controls

The auditor must ensure that controls such as procedures are adequate and are being followed, that there is conformance to specifications, and that any relevant laws or regulations are adhered to. In addition, data systems must maintain and be able to convey accurate and adequate information on quality for the organization.

If tasks such as these are followed, the organization will more easily be able to identify any deficiencies, and the corrective actions that need to be taken and opportunities for continuous improvement will be identified.

Evidence

The data gathered in a quality audit provides management with the necessary information to, among other things:

- Recognize actual or potential risks.
- Make appropriate decisions so the costs of quality problems can be prevented or rectified.
- Identify areas of opportunity for continuous improvement.
- Assess the quality of staff training.
- Verify compliance with the organization's processes and procedures as well as any regulatory or legal requirements.
- Justify the expenditures on quality activities by assessing the actual savings achieved (which are more difficult to identify and track).
- Eliminate outdated activities and unnecessary controls.

This information is intended for the organization to use for continuous improvement of their controls and standards.

Due diligence audits

Due diligence is the process of investigating a person, business, or financial transaction to establish the value of an entity or transaction and the cost of any associated liabilities. The investigation should identify the presence of certain risks and/or confirm the absence of such risks. A due diligence audit may refer to either an investigation of an entity/transaction or an audit of the due diligence investigation process itself.

The most common situations for performing due diligence audit are:

- Financial (banking, securities, mergers or acquisitions).
- Real estate (property, structures).
- Intellectual property.

Objectives

Due diligence investigations are often undertaken by persons or organizations when they are interested in acquiring another business or property or are otherwise becoming involved in a financial transaction. The results of the investigation are used to decide whether or not to hire an individual or enter into a business partnership, joint venture, merger, consolidation, or other similar arrangement.

Most of the time, due diligence audits are at management's discretion. It is simply best practice to ensure that the proposed action will enhance the value of the organization and avoid hidden liabilities. In some instances, such as a violation of a company policy that restricts copying proprietary software or theft of intellectual property, a due diligence audit may be required by law.

Stakeholders

Stakeholders to a due diligence audit include the person or entity being reviewed, because the process could reveal potentially damaging information that should be handled with extreme sensitivity so as not to provoke harm to that person or entity's reputation. Other key stakeholders include the management decision maker involved in the potential new relationship or merger/acquisition, the board, the legal department, related business process owners, and any consultants or advisors.

Audit team composition

Typical due diligence engagement teams include three types of personnel:

- Internal auditors
- Lawyers
- External auditors

Each of these have specific areas of responsibility in a due diligence engagement. For example, if a department store is considering acquisition of a clothing design firm:

- The internal auditor might evaluate their ability to bring appropriate apparel to market rapidly.
- The external auditor might evaluate the transactions involved in developing new lines of apparel.
- The lawyer might investigate any legal problems with lawsuits related to trademarks or workplace safety.

The goal is to ensure that the information gathered is accurate and timely and covers all areas of risk and opportunity.

Risks

Whenever due diligence is talked about, "standard of" or "due care" is also mentioned. Due care is the level of caution that an individual exercises when performing the due diligence audit and reporting the results. Basically, did the internal auditor do what any reasonable person would do? This concept is especially important when the risk of civil litigation is involved. Civil litigation could occur if due diligence reveals information that the other party denies to be true and claims is damaging to its livelihood or reputation (assuming the information was disclosed in some way).

Other risks related to poor due diligence include harm to the organization's reputation if it is associated with an individual or entity that is later found to have engaged in illegal or unethical activities that should have been discovered earlier. Another risk is harm to the organization's revenue and profits if an organization to be acquired inflated its revenues and profits. The latter allegedly occurred in November 2012 when Hewlett Packard (HP) accused the organization it acquired, Autonomy, of inflating its revenues and profits prior to the acquisition, which HP claims required it to make a US $5 billion write-down despite having conducted a due diligence audit with 300 team members. Autonomy has denied the allegations.

Audit methods

A due diligence audit can be as complex as purchasing another business or as simple as a home buyer performing a title search. Therefore, due diligence audits will similarly have a broad range in scope. Taking a merger or acquisition as an example, audit methods for this type of due diligence include pre-acquisition due diligence audits from the perspective of the buyer and of the seller and post-acquisition due diligence audits.

Pre-acquisition due diligence (buyer perspective)

Due diligence audits from the perspective of the buyer start by ensuring that a key executive is sponsoring the acquisition and is promoting buy-in and the due diligence process itself. Internal auditors often follow checklists for this complex activity, including a controls checklist and an accounting checklist.

A controls checklist may include the following analyses related to the potential merger or acquisition:

- Analysis of the internal control environment and risk appetite (actual versus expected)
- Any significant inherent/residual risks that exceed the acquirer's risk appetite
- The cost of improving controls to address significant inherent/residual risks
- Relative difficulty of integration with the candidate's information systems

An accounting checklist may include analysis of the following items:

- Earnings quality
- Cash flow
- Quality of assets
- Valuation of liabilities and potential for unrecorded or underestimated liabilities
- How the organization accounts for any business losses
- Pro forma financial statements (analysis of whether financial projections are likely to be achieved)
- Potential for fraud

Organizations use the results of these analyses to adjust the relative value of the potential acquisition or merger. Added costs such as for improving controls are accounted for as a cost of acquisition.

Pre-acquisition due diligence (seller perspective)
An organization wishing to sell a business unit or business may wish to conduct its own due diligence prior to attempting to find a buyer, especially if the unit was recently acquired and is not fulfilling its potential. The purpose of this type of audit is to avoid a situation where a business unit is rejected by potential buyers after their own due diligence and the unit becomes difficult to sell at a fair price. In general, organizations conducting this type of audit should adopt the perspective of a buyer. Therefore the methods for this process are the same as previously described from the buyer perspective. However, the internal auditor is expected to provide management with any information that could cause due diligence concerns as well as recommendations for remediation.

Post-acquisition due diligence
Once an organization is acquired, it often becomes possible to review much more detailed records than was possible prior to the acquisition. Therefore, it is important to perform a post-acquisition due diligence audit to check for internal control weaknesses, financial reporting fraud, and actual versus planned progress toward organizational objectives. This type of audit should be conducted as soon as possible because it could reveal areas where immediate action could be taken to correct course or stop losses.

Key stakeholders for this type of audit are a transition manager and various experts in relevant business processes. A transition manager is a financial expert who reports to the CFO. This position does not run the business unit but works to achieve financial integration. Similarly, the other experts also help with integration of their business functions. Internal audit works with these individuals to perform a due diligence audit of internal controls and business process integration.

Controls

Controls in a due diligence audit relate to the entire spectrum of controls when considering a merger or acquisition, but key controls related to financial accounting accuracy (especially business valuation) and prevention of fraud are the first concern. IT controls and integration are also a key concern. Post-acquisition audits are run similarly to an audit of any business unit, except that any observations that lead to negative or unexpected results (from expectations developed at the time of acquisition) should be closely examined to determine how long these control deficiencies existed without being addressed by the acquired organization's management. This may result in disciplinary actions.

Evidence

The information and documentation used in a due diligence audit varies from country to country. In the United States, only public documents such as SEC filings, court records, and press releases can be reviewed. In other countries, private information can be collected, although this is usually covered by confidentiality agreements.

The final report to management should focus only on facts and maintain a neutral, objective tone. In an article in *Internal Auditor* titled "The Art of Coordination," Charles Zhang provides some suggestions for avoiding subjectivity in the report:

- Include an executive summary with bullet points highlighting aspects that could favor the negotiation of a better deal.
- Structure the report by cycles of business as defined by the acquiring organization; for example, categories could include finance and administration, sales and marketing, human resources, management, purchasing, production, and treasury.
- Index all supporting documents and work papers.

There are a number of different formats that can be used for final reports of audit engagements. The key for the team is determining how to convey the information they have collected in a way that will best communicate the results.

Once the report is presented to senior management, an organization can decide if they want to:

- Continue with the deal—No problems or liabilities have been discovered.
- Revalue the transaction—The price is adjusted, usually downward, based on the internal auditor's findings.
- Correct the problem—There is a way to resolve an issue before the final deal is concluded.
- Cancel the deal—There is no remedy for the problems or liabilities or the remedy may be too costly.

In the business world today, it is critical that due diligence audits are performed with the utmost care.

Security audit engagements

Security is increasingly an important part of internal auditing. Standard 2120.A1 states that:

> The internal audit activity must evaluate risk exposures relating to the organization's governance, operations, and information systems regarding the:
> - Reliability and integrity of financial and operational information.
> - Effectiveness and efficiency of operations and programs.
> - Safeguarding of assets.
> - Compliance with laws, regulations, policies, procedures, and contracts.

Objectives

Security audits primarily focus on risk assessment, controls, and governance in regard to safeguarding of assets and reliability and integrity of information.

Stakeholders

Security audits can span the operations and facilities or can be focused on one subject, such as information technology security or head office security. Therefore, stakeholders will include all parties directly responsible for the security of the area to be audited, including physical security guards, if any, and IT professionals. The board and management have ultimate responsibility and are the stakeholders to whom the CAE reports all security issues and recommendations.

Audit team composition

Security audit team composition will depend on the focus of the security audit. Physical security audits should have an internal auditor who has experience in physical access control and provisioning of rights to various job roles or individuals. Logical or other information system security audits should have team members who are generally conversant with information systems as well as a specialist in information systems auditing if the project complexities require it.

Risks

A security policy might include control systems and standards to manage security within acceptable risk limits in regard to the following risks:

- Unauthorized physical access to or attack on a facility or a person
- Theft of or willful damage to products, inventory, supplies, assets, or information
- Fraud by employees or third parties

These concerns can be influenced by other industry- or region-specific risks:

- Inherent industry risks
- Inherent social and political risks
- Market and economy pressures
- Location and facility risks
- Natural hazards, such as fire, flood, earthquake, animals, and biohazards

The policy could include standards and guidance in regard to risks and issues such as:

- Bomb threats.
- Addictions (e.g., drugs, alcohol, gambling).
- Weapons.
- Kidnap and extortion.
- Travel risk.
- Executive protection.
- Access and egress.
- Crisis management.
- Cameras and electronic monitoring.
- Intrusion detection.
- Facility design and construction.
- Investigations.
- Searches.
- Use of third-party security services.
- Relationship with law enforcement.
- Other issues specific to the risks of the organization.

Audit methods

Internal auditing for security differs depending on whether it is done as part of the design of a facility or information system or if it is conducted for ongoing operations and systems.

Auditing security for new facilities and/or information systems
Facility design is often developed from an operating need, and security features may be added on rather than integrated into the design. Internal auditors can help organizational design teams consider items such as video surveillance; clear lines of sight; electronic controls over access, egress, and movement (e.g., elevators); lighting; heating, ventilation, and air conditioning systems; patrols; emergency response; and weapons management during the design phase of a facility and during an audit of security.

As noted in *Sawyer's Internal Auditing,* physical security in regard to information technology can be achieved, in most cases, by careful planning. Factors that impact security can be mitigated by:

- Selecting an inconspicuous location for data centers.
- Providing for continued operation during floods, fires, earthquakes, and other disasters.
- Putting computers in a room with only interior walls.

- Storing tapes and other media in fire-rated vaults.
- Minimizing entry points to computer rooms. (Make sure that the limited entry points meet fire codes.)
- Eliminating entry points such as false ceilings and crawl spaces by using slab-to-slab construction in highly sensitive areas.
- Locking emergency exits from the outside and installing alarms.
- Using closed-circuit TV to monitor visitors in sensitive areas.
- Installing motion sensors in areas such as tape vaults to monitor access before and after business hours.
- Ensuring that air temperature and humidity are controlled and monitored.
- Minimizing exposed wiring.

Auditing security for existing facilities and/or information systems
Internal auditors must evaluate the effectiveness of the organization's security controls. The auditor must be able to explain, in reports to management, the extent of the risk or exposure resulting from any deficiencies found in the security controls. The auditor should be able to recommend alternatives to the current system or control. These alternatives may include, but are not limited to, a different security system, changes to procedures or controls, and enhanced training for relevant employees.

IT security is so important for financial information that many organizations audit IT security every year. The increasing use and constant release of new hardware and software requires continuous training for the auditor to remain proficient in security issues. The *GTAG* series of Practice Guides and *GAIT* methodologies are important learning tools for this type of audit.

For other records, the internal auditor should consider both on-site and off-site storage equipment and facilities, record retention and destruction policies and procedures, and recycling activities (to ensure that recycled documents do not contain confidential information).

Internal auditors are also expected to comply with security requirements when working at various locations and while traveling in order to protect themselves and the information they have. Laptops and cell phones are attractive items for theft.

Controls

Controls include the following types:

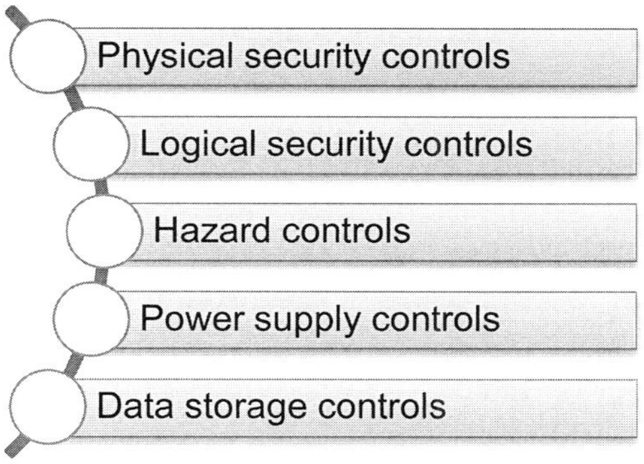

Physical security controls

Physical security of assets is one of the most basic and important controls for an organization, and it is the responsibility of management to ensure that the controls are appropriate and complied with. Physical security measures are manual and physical in nature, such as doors, locks, guards, and policies and procedures.

Within each area, there are many types of risks that must be addressed, and controls should include preventive, detective, and mitigating measures.

Organizations have areas such as building entries, common areas, data centers, storage sites, and hazardous areas where access should be restricted in layers of higher and higher security based on role, with visitors being one of the designated roles (minimal access). There are several ways to limit access to authorized personnel. Locks and keys are an obvious example, but swipe or proximity cards/badges can be used as well as biometric access systems for high security such as fingerprint scanners. Physical barriers such as bullet-proof glass or concrete barriers for cars are also access controls. Access control requires good monitoring controls, including cameras and good lighting and lines of sight for security guards.

Logical security controls

Logical security is electronic in nature, and it is designed to achieve the same results as physical controls. Examples include password protection, edit checks, and system lockdown. This includes assurance that:

- Only authorized users have access to data.
- Level of access is appropriate to need and role.
- Modifications to data leave a complete audit trail.
- Unauthorized access is denied and the attempt is reported.

Passwords are the most common means of authenticating users. They are also the most common way for unauthorized persons to access electronic information, usually because an employee protects their password poorly. For example, the employee uses a personal piece of information (home address or spouse's name) or writes the password down and leaves it in a location where others may see it. Some organizations use software that encrypts passwords, forces a periodic change of passwords, or requires a particular password structure (for example, a designated number and type of characters).

Data security software may also control access to resources by, for example, permitting access only to certain departmental users or suspending a user ID after a set number of invalid entry attempts.

In addition, security codes can be required for various levels of access. For example, one ID code may be necessary to access all data except salary and a second ID code may be necessary to access salary information. Biometric systems can be used for high-security information system access control.

Hazard controls

For many hazards, security is primarily a factor of adequate control design and crisis management programs. Some of these risks and controls may also be evaluated as part of a health and safety audit.

Fire, smoke, and water are frequent sources of damage for organizations. Because disaster prevention is preferable to disaster recovery, an organization needs to develop fire and flood prevention techniques that will mitigate their risks. Some examples of safeguards are:

- Early warning systems, such as fire alarms and smoke detectors throughout the facility.
- Installing appropriate fire suppression systems in facilities and/or vehicles.
- Conducting drills.
- Acquiring fire- and water-resistant storage for important documents.
- Ensuring that relevant third parties have adequate controls.

These systems must be constantly monitored and periodically tested.

Earthquake loss prevention involves adequate design of construction of facilities, quality control over materials, site location, emergency preparedness and drills, insurance coverage, and business interruption plans.

Power supply controls
Organizations that would be severely damaged by a power shortage or outage (for example, loss of valuable data or a window of opportunity for security breaches) can provide an alternative source of power. Depending on the organization's needs, they can use a long-term solution or a short-term solution.

A long-term solution such as a generator will provide power for longer periods. This solution tends to have a higher cost, both in installation and maintenance, and is most commonly used for large systems and critical applications or for facilities in countries with unreliable electrical grids.

Short-term solutions such as uninterruptible power supply (UPS) systems and surge protectors are less costly sources of temporary power that allow an orderly shutdown of electronic equipment, such as computers, during brownouts or blackouts.

Data storage controls
Organizations are constantly generating data. Depending on the type of organization, sometimes an enormous amount of data is produced and retained. There are a number of ways to store this data. If the media are kept only on site, or only one copy is kept, there is a tremendous exposure for it to be damaged or lost. Most organizations have a system where a backup copy of the media is also kept off site.

Data can be lost through mislabeling, mishandling, repeated use, magnetic disruption, or natural disasters. Organizations have different ways of dealing with these kinds of exposures, such as using systems that automatically label a file with an internal code. This eliminates the possibility of external labels being lost or removed or becoming unreadable through time.

For electronic data storage, the auditor might:

- Determine that internal and external labels are used appropriately.
- Determine whether or not tape, disk, and file management systems are available.
- Audit third-party distributed storage methods such as a cloud, including that the organization has done due diligence of any third-party storage organization, understands the intellectual property risks of the countries in which the data may be stored, and has appropriate contractual controls over these solutions.

- Assess the frequency of abnormal terminations of stored data because of inadequate disk space.
- Assure that data has been sufficiently backed up to allow recovery of lost files.
- Evaluate the housing of data and determine whether off-site storage exists as well as on-site storage.
- Assess temperature and humidity controls.
- Evaluate file-naming conventions to determine whether they provide sufficient information to allow proper handling.

Physical records may be stored in locked file rooms; fire-, smoke-, or water-resistant cabinets; rooms using waterless fire suppression techniques; safes; etc. There may be duplicate imaged or microfilmed copies stored as a backup should the original be damaged. Off-site storage of archived records should be evaluated for similar risks, as should controls over information held by third parties.

Evidence

Evidence will consist of reporting on physical or logical control weaknesses that have been observed. Internal auditors can provide value in this area by describing risk and control implications and potential losses from risk exposures, preferably in monetary terms when this is feasible.

Privacy audit engagements

The issues of privacy and the protection of private information are covered by Standard 2100: "The internal audit activity must evaluate and contribute to the improvement of governance, risk management, and control processes using a systematic and disciplined approach."

As noted in Practice Advisory 2130.A1-2, "Evaluating an Organization's Privacy Framework," privacy can mean many things to many people.

> Privacy definitions vary widely depending upon the culture, political environment, and legislative framework of the countries in which the organization operates . . . . Personal information generally refers to information associated with a specific individual, or that has identifying characteristics that, when combined with other information, can then be associated with a specific individual. It can include any factual or subjective information—recorded or not—in any form of media. Personal information could include:
>
> - Name, address, identification numbers, family relationships;
> - Employee files, evaluations, comments, social status, or disciplinary actions;
> - Credit records, income, financial status; or
> - Medical status.

Objectives

There are some overall expectations for performing a privacy audit. Practice Advisory 2130.A1-2 states:

> The internal audit activity can contribute to good governance and risk management by assessing the adequacy of management's identification of risks related to its privacy objectives and the adequacy of the controls established to mitigate those risks to an acceptable level. The internal auditor is well positioned to evaluate the privacy framework in their organization and identify the significant risks, as well as the appropriate recommendations for mitigation.
>
> The internal audit activity identifies the types and appropriateness of information gathered by the organization that is deemed personal or private, the collection methodology used, and whether the organization's use of that information is in accordance with its intended use and applicable legislation.

Stakeholders

Stakeholders to privacy issues start with the board and audit committee, who are ultimately accountable for assessing risks and implementing privacy controls. Other stakeholders include anyone who could be affected by a breach in privacy controls, including customers, employees, the organization, and business partners. Also, other oversight groups may exist.

Audit team composition

Practice Advisory 2130.A1-2 states: "Given the highly technical and legal nature of privacy issues, the internal audit activity needs appropriate knowledge and competence to conduct an assessment of the risks and controls of the organization's privacy framework."

Internal auditors will also work with in-house legal counsel, information technology specialists, and privacy professionals.

Risks

Protection of privacy is a very serious risk management issue for organizations. Practice Advisory 2130.A1-2 states:

> The failure to protect personal information with appropriate controls can have significant consequences for an organization. The failure could damage the reputation of individuals and/or the organization, and expose an organization to risks that include legal liability and diminished consumer and/or employee trust.
>
> Risks associated with the privacy of information encompass personal privacy (physical and psychological); privacy of space (freedom from surveillance); privacy of communication (freedom from monitoring); and privacy of information (collection, use, and disclosure of personal information by others).

Privacy risks may also include impairment of the organization's brand and public image, followed by potential losses of market share and customers, leading to potential losses for investors or the organization. Also, in addition to legal liability, regulators could impose sanctions and they or other parties could allege that the organization uses deceptive practices. Organizations could earn the distrust of customers, employees, or society or damage relationships with business partners.

Audit methods

Practice Advisory 2130.A1-2 discusses how to conduct an evaluation of the management of the organization's privacy framework, stating that the internal auditor:

- Considers the laws, regulations, and policies relating to privacy in the jurisdictions where the organization operates;
- Liaisons with in-house legal counsel to determine the exact nature of laws, regulations, and other standards and practices applicable to the organization and the country/countries in which it operates;
- Liaisons with information technology specialists to determine that information security and data protection controls are in place and regularly reviewed and assessed for appropriateness;
- Considers the level or maturity of the organization's private practices. Depending on the level, the internal auditor may have differing roles. The auditor may facilitate the development and implementation of the privacy program, evaluate management's privacy risk assessment to determine the needs and risk exposures of the organization, or provide assurance on the effectiveness of the privacy policies, practices, and controls across the organization. If the internal auditor assumes any responsibility for developing and implementing a privacy program, the internal auditor's independence will be impaired.

An important step in evaluating an organization's privacy framework is to determine the maturity level of the organization. This is often done using a Capability Maturity Model (CMM). As described in *Privacy: Assessing the Risk* by Hargraves, Lione, Shackelford, and Tilton, there are five levels of an organization's maturity concerning privacy protection:

- **Level 1—Initial.** Organizations at this level have no defined policies or procedures that control the security of private information. There is a lack of interest in or involvement by management and employees.
- **Level 2—Repeatable.** These organizations have a defined policy and at least some commitment on the part of management and employees.

- **Level 3—Defined.** A privacy policy has been established and senior management is committed to it. Risk assessments, priorities, resource allocation, and activities have been performed or developed to ensure consistent privacy controls.
- **Level 4—Managed.** Privacy requirements and controls are an integral part of the organization's framework. There is commitment by all parties in the organization.
- **Level 5—Optimizing.** Continuous improvement is achieved through monitoring of the privacy framework. Any corrective action is addressed by all relevant parties in the organization, and no change is made without extensive coordination.

At each level, the internal auditor can help the organization to achieve the next level. This is done by identifying significant risks and making recommendations to mitigate them.

Additional audit procedures include liaising with privacy professionals to help understand internal and customer-oriented privacy policies and organizational maturity in these areas. When liaising with IT specialists, some information sources to audit include system controls, information flows, storage controls, and incident response programs.

Privacy audits may also review the following topics according to the Practice Guide "Auditing Privacy Risks," second edition:

- Governance/management oversight.
- Privacy policies and controls.
- Applicable privacy notices.
- Types and appropriateness of information collected.
- Systems that process, store, and transmit personal information.
- Collection methodologies.
- Consent and opt-in/opt-out management.
- Use of personal information for compliance with stated intent, applicable laws, and other regulations.
- Security practices, operations, and technical controls in place to protect personal information.
- Retention and disposal practices for personal information.

Controls

Practice Advisory 2130.A1-2 states: "Effective control over the protection of personal information is an essential component of the governance, risk management, and control processes of an organization. The board is ultimately accountable for identifying the principal risks to the organization and implementing appropriate control processes to mitigate those risks. This includes establishing the necessary privacy framework for the organization and monitoring its implementation."

While there are many privacy frameworks an organization can adopt, a best practice is to adopt a framework that is both principles-based and that balances the individual right to privacy against the legitimate information rights of the organization. A principles-based framework usually starts with a set of generally accepted privacy principles and works to make them easier to understand and implement. For example, the AICPA and the Canadian Institute of Chartered Accountants has issued a set of ten Generally Accepted Privacy Principles (GAPP), as shown in Exhibit I-26.

Exhibit I-26: AICPA/CICA Generally Accepted Privacy Principles

Management	Privacy policies and procedures are defined, documented, communicated, and accountable.
Notice	Policies, procedures, and purpose of collection, use, retention, and disclosure are provided in a notice.
Choice and consent	Individuals are told available choices and the organization gets explicit or implicit consent to collect, use, and disclose personal information.
Collection	Collection is limited to the purpose identified in the notice.
Use, retention, and disposal	Use is limited to the purposes in the notice. Retention is limited to the need stated in the notice or as required by law.
Access	Individuals can access and correct personal information.
Disclosure to third parties	Disclosure is limited to parties in the notice.
Security for privacy	Physical and logical access controls exist.
Quality	Personal information is maintained, complete, and accurate.
Montoring and enforcement	Compliance and complaint resolution systems exist.

The privacy framework should also enable easier compliance with privacy-related laws, regulations, and policies. An internal auditor must be aware of and up-to-date on privacy-related laws, regulations, and policies in jurisdictions where the organization operates. Some examples of these are:

- The European Union (EU) Directive on Data Protection.
- The EU E-Privacy Directive.
- OECD Guidelines.
- The Canadian Personal Information Protection and Electronic Documents Act.
- The US Health Insurance Portability and Accountability Act of 1996.
- Japan's Personal Information Protection Act of 2003.
- Australia's Privacy Act of 1988.

Note that some of the above directives or acts also contain their own versions of generally accepted privacy principles, and most are very similar to those listed above. The internal auditor should work with either in-house or external counsel to determine the exact nature of such laws or regulations and whether they impact the organization or expose it to risks.

Evidence

Audit evidence may take the form of observed control weaknesses or evidence of past control failures. Internal auditors should make timely recommendations if they identify a significant risk of a large control failure, such as the theft of data from a database containing customers' credit card information, because this type of breach will have immediate severe consequences such as negative press and scrutiny from regulators and privacy watchdogs. Other types of control weaknesses include inadequate access controls; excessive collection, sharing, disclosure, or retention of data; incomplete, outdated, or damaged data; poor or incorrect data processing; or ineffective use of data.

The auditor should have legal counsel review the evidence before disclosing it in official audit communications that discuss potential privacy violations. This will balance the auditor's need to disclose findings against the counsel's legal requirement to defend the organization.

More information on privacy auditing is provided in "Auditing Privacy Risks."

Performance audit engagements

It is important to realize that not all aspects of an organization can be efficiently and effectively tracked. Standards should be designed and written in a way that will allow personnel to measure progress toward meeting the organization's most important objectives. As noted earlier, these standards are often called key performance indicators (KPIs). They are also referred to as targets, goals, or business objectives.

Objectives

The key to successful management is establishing controls that are appropriate and effective. In order to achieve this, a manager must create standards that include the ability to measure performance, analyze deficiencies to determine their causes, and perform corrective actions that enable the organization to adhere to the standards.

Stakeholders

Stakeholders include the board and management who require accurate and timely performance information to make corrections as well as any internal or external party or entity that is being measured. Stakeholders who are being measured for performance have an interest in being measured against things that they can personally control to some degree. They also want to know how they are being measured so they can have a reasonable chance of success and improvement.

Audit team composition

Audit team composition will vary depending on the business unit or process for which the KPIs are being audited. Similarly, required competencies will vary and must be assessed by the CAE depending on the situation.

Risks

What can be measured can be managed, so failure to measure performance introduces the risk that the performance cannot be managed. Other risks include measuring the wrong KPIs so that workers or processes fail to work toward organizational goals or objectives, receiving information too late to be of use, and measuring too many performance indicators rather than just the key ones. Measuring too many performance indicators can increase measurement costs while reducing the effectiveness of the indicators as a management tool. Persons and processes that are not managed can quickly get out of control, and the results can include missed budgets or deadlines, accidents, lawsuits, increased insurance premiums, and loss of worker productivity.

Audit methods

While management should exercise control by creating and applying KPIs, auditors should perform efficient and cost-effective audits by focusing on the KPIs. KPIs are based on plans and not on policies or rules. Types of KPIs include the following:

- **Quantity of output standards** measure quantitative performance, such as units produced per day or week.
- **Accuracy of quality standards** measure quality performance, such as the number of sold items returned.
- **Cost standards** specify benchmarks, such as material costs per unit.
- **Timeliness standards** are associated with things such as production schedules or project completion.

- **Capital standards** deal with capital investment such as return on investment (not operating costs).
- **Revenue standards** measure the monetary values assigned to sales, such as revenue per airplane passenger mile.

KPIs might include accident reduction, reduced machine downtime caused by accidents, or lower workers' compensation insurance premiums.

Controls

The auditor should assess considerations such as the following:

- Does the organization have KPIs?
- Are the KPIs appropriate, i.e., can they really measure the organization's success in meeting its objectives?
- Do the KPIs include the human factor, i.e., will they create frustration or confusion for employees?
- Are measurements taken and reported at appropriate times, i.e., early enough in the process to correct course?
- Are measurements used effectively in controlling performance by identifying deficiencies and correcting them?

Evidence

Audit evidence starts by indicating whether KPIs are being used in a given area for measurement, analysis, and feedback. Analysis of KPIs should show a cause-and-effect link between the KPIs and the actual behavior they promote using real examples of observed behavior when feasible. Recommendations should be linked to organizational objectives by indicating whether the existing KPIs are adequate to promote achievement of these objectives or if a different set of KPIs would be more efficient or effective in achieving objectives.

Operational (efficiency and effectiveness) audit engagements

Operational audits are not finance- or compliance-focused but may include some financial and compliance risks. They are focused on providing assurance on the governance, risk management, and controls in regard to the effectiveness and efficiency of operations. Operational (efficiency and effectiveness) audit engagements are referred to as management audits in government environments.

Objectives

There are three key considerations in reaching an evaluation of the overall effectiveness of the organization's risk management and control processes:

- Were significant discrepancies or weaknesses discovered from the audit work performed and other assessment information gathered?
- If so, were corrections or improvements made after the discoveries?
- Do the discoveries and their consequences lead to the conclusion that a pervasive condition exists resulting in an unacceptable level of business risk?

Stakeholders

Stakeholders include the board and management who are ultimately responsible for oversight and specific business process owners who will be responsible for addressing audit recommendations.

Audit team composition

The audit team composition should include auditors familiar with the business process being audited.

Risks

Risks related to operational effectiveness include business processes that fail to work toward organizational objectives or are counterproductive to the overall objectives, perhaps due to suboptimization. Suboptimization involves focusing on optimizing a particular business process or business unit at the expense of the overall organizational goals, often caused by a departmental "silo" mentality. Risks related to inefficiency involve achieving goals in a manner that is more costly than the value that is added or more costly than a selected benchmark. Suboptimization can affect both efficiency and effectiveness. For example, a repair department could decide to ground an airplane for several days so that the repair department can avoid the travel cost of rushing personnel to the site. The repair department may meet its budget but the overall organizational opportunity cost is much greater. The event is also ineffective because it will inconvenience passengers. An audit recommendation that focused on root causes would recommend redesigning the repair department manager's incentives (currently too much weight on meeting the department budget).

Audit methods

Operational audit subjects could include manufacturing plants, marketing activities, human resources, engineering, cafeteria services, housekeeping, fleet management, facility management, etc. Operational information may include production volumes, reserves, personnel head counts, emission or effluent statistics, productivity rates, weights and measures, etc. See Part 3, Section III, Chapter B, for information about procurement audits.

The temporary existence of a significant risk management and control discrepancy or weakness does not necessarily lead to the judgment that it is pervasive and poses an unacceptable residual risk. The pattern of discoveries, degree of intrusion, and level of consequences and exposures are factors to be considered in determining whether the effectiveness of the whole system of controls is jeopardized and unacceptable risks exist.

Controls

COSO's *Internal Control—Integrated Framework* describes internal control as a process designed to provide reasonable assurance of achieving objectives in three areas:

- Effectiveness and efficiency of operations
- Reliability of financial reporting
- Compliance with applicable laws and regulations

Therefore, evaluating the internal control framework for the area being audited is an important audit step, including audits of "soft controls" such as the "tone at the top," the ethical environment, or the corporate culture.

Operational auditing goes beyond traditional concerns with reliability of financial statements to consider how efficiently and effectively the various operations in an organization are meeting their objectives. This may include, among other goals:

- A review of policies, procedures, and systems.
- Quality of management.
- The use of resources to achieve organizational goals efficiently and effectively and the safeguarding of assets.

Evidence

The internal auditor should be able to reach a conclusion about how effectively the subject area supports organizational goals and objectives.

Financial audit engagements

Financial audits performed by external auditors focus on an organization's financial statements; financial audits performed by internal auditors focus on an organization's internal controls.

Objectives

The objective of external financial reporting is preparing relevant and reliable financial statements that fairly and accurately represent the activities of the organization. Financial reporting objectives should form the basis for the majority of internal controls. The internal controls set reliable financial reporting as a key objective because of its importance not only in satisfying legal and regulatory issues but also in ensuring efficiency and stewardship over the organization's resources.

The objective of internal control assurance is to ensure that the organization is adhering to the processes and procedures that control any type of financial activity.

The US Sarbanes-Oxley Act and related US Securities and Exchange Commission rules clearly provide considerable incentive for principal executives and financial officers to seek assurance that controls are in place to support their certifications in regard to financial statements, controls, and disclosures, for the laws make them personally responsible for these matters. Internal auditors might provide "value-added services" to those executives (and, of course, to the organization and the investing public).

Such legislation and regulations, around the world, have increased focus on internal auditor responsibilities in the area of financial audits.

Stakeholders

Stakeholders include the board, the audit committee, and senior management, especially the CEO and the CFO due to their personal accountability. Other stakeholders include regulators such as the SEC, rating agencies, current and potential stockholders and investors, external auditors, and interested parties.

Audit team composition

Senior management, external auditors, and internal auditors have the following roles:

- Executive management is the owner of the control environment and financial information, including the notes accompanying the financial statements and the accompanying disclosures in the financial report.
- The external auditor assures the financial report user that the reported information fairly presents the financial condition and result of operations of the organization in accordance with Generally Accepted Accounting Principles.
- The internal auditor performs procedures to provide a level of assurance to senior management and the audit or other committee of the governing board that controls surrounding the processes supporting the development of the financial report are effective. Internal auditing should be done in conformance with the *Standards*.

Risks

The internal audit activity's work plans and specific assurance engagements begin with a careful identification of the exposures facing the organization, and internal audit's work plan is based on the risks and the assessment of the risk management and control processes maintained by management to mitigate those risks.

Among the events and transactions included in the identification of risks are:

- New businesses—including mergers and acquisitions.
- New products and systems.
- Joint ventures and partnerships.
- Restructuring.

- Management estimates, budgets, and forecasts.
- Environmental matters.
- Regulatory compliance.

Audit methods

The IIA believes that internal control should be broadly defined and that the best guidance available currently is contained in COSO's *Internal Control—Integrated Framework* and *Internal Control Over Financial Reporting—Guidance for Smaller Public Companies.*

The assessment of a system for internal control of an organization should employ a broad definition of control. While use of the COSO model is widely accepted, it may be appropriate to use some other recognized and credible model. Sometimes, regulatory or legal requirements will specify the use of a particular model or control design for an organization or industry within a country.

Several conclusions in the *Internal Control—Integrated Framework* report are relevant to this discussion:

- Internal control is defined broadly; it is not limited to accounting controls and is not narrowly restricted to financial reporting.
- While accounting and financial reports are important issues, there are other important aspects of the business, such as resource protection; operational efficiency and effectiveness; and compliance with rules, regulations, and organization policies. These factors also have an impact on financial reporting.
- Internal control is management's responsibility and requires the participation of all persons within an organization if it is to be effective.
- The control framework is tied to the business objectives and is flexible enough to be adaptable.

The CAE should provide internal audit's assessment of controls, including the design or model, to the audit committee. The governing board must rely on management to maintain effective controls, and it (or the audit or other designated committee) should ask questions that include the following.

- Is there a strong ethical environment and culture in the organization?
  - Do board members and senior executives set examples of high integrity?
  - Are performance and incentive targets realistic, or do they create excessive pressure for short-term results?

  - Is the organization's code of conduct reinforced with training and top-down communication? Does the message reach the employees in the field?
  - Are the organization's communication channels open? Do all levels of management get the information they need?
  - Is there zero tolerance for fraudulent financial reporting at any level?

- How does the organization identify and manage risks?
  - Is there a risk management process, and is it effective?
  - Is risk managed throughout the organization?
  - Are major risks candidly discussed with the board?

- Is the control system effective?
  - Are the organization's controls over the financial reporting process comprehensive, including preparation of financial statements, related notes, and other required and discretionary disclosures that are an integral part of the financial reports?
  - Do senior and line management demonstrate that they accept control responsibility?
  - Is there an increasing frequency of "surprises" occurring at the senior management, board, or public levels from the organization's reported financial results or in the accompanying financial disclosures?
  - Is there good communication and reporting throughout the organization, especially for timely disclosure of bad news?
  - Are controls seen as enhancing the achievement of objectives or as a "necessary evil"?
  - Are qualified people hired promptly, and do they receive adequate training?
  - Are problem areas fixed quickly and completely?

- Is there strong monitoring?
  - Is the board independent of management, free of conflicts of interest, well informed, and inquisitive?
  - Does internal audit have the support of senior management and the audit committee?
  - Do the internal and external auditors have and use open lines of communication and private access to all members of senior management and the audit committee?
  - Is line management monitoring the control process?
  - Is there a program to monitor out-sourced processes?

Controls

Internal controls, no matter how effective, cannot ensure success against all contingencies. Bad decisions, poor managers, or environmental factors can negate controls. Also, dishonest management may override controls and ignore or stifle communications from subordinates. An active and independent governing board that is coupled with open and truthful communications from all components of management and is assisted by capable financial, legal, and internal audit functions is capable of identifying problems and providing effective oversight.

Best practices indicate that internal auditors recommend improvements to policies, procedures, and the process for quarterly reporting and suggest that internal controls include:

- Properly documented policies, procedures, controls, and monitoring reports.
- Quarterly checklists of procedures and key control elements.
- Standardized control reports on key disclosure controls.
- Management self-assessments (such as CSA).
- Review of draft regulatory filings prior to submission.
- Process maps to document the source of data elements for regulatory filings, key controls, and responsible parties for each element.
- Follow-up on previously reported outstanding items.
- Consideration of internal audit reports issued during the period.
- Special or specifically targeted reviews of high-risk, complex, and problem areas, including material accounting estimates, reserve valuations, off-balance-sheet activities, major substitutions, joint ventures, and special purpose entities.
- Observation of the closing process for the financial statements and related adjusting entries, including waived adjustments.
- Conference calls with key management from remote locations to ensure appropriate consideration of and participation by all major components of the organization.
- Review of potential and pending litigation and contingent liabilities.
- CAE report on internal control, issued at least annually and possibly quarterly.
- Regularly scheduled disclosure and audit committee meetings.

Evidence

An organization's audit or other board committee and internal auditing activity have interlocking goals. The core role of the chief audit executive is to ensure that the audit committee receives the support and assurance services it needs and requests. One of the primary objectives of the audit committee is oversight of the organization's financial reporting processes to ensure their reliability and fairness. The committee and senior management typically request that the internal audit activity perform sufficient audit work and gather other available information during the year to form an opinion on the adequacy and effectiveness of the internal control processes. The CAE normally communicates that overall evaluation, on a timely basis, to the committee. The committee will evaluate the coverage and adequacy of the CAE's report and may incorporate its conclusion in the committee's report to the governing board.

Ratio analysis

Ratio analysis—the comparison of two sets of data—is an important part of financial analysis.

Ratios, by definition, measure relationships between quantities. The objective of ratio analysis is to detect unexpected relationships compared to what the internal auditor would normally expect to see, based on historical trends, expected cause-and-effect relationships among several ratios or inputs and outputs, or various benchmarks.

Stakeholders to ratio analysis include the board and management, who want analysis results to highlight just the key drivers that indicate significant risk or impact achievement of organizational objectives. Other stakeholders include various analysts who produce and analyze ratios as well as any persons who have their performance assessed by or provide inputs to ratios.

Audit team composition will vary depending on the complexity of the ratios being analyzed. Specialists for a given area may be needed to provide sufficient expertise.

Risks relate to the drawbacks of financial ratio analysis, which include the difficulty of comparing financial statements between organizations due to the differences in accounting methods and management's ability to adjust estimates and assumptions, the difficulty in comparing long-term historical information due to inflation, and the ability to misinterpret some ratios because the wrong ratio is being used or the ratio fails to show other contributing factors to a relationship, such as a ratio that fails to account for the time value of money.

Setting and monitoring targets for financial or operating ratios can be used as KPIs to show when controls are operating effectively and when they are out of control.

Audit evidence related to ratio analysis can be used to show whether the current set of KPIs is sufficient. Recommendations may include the use of different ratios, adding ratios, or reducing the number of ratios used. The set as a whole should enable timely management decision making without providing too much information, which can often obscure key relationships.

Auditors employ several types of ratio analysis: common-size statements, nonfinancial ratios, and financial ratios.

Common-size statements

Common-size statements express all account balances as percentages of one relevant aggregate balance, usually sales revenues for the income statement or total assets for the balance sheet. For instance, expressing all items on the income statement as percentages of sales revenues makes all income statements to be compared a common size, no matter how large or small the particular numbers in them might be. And this in turn enables comparisons among statements containing very different absolute values. If marketing expenses, for example, are expressed as 0.50% of sales revenues, it doesn't matter if expenses are US $1,000 and revenues are US $200,000 or expenses are US $10,000 and revenues are US $2,000,000. On both statements, sales revenues will be 100% and marketing expenses will be 0.50%. Thus, the two can be compared to look for trends or variances. Converting all income statement items to percentages of sales revenues is also called vertical analysis.

Nonfinancial ratios

Nonfinancial ratios compare relationships between two measurable and correlated business elements. For example, internal auditors could calculate the ratio of sick days taken to the total accrual of sick days and compare these ratios by department. Like any ratio, nonfinancial ratios make data comparable or of a common size. These ratios are often used as key performance indicators to measure and manage achievement of objectives and mitigation of key risks. For example, the ratio of orders processed without error or delay to the total number of orders shipped might be a supply chain management KPI.

Nonfinancial ratios can be reviewed from period to period or assessed against an internal or external benchmark. Exception reports may highlight nonfinancial ratios that require scrutiny.

Financial ratios

Financial ratios are used to compare the relationships between various items in financial statements or other financial accounts. There are numerous specific ratios used by auditors, managers, lenders, and investors to determine the health of an organization. These ratios can be used to compare performance of units within an organization, and they can be used to compare organizations to one another or to a common standard, such as overall ratios in an industry.

Financial ratios are often categorized according to the type of information they provide as activity, liquidity, leverage, or profitability ratios.

- **Activity ratios.** Activity ratios are used to measure an organization's efficiency in turning various balance sheet accounts into sales or cash. Common activity ratios appear in Exhibit I-27.

Exhibit I-27: Commonly Used Activity Ratios

Ratio	Calculation	What It Measures
Inventory Turnover	$\frac{\text{Cost of Goods}}{\text{Average Inventory}}$	Inventory turnover measures the number of times during the year inventory is replaced. It is useful in comparing one organization to others in the same industry or measuring the trend in the organization. A higher number indicates greater efficiency.
Days' Sales Outstanding	$\frac{\text{Accounts Receivable}}{\text{Sales / 360 Days}}$	Days' sales outstanding is a measure of a company's effectiveness in collecting accounts receivable. A smaller number for the ratio indicates greater effectiveness in managing and collecting money from customers. (Some accountants use 365 days in the denominator rather than 360.)
Accounts Payable Turnover	$\frac{\text{Purchases}}{\text{Average Accounts Payable}}$	The accounts payable turnover ratio indicates how many times a company's accounts are generated and paid in a year. A lower ratio is preferable (as long as accounts are paid in a timely fashion). To calculate purchases, the cost of goods sold is adjusted by the change in inventory. (Purchases = COGS + Ending Inventory – Starting Inventory)
Fixed Assets Turnover	$\frac{\text{Net Sales}}{\text{Average Net Fixed Assets}}$	Fixed assets turnover is a measure of how efficiently a company uses its fixed assets (property, plant, equipment) to generate sales. The higher the number, the more efficiently fixed assets are being used. Fixed assets turnover might be used to measure the effectiveness of significant investments in PPE. (Net Sales = Sales – Sales Discounts – Sales Returns – Sales Allowances)
Total Assets Turnover	$\frac{\text{Net Sales}}{\text{Average Total Assets}}$	Total assets turnover is a measure of how well assets are being used to produce revenues. The higher the number, the more efficiently all assets are being used. (Net Sales = Sales – Sales Discounts – Sales Returns – Sales Allowances)

- **Liquidity ratios.** Liquidity ratios measure an organization's solvency by comparing assets to liabilities. These ratios are explained in Exhibit I-28.

Exhibit I-28: Commonly Used Liquidity Ratios

Ratio	Calculation	What It Measures
Current Ratio	$\frac{\text{Current Assets}}{\text{Current Liabilities}}$	The current ratio measures an organization's potential for paying down current liabilities. A larger number for the ratio indicates more assets in relation to debt and therefore signals greater ability to pay holders of short-term debt.
Quick Ratio	$\frac{\text{Current Assets} - \text{Inventory}}{\text{Current Liabilities}}$ *or* $\frac{\text{Cash, Cash Equivalents, and Receivables}}{\text{Current Liabilities}}$	The quick ratio is similar to the current ratio, but it eliminates inventory, which is considered the least liquid portion of current assets and therefore the least available for reducing current debts. It is the proportion of the most liquid sources of funding (cash, cash equivalents, receivables) to liabilities. Since inventory is excluded, a stable current ratio but declining quick ratio could indicate an increase in inventory.
Net Working Capital	Current Assets – Current Liabilities	Not actually a ratio, net working capital measures the relationship of short-term debt to short-term assets by simply subtracting liabilities from assets. A larger number indicates a greater ability to pay current debts—greater liquidity, in other words.

- **Leverage (or debt) ratios.** Leverage ratios (also called debt ratios) are similar in intent to liquidity ratios in that they measure an organization's assets against its liabilities to ascertain ability to pay down debt. Leverage, however, is a longer-term measure of the organization's solvency. While an organization can sustain a high rate of short-term indebtedness (start-ups are invariably in this position), a high level of indebtedness in relation to equity cannot be sustained over the long term without reducing the organization's ability to attract lenders and investors. Leverage ratios are generally used to track one organization's changing solvency from period to period. Examples of commonly used leverage ratios appear in Exhibit I-29.

Exhibit I-29: Commonly Used Leverage (Debt) Ratios

Ratio	Calculation	What It Measures
Debt Ratio	$\frac{\text{TotalLiabilitie}}{\text{TotalAssets}}$	The ratio of all the organization's debt to all of its assets provides a general measure of its ability to repay creditors. The higher the number, the greater the firm's leverage (amount of borrowed money in relation to equity). Reasonable debt ratios vary among industries and with the age of the organization (or its products). In general, however, higher debt ratios indicate higher risk for investors and creditors.
Debt to Equity Ratio	$\frac{\text{Total Liabilities}}{\text{Total Equity}}$	The debt to equity ratio measures an organization's proportion of liabilities (what is owed) to equity (residual ownership of assets). A reasonable ratio of debt to equity varies among industries, with capital-intensive organizations generally carrying more debt in relation to owners' equity. A percentage under 100% is desirable.
Times Interest Earned Ratio	$\frac{\text{Earnings Before Interest and Taxes (EBIT)}}{\text{Interest Expense}}$	Times interest earned measures the organization's ability to service all of its liabilities. As the name indicates, the ratio indicates the number of times a company can cover fixed obligations with earnings before interest and taxes. A higher number indicates greater ability to pay creditors. The interest number used in EBIT refers to the organization's obligations related to long-term financing during the period measured.
Fixed Payment Coverage Ratio	$\frac{\text{Earnings Before Interest and Taxes (EBIT)}}{\text{Interest} + (\text{Principal} + \text{Preferred Dividends}) \times [1 / (1 - \text{Taxes})]}$	The fixed payment coverage ratio measures an organization's ability to pay fixed obligations within a set period of time. The denominator includes principal, interest, and preferred dividends owed to investors.

- **Profitability ratios.** Profitability ratios indicate ability to make a profit. They involve various comparisons of earnings (revenues reduced by expenses) in the numerator to revenues in the denominator. Earnings and revenues can be measured in several different ways, so there are a number of different profitability ratios, as shown in Exhibit I-30.

Exhibit I-30: Commonly Used Profitability Ratios (continued on next page)

Ratio	Calculation	What It Measures
Gross Profit Margin	$\frac{\text{Gross Profit}}{\text{Net Sales}}$ *or* $\frac{\text{Net Sales} - \text{Cost of Goods Sold}}{\text{Net Sales}}$	Gross profit is the money remaining from sales revenues after deduction for the cost of goods sold; the gross profit margin is the proportion of net sales minus cost of goods sold to net sales. When used as a comparison of organizations, a higher ratio indicates more effective management of pricing and control of costs. When used to track one organization's profitability over time, a rising trend indicates increases in operational efficiency.
Operating Profit Margin	$\frac{\text{Operating Profit}}{\text{Net Sales}}$ *or* $\frac{\text{Net Sales} - (\text{Cost of Goods Sold} + \text{Operating Expenses})}{\text{Net Sales}}$	The operating profit margin measures the proportion of net sales less cost of goods sold plus operating expenses (i.e., selling, general, and administrative expenses) to net sales. The higher the operating profit margin, the greater the company's operating efficiency.
Net Profit Margin	$\frac{\text{Net Profit}}{\text{Net Sales}}$ *or* $\frac{\text{Operating Profit} - (\text{Interest} + \text{Taxes})}{\text{Net Sales}}$	Net profits are calculated by subtracting interest and taxes from operating profits. The net profit margin, therefore, is the portion of sales remaining after covering net profits. It provides a measure of the effectiveness of debt and tax management as well as effective management of operations, pricing, and cost controls.

Exhibit I-30: Commonly Used Profitability Ratios (concluded)

Ratio	Calculation	What It Measures
Return on Investment (ROI)	Total Asset Turnover × Net Profit Margin	Known as the DuPont formula, this measure of return on investment is the product of the net profit margin (see above in this table) multiplied by total asset turnover. This calculation measures an operation's effectiveness in using assets to generate profits. Efficiency in turning over assets, therefore, may compensate for a relatively low net profit margin. A reasonable ROI depends in part on the industry in which the operation functions.
Return on Equity (ROE)	$\frac{\text{Net Profits}}{\text{Shareholders' Equity}}$	Return on equity (ROE) measures the operation's relative success in generating net profits (profits after subtracting cost of goods sold, operating expenses, interest, and taxes) from a given amount of shareholders' equity.
Return on Capital	$\frac{\text{Return on Equity (ROE)}}{(1 + \text{Debt to Equity Ratio})}$ or ROE x (1 – Debt to Capital)	Return on capital measures an operation's effectiveness in using debt and equity to generate earnings. In heavily leveraged operations (high ratio of debt to equity), return on capital generally provides a more meaningful measure of success than return on equity (ROE) alone.
Earnings per Share	$\frac{\text{Total Earnings}}{\text{Number of Shares Outstanding}}$	The ratio of total earnings to number of shares outstanding provides a commonly used measure of a company's value to investors.

Compliance audit engagements

As referenced earlier, the COSO internal framework states that controls focus on three areas: operational efficiency and effectiveness, financial reporting, and compliance. According to the Open Compliance and Ethics Group, "Compliance is the act of adhering to, and the ability to demonstrate adherence to, mandated requirements as defined by laws and regulations as well as voluntary requirements resulting from contractual obligations and internal policies." Compliance audits evaluate the adequacy and effectiveness of controls that keep the organization in compliance with applicable laws and regulations, contracts, and the organization's own policies.

Objectives

The objectives of an effective compliance program is to:

- Identify and discourage intentional and unintentional violations.
- Detect illegal activities.
- Assist in proving insurance claims.
- Encourage proper behavior by providing incentives.
- Enhance and create corporate identity.

The organization should establish compliance standards and procedures that are reasonably capable of reducing the prospect of criminal conduct by employees and other agents, and compliance audits should review and assess them.

Stakeholders

Stakeholders include the board and management, compliance professionals, and process owners and workers who are responsible for day-to-day compliance. Large organizations, especially those in heavily regulated industries, often have a chief compliance officer.

Audit team composition

Internal auditors may not directly conduct compliance audits, as this is often the role of compliance professionals. However, internal auditors may audit the compliance process and the effectiveness of compliance professionals. In this case, internal auditors on the team should understand the compliance framework being used and specific laws, regulations, and policies for the area.

Risks

Risks of noncompliance include regulatory fines and sanctions, individual and/or corporate legal liability, financial losses from mismanagement, damage to reputation, and possibly damage to the environment, worker health or safety, or the health and safety of customers and the community. While there are many types of regulations and policies, each with their own risks, environmental compliance risks can be used as a representative example. Environmental, health, and safety (EH&S) risks to consider in audit planning include ineffective organizational reporting structures; likelihood of causing environmental harm; fines and penalties; expenditures mandated by environmental or health and safety agencies; history of injuries and deaths; records of losing customers; and negative publicity, loss of reputation, and public image.

Audit methods

Internal auditors should start an audit of the compliance process by developing a working knowledge of the framework that compliance professionals use to assess compliance.

There are two compliance frameworks that have become generally accepted:

- **Australian Standard (AS) 3806—2006 Compliance Program.** This is a global compliance framework for public and private organizations based on comprehensive principles (i.e., it is not rules-based) that, according to AS 3806, is "intended to help organizations identify and remedy any deficiencies in their compliance with laws, regulations, and codes, and develop processes for continual improvement in this area."

- **US Federal Sentencing Guidelines for Organizations (USFGO).** This is also a principles-based framework, originally intended to guide US federal judges when imposing sentences on organizational defendants, but it has become a de facto standard for compliance. It has seven principles that are intended to guide human behavior toward clear accountability and ethical conduct. It also promotes compliance training and leadership.

The role of internal auditing in compliance is to provide assurance that compliance professionals, processes, and systems are effective. To audit the effectiveness of these people, processes, and technologies, internal auditors should start by forming a basic knowledge of the roles and responsibilities of compliance professionals and the frameworks and systems they use and then determine how well these professionals are using these tools and techniques to ensure compliance against the specific laws, regulations, and policies that they are responsible for assessing.

Specific areas for internal auditors to verify include that standards and procedures should include written policies that clearly identify required and prohibited activities (and which may be incorporated in a code of conduct). There should be an organization chart that identifies personnel who are responsible for implementing compliance programs. Responsibility for oversight of regulatory compliance programs should be assigned to high-level personnel in the organization. Due care should be taken not to assign compliance responsibilities to persons who are or should be known to have a tendency to break the law.

International companies should create a global compliance program with codes that reflect appropriate laws, regulations, and local conditions.

The organization should take steps to communicate standards and procedures to all employees through training, publications, etc. The development of an effective "tone at the top" governance program will help in the implementation of standards and procedures.

There should be hotlines for reporting suspect activities (without fear of reprisal). Studies show that hotlines work best when they connect to an in-house representative who is not a member of the legal department and when they are backed by nonretaliation policies. Write-in reports and off-site ombudspersons inspire less confidence than on-site hotlines.

The organization should take responsible steps to achieve compliance through promoting monitoring and auditing systems that have a reasonable chance of detecting noncompliant behavior and encouraging the reporting of such behavior without fear of retribution.

Note that resources devoted to the internal audit plan should be proportional to the size of the organization and the demands of the audit task.

Controls

Controls will differ depending on the area for which the rules, regulations, and policies apply. Controls related to compliance with environmental laws and regulations are used as a representative example. Types of environmental audits include the following:

- Environmental management systems audits that focus on systems in place to ensure that they are operating properly to manage future environmental risks
- Due diligence audits used as a risk management tool by organizations purchasing land
- Treatment, storage, and disposal facility audits that track hazardous substances "from cradle to grave"
- Pollution prevention audits that assess operations to identify ways to minimize waste and pollution at the source
- Environmental liability accrual audits that quantify and report accrued liabilities for environmental issues
- Product audits that assess a facility's production process to assure compliance

The majority of environmental compliance audit functions report to the organization's environmental component or the general counsel rather than to the CAE. Reporting to the EH&S executive may result in a loss of the independence required for an effective audit function. The EH&S executives are typically responsible for the facilities being audited and therefore have a potential conflict of interest that may tempt them to suppress information about problems.

IIA studies have shown that environmental auditors seldom meet with governing boards and a majority of them have no contact with the CAE, a substantial majority of organizations never include environmental issues in their agendas, and a significant number of organizations have incurred penalties recently and describe their environmental risks as material.

The CAE should foster a close working relationship with the chief environmental officer and coordinate the audit plan with environmental auditing activities. Periodically, the CAE should schedule an EH&S audit, which could focus on compliance, management systems, or both.

The CAE should evaluate whether environmental auditors outside the CAE's organization are in compliance with audit standards and/or a code of ethics.

The CAE should evaluate the organizational placement and independence of the environmental audit function to ensure that significant information about risks is being reported to the audit committee or other board committee.

Evidence

The audit report should include a review of the compliance programs to see if written materials are effective, employees have received communications, detected violations have been handled appropriately, discipline has been even handed, whistleblowers have not suffered retaliation, and the compliance unit has fulfilled its responsibilities.

After an offense has been detected, the internal auditor should observe whether the organization takes all reasonable steps to prevent further offenses of the same type. This might include appropriate discipline or a requirement to self-report to the government. Detecting a violation that was not prevented by the compliance program signals a need to review the program to see if it needs changing. Adequate discipline of violators is necessary and should be appropriate to the individual case. If the CAE uncovers exposures that are not properly managed, he or she would normally change the schedule of engagements to evaluate those risks further prior to presenting recommendations. The CAE should identify needed improvements and solicit employee contributions to that effort.

Topic 9: Conduct Consulting Engagements (Level P)

Internal control training

Internal controls are a fundamental part of any system. They are used to standardize and guide operations and are designed to improve performance in order to accomplish an organization's goals and objectives. Internal auditors are natural facilitators of internal control presentations and classes. The auditors themselves should have ongoing training in controls.

From the perspective of COSO's *Internal Control—Integrated Framework,* internal control naturally involves everyone in an organization; therefore, everyone (and the organization itself) can benefit from wider awareness of control procedures and their importance.

Relationship of training and the engagement process

Audits go more smoothly if those being interviewed during the engagement are willing and cooperative participants. Providing audit clients the opportunity to attend a well-structured workshop on COSO controls can help them understand the importance of audits and, perhaps, make them more comfortable with the process and more willing to provide useful, complete information.

COSO training would give the audit clients a full understanding of the five components of the framework:

- **Control environment.** Everyone is doing the right things in their job.
- **Risk assessment.** Risks are considered for all objectives.
- **Control activities.** Controls are in place because of identified risks.
- **Information and communication.** Data is available and discussed.
- **Monitoring.** Achievement of objectives is being monitored.

Knowledge of these components and the related factors help the clients to understand the necessary management activities to be evaluated in making a conclusion on the quality of internal controls.

The performance of this type of training helps the audit clients to provide better performance in their job responsibilities, which helps the organization achieve its objectives. This type of training also helps the internal audit activities be understood and be well received by the clients being audited.

Project team advisor

Internal auditors may consult with teams working on business process reengineering, new business development, post-investment reviews, and similar projects, providing advice on risk management, governance, and controls, but they are constrained from making management decisions and implementing such decisions.

Business process mapping

Business process mapping is often used in consulting engagements as the equivalent of an operational audit. Business process mapping often begins by getting a process owner to lead the internal auditor on a walk-through and then conducting a flowcharting activity to map the process and identify where value is added and where business process improvements could be made, such as by simultaneously performing some activities or by eliminating non-value-added activities. It can also reveal where controls are used and whether they are functioning as intended. Many other methods of business process mapping can also be performed. See Part 1, Section III, for other methods.

Walk-throughs

Walk-throughs are step-by-step demonstrations or explanations of a process or task conducted by the process or task owner in the presence of the internal auditor. Internal auditors use walk-throughs to better understand a process flow and to verify the actual state of controls in an organization: which controls are included in normal activities and which controls are effectively executed in the real world.

Exhibit I-31 shows that walk-throughs can help reveal the root cause of a control weakness or failure.

Exhibit I-31: What Walk-Throughs May Reveal

Walk-Through Reveals . . .	Potential Root Cause(s)	Potential Recommendation
The employee is not executing the control.	The employee has an incomplete understanding of the control procedure or its purpose.	Recommend better training on the control.
	The employee is deliberately omitting the control due to time, cost, or other motives.	Report the issue to local management.
The employee performs the control correctly despite evidence of control failures.	The employee does not usually perform the control and is doing it only when observed.	Discuss the potential problem with local management.
The employee is attempting to execute the control but is not following the proper procedure.	The employee has an incomplete understanding of the procedure or is deliberately modifying it.	Implement better training or management discipline.
	The procedure does not work well in practice despite being theoretically sound, either because the environment has changed since the procedure was designed or because the worker had no input in control design and it is impractical to implement as written.	Recommend that the control be revised or redesigned with worker input to be more effective and/or efficient.

Separating failures in the design of controls from failures in their execution can help internal auditors add value. When employees are better educated on controls, they will be more proactive in implementing them. When controls are designed more effectively, especially when the worker participates in the design of procedures, it reduces worker frustrations, promotes buy-in, and helps motivate good behavior.

Flowcharting

Next to personal inspection, process documentation is most commonly achieved through the use of flowcharts. A flowchart is a graphical representation of the actual or ideal path followed by any service or product. It provides a visual sequence of the steps in a process, illustrates the relationship between parts, and identifies what the process does or should do.

Flowcharts can be created in a variety of ways, from highly informal pencil drawings on scraps of paper to technically sophisticated computer graphics. One effective way to construct a flowchart is to gather all stakeholders in the process together to identify the steps. Each step can be described on a Post-it™ note, and the notes can be arranged and rearranged to create a map of the sequence all can agree upon. Flowcharting software ranges from Microsoft Word or Excel (which include standard flowcharting symbols) through various graphics programs to specialized charting applications such as Microsoft Visio, SmartDraw, Edraw, and numerous others.

The auditor can develop a flowchart of any process, from the process of the audit itself to the processes to be audited. In any case the benefits are the same: Drawing out each step of a process provides an easy-to-follow, start-to-finish map. When each proposed or existing step has been placed on the "map," the auditor and other reviewers can more readily assess which steps are crucial, which can be omitted, and which should be sequenced differently—as well as identifying places where new steps should be added.

Flowcharts have multiple uses—developing processes, refining processes, and auditing processes among them. In the process of creating the flowchart, participants may discover points of weakness in controls—lack of supervision, assignment of responsibilities to the wrong level of the organization, failure to segregate functions to avoid conflict of interest, and so on. In other instances participants may all agree that a flowchart provides an accurate description of what happens in reality, but when comparing it against field observations the auditor may find that in fact it does not reflect what actually happens.

Flowcharting a process helps to provide a complete picture of what is happening in the process from beginning to end, including the control points. A flowchart eliminates abstractions about how work flows through a system.

During the planning phase of an engagement, internal auditors may review existing flowcharts or they may prepare new flowcharts. When reviewing an existing flowchart, an internal auditor can make a preliminary assessment about identification of risks, the adequacy of controls, or if there are unnecessary controls in the process. The internal auditor should also verify that the flowchart is current and accurately reflects the process. The reality is that processes change but flowcharts are not always updated.

Because flowcharting has been so widely used in so many organizations, it has its own vocabulary of standard symbols to represent the typical parts of a process, such as operations, documents, data storage, decision points, and many other procedural milestones. Common symbols internal auditors use are shown in Exhibit I-32.

Exhibit I-32: Standard Flowchart Symbols

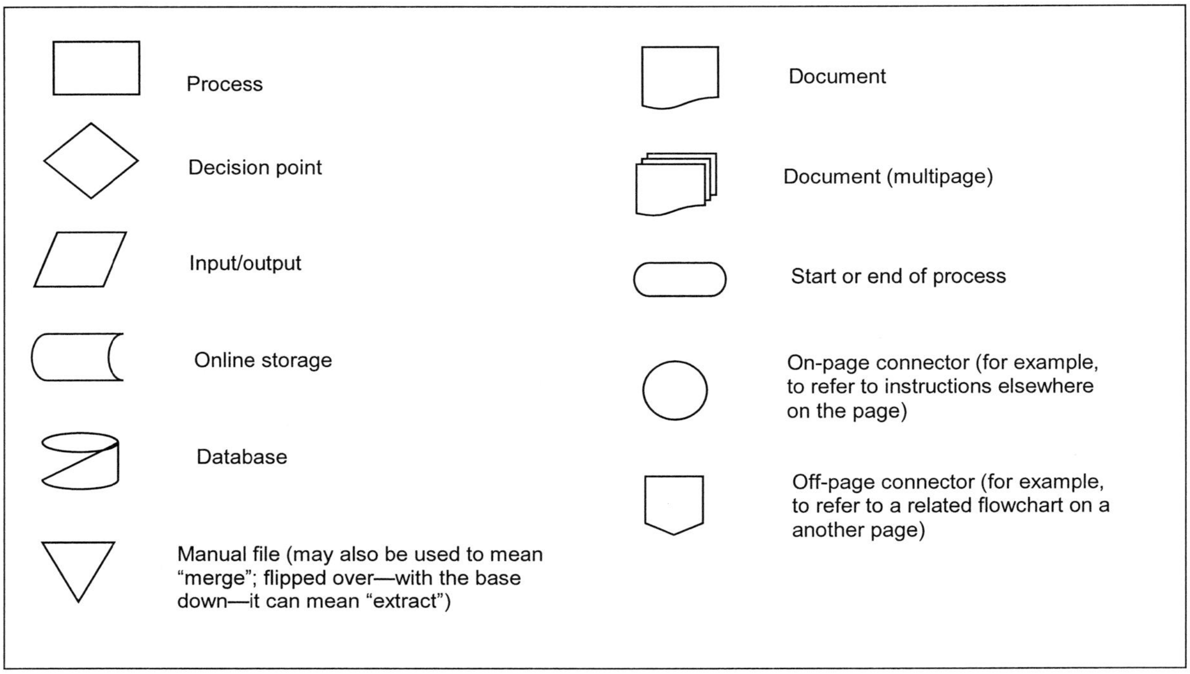

Flowcharts range from simple to complex depending on the level of detail shown. There are also several formats for different types of flowcharts. Each type can be used to highlight different aspects of a process or task.

An example of a flowchart using a vertical format is shown in Exhibit I-33 on the next page. (Other formats are presented in Part 1.) The process charted includes the scheduling, pressing, assembly, and inspection of components. Note that the inspections function appears at two different points in the process, complicating the map.

Flowcharts can yield much useful information for internal auditors. They provide a clear picture of how a process works by illustrating the relationship of various steps and control points. They provide a common reference point and standard language for talking about an existing process or project during an audit engagement.

Exhibit I-33: Vertical Flowchart

Vertical format emphasizing flow through departments

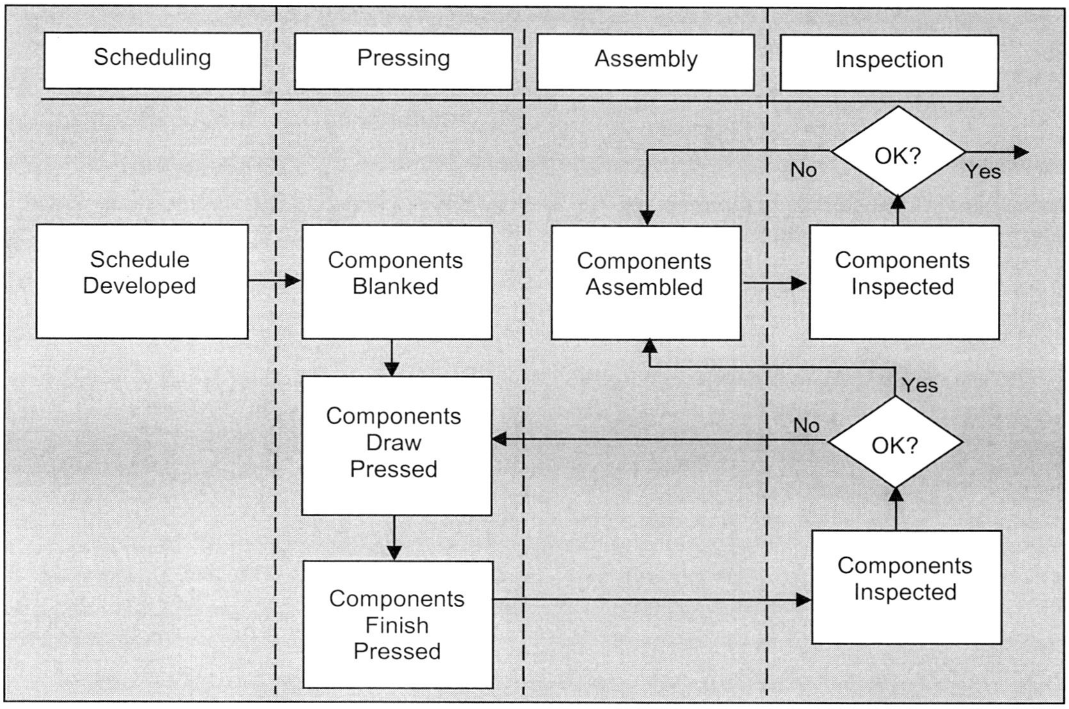

Benchmarking

A benchmark is simply a goal that an organization (or person) aims to achieve. It is measured against an internal or external group for the purpose of determining areas for potential improvement and to identify best practices. Internal benchmarks include historical data as well as goals and objectives; external benchmarks include industry standards or best practices. Regulatory requirements are another external standard of comparison.

Effective benchmarking depends upon the care and intelligence invested in selecting the goal. A benchmark that can't be measured, can't be reached, or can be reached too easily has little or no value. Evaluating the benchmarks set by clients within the organization is a service appropriate for internal auditors to provide. Benchmarking is especially appropriate in performance audits and in total quality audits. (Benchmarking is in fact associated with TQM.)

Benchmarking also assumes that reaching the benchmark set for the organization will help it grow, gain market share, improve customer satisfaction, or otherwise achieve a significant goal. A department might benchmark the performance of its employee rugby team, but that's unlikely to be a mission-critical matter.

Classifications of benchmarking

There are several widely accepted ways of selecting benchmarks that are measurable, precise, meaningful, and realistic. Exhibit I-34 describes common classifications for benchmarking activities.

Exhibit I-34: Classifications of Benchmarking

Description	Example	Advantages	Disadvantages
Internal benchmarking			
Comparing similar information within process or entity, either achievable performance above current baseline or stellar practice.	Historical comparison of manufacturing processes, services, or types of reports: • Across divisions. • Between different locations. • With another function.	Fairly easy to collect data.	Focus is somewhat limited and possibly biased.
Competitive benchmarking			
Comparing measures with similar measures of direct competitors, locally, nationally, or worldwide.	Review of practices, policies, procedures, services, and timeliness of market share leader in hi-tech electronics industry with goal of surpassing that leader.	Comparisons with organizations in same industry typically yield valuable, relevant information.	• Data may be difficult to collect; may encounter resistance with direct competitors. • Ethical/legal issues may be concern.
Industry benchmarking			
Comparing processes to those with similar processes in the same industry.	Steel manufacturer reviewing other steel manufacturers to determine average spending on pollution control equipment.	Likely to create realistic benchmark.	Can be limiting or unambitious.
Functional benchmarking			
Compares organizations with related functions in same technical area to show what is being achieved in other industries.	Comparison of billing and collection procedures between hospital and credit card company.	Typically little resistance encountered in partnering and collecting data.	Relevance across industries may be limited.
Generic benchmarking			
Comparing process in one operation against process with similar features but in another industry.	Comparison of customer service wait times among various call centers in home country and in other countries.	Spurs innovation.	May be problems and/or high costs associated with translating practices from one organization to another.
Best-in-class benchmarking			
Comparing measures with those of organizations that are best in class for function.	Comparison of process management between American companies and a Malcolm Baldrige National Quality Award winner.	• Spurs innovation. • Typically little resistance encountered in partnering and collecting data.	May be problems and/or high costs associated with translating practices from one organization to another.

Systems development life cycle review

Organizations need to control information system resources as they do human resources or any other precious organizational resource. For this reason, the process of systems development has a unique methodology and discipline.

Sawyer notes that the systems development life cycle (SDLC) should involve all stakeholders in the system being created or overhauled. Stakeholders encompass all those who have an organizational interest in the day-to-day operations of the system. The auditor has significant responsibilities during the SDLC:

- Ensuring that stakeholder interests are at the forefront of the development objectives
- Ensuring that the development project follows the organization's standards for systems development

Exhibit I-35 shows a typical systems development life cycle. (Other models exist.)

Exhibit I-35: Systems Development Life Cycle

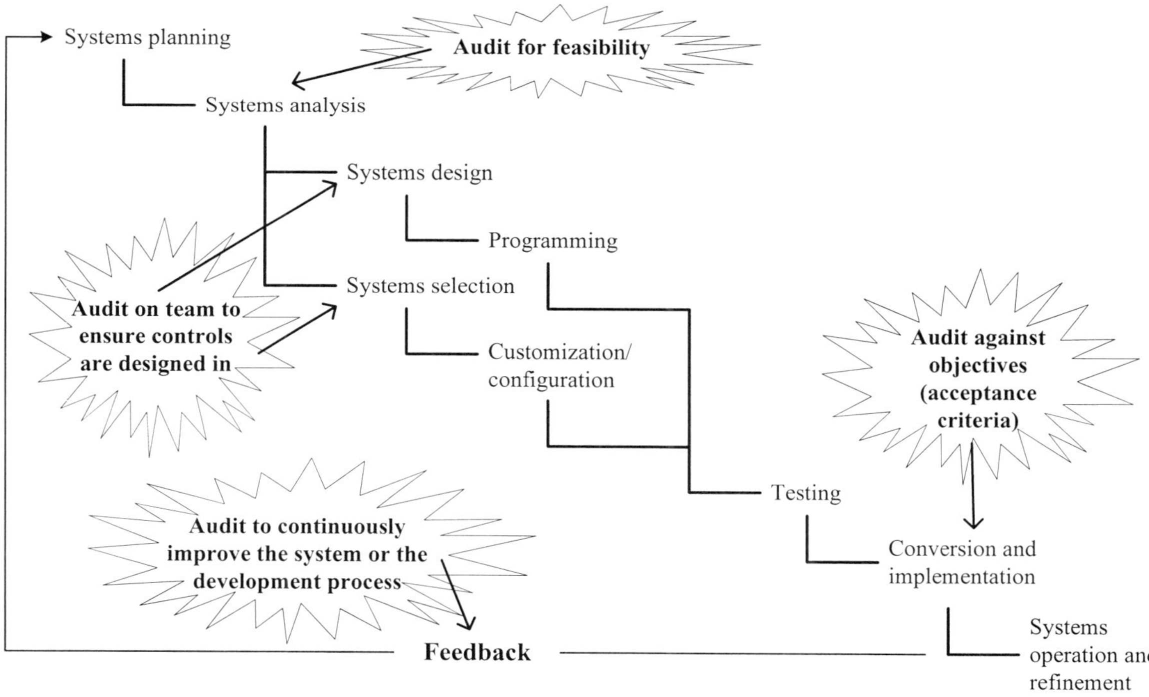

Auditors could be involved in a design review at several places in this cycle:

- During systems analysis as a project team member to evaluate the feasibility of proposed systems or the process used to assess feasibility
- During system design or system selection as a project team member to ensure that controls are designed in

- During conversion and implementation to ensure that the project meets objectives and acceptance criteria
- During feedback as part of a post-project design or acquisition review for continuous improvement of the system and/or the process in general

For example, during systems analysis, the internal auditor's consulting role for a feasibility study (a study to determine if a project will add value and satisfy objectives at a reasonable cost) could include ensuring that:

- The team includes appropriate stakeholder representation.
- The team has sufficient hardware and software expertise.
- A thorough analysis of the preexisting manual or automated system is conducted.
- Control deficiencies identified through audits are considered.
- Specifications for the new system consider anticipated growth, not just current volume.
- Risk of fraud or the loss of control is considered.
- Users agree on the proposed system.
- Budget estimates are reasonable and supportable.
- Input and output requirements are clearly defined.
- Reasonable conversion plans are formulated.
- Proper written authorization is obtained for each phase of the SDLC.

A more detailed review of the components of the SDLC is presented in Part 3.

Review of performance audits

The earlier discussion of performance audit engagements explained the use of key performance indicators by management to measure progress. KPIs should be measurable, selective (you can't efficiently measure every activity), and tied to the organization's major objectives (hence, "key"). Internal audit can work with clients to develop performance measures as well as review them in an audit.

Next Steps

You have completed Part 2, Section I, of The IIA's CIA Learning System®. Next, check your understanding by completing the online section-specific test(s) to help you identify any content that needs additional study.

Once you have completed the section-specific test(s) and feel confident that you have mastered the information, you can advance to studying Section II.

Section II: Managing Individual Engagements

This section is designed to help you:

- *Establish engagement objectives/criteria and finalize the engagement scope.*
- *Plan engagements to ensure identification of key risks and controls.*
- *Complete a detailed risk assessment of each audit area.*
- *Use a risk control matrix to ensure that all significant risks are addressed in the audit.*
- *Determine engagement procedures.*
- *Prepare an engagement work program.*
- *Target audit-related sources of evidence and select appropriate audit tests.*
- *Determine staffing and resources needed for the engagement.*
- *Construct an audit staff schedule for effective use of time.*
- *Direct/supervise individual engagements.*
- *Create an audit work plan.*
- *Nurture instrumental relations, build bonds, and work with others toward shared goals.*
- *Coordinate work assignments among audit team members when serving as auditor-in-charge of a project.*
- *Review work papers.*
- *Conduct exit conferences.*
- *Complete performance appraisals of engagement staff.*
- *Initiate preliminary communication with engagement clients.*
- *Communicate interim progress.*
- *Develop recommendations when appropriate.*
- *Prepare a report or other communication.*
- *Describe the characteristics of an effective report.*
- *Approve the engagement report.*
- *Determine distribution of the report.*
- *Obtain management response to a report.*
- *Report outcomes to appropriate parties.*
- *Identify appropriate methods to monitor engagement outcomes.*
- *Monitor engagement outcomes and determine appropriate follow-up by the internal audit activity.*
- *Conduct follow-up and report on management's response to internal audit recommendations.*
- *Escalate issues if auditor-in-charge believes management is accepting too much risk.*
- *Report significant audit issues periodically to senior management and the board.*

The Certified Internal Auditor (CIA) exam questions based on content from this section make up approximately 40% to 50% of the total number of questions for Part 2. All topics are covered at the "P—Proficiency" level, meaning that you are responsible not only for comprehension and recall of information but also for higher-level mastery, including application, analysis, synthesis, and evaluation.

Section Introduction

Section II moves from the general work of internal auditing to the specific processes used to:

- **Plan engagements,** which includes establishing engagement objectives, developing an audit program that incorporates activities aimed at meeting the organization's risk management objectives, allocating staff and resources, and scheduling (Chapter A).

- **Supervise engagements,** which calls upon the audit leader to manage the audit team and its work product, to assess client understanding and satisfaction with the audit, and to evaluate staff performance on the audit engagement (Chapter B).

- **Communicate effectively** throughout the engagement process with operational management, senior management, and the board, which includes preliminary and interim communication and preparation and distribution of the final audit report (Chapter C).

- **Monitor engagement outcomes,** which involves both planning—deciding what will be monitored and how—and implementation of monitoring activities and may also include following up on management's response to audit recommendations, escalating audit issues to senior management and the board if necessary, and reporting on significant audit issues to senior management and the board (Chapter D).

This section of Part 2 focuses on the issue of what follows an audit engagement and the delivery of the engagement report. The results noted in the engagement report have the potential to increase the effectiveness of controls and management of risk throughout the organization but only if they are translated by management into actions and if the success of implemented changes is monitored. Internal auditing may facilitate this process of continual organizational improvement by providing specific observations, conveying the potential benefits of remedial action, ensuring response to significant risks, and conducting appropriate follow-up and monitoring activities. These tasks can be supported by the development of a culture that recognizes and addresses the obstacles to the implementation of audit findings, the reduction of organizational risk, and the implementation of a system for conducting follow-up. This section describes the four steps in this system, from determining appropriate follow-up to communicating the results of follow-up activity, and relates to the following standards:

- 2500—"Monitoring Progress"
- 2060—"Reporting to Senior Management and the Board"
- 2600—"Resolution of Senior Management's Acceptance of Risks"

Chapter A: Plan Engagements

Chapter Introduction

An engagement is "a specific internal audit assignment, task, or review activity, such as an internal audit, control self-assessment review, fraud examination, or consultancy" (*Standards* Glossary). An engagement that is carefully thought out and planned has a high probability of success. The planning process helps to ensure that meaningful work is performed, audit deliverables add value to the organization, and audit resources are used efficiently and effectively during the engagement.

This chapter focuses on the engagement planning process. Topics include:

1. Establish engagement objectives/criteria and finalize the scope of the engagement.
2. Plan the engagement to assure identification of key risks and controls.
3. Complete a detailed risk assessment of each audit area, prioritizing or evaluating risk/control factors.
4. Determine engagement procedures and prepare an engagement work program.
5. Determine the level of staff and resources need for the engagement.
6. Construct an audit staff schedule for effective use of time.

While many organizations have documented audit programs or suggested practices for many audit activities, it is important that the work/audit program for each engagement be developed.

Related *Standards* and Practice Advisories

The *Standards* and Practice Advisories related to engagement planning are listed in Exhibit II-1.

Exhibit II-1: Engagement Planning–Related *Standards* and Practice Advisories (continued on next page)

Standard	Related Guidance
Performance Standard 2200, "Engagement Planning" Internal auditors must develop and document a plan for each engagement, including the engagement's objectives, scope, timing, and resource allocations.	Practice Advisory 2200-1, "Engagement Planning"
Performance Standard 2201, "Planning Considerations" In planning the engagement, internal auditors must consider: • The objectives of the activity being reviewed and the means by which the activity controls its performance; • The significant risks to the activity, its objectives, resources, and operations and the means by which the potential impact of risk is kept to an acceptable level; • The adequacy and effectiveness of the activity's governance, risk management, and control processes compared to a relevant control framework or model; and • The opportunities for making significant improvements to the activity's governance, risk management, and control processes.	
Implementation Standard 2201.A1 (Assurance Engagements) When planning an engagement for parties outside the organization, internal auditors must establish a written understanding with them about objectives, scope, respective responsibilities, and other expectations, including restrictions on distribution of the results of the engagement and access to engagement records.	
Implementation Standard 2201.C1 (Consulting Engagements) Internal auditors must establish an understanding with consulting engagement clients about objectives, scope, respective responsibilities, and other client expectations. For significant engagements, this understanding must be documented.	
Performance Standard 2210, "Engagement Objectives" Objectives must be established for each engagement.	Practice Advisory 2210-1, "Engagement Objectives"
Implementation Standard 2210.A1 (Assurance Engagements) Internal auditors must conduct a preliminary assessment of the risks relevant to the activity under review. Engagement objectives must reflect the results of this assessment.	Practice Advisory 2210.A1-1, "Risk Assessment in Engagement Planning"
Implementation Standard 2210.A2 (Assurance Engagements) Internal auditors must consider the probability of significant errors, fraud, noncompliance, and other exposures when developing the engagement objectives.	

Exhibit II-1: Engagement Planning–Related *Standards* and Practice Advisories (continued on next page)

Standard	**Related Guidance**
Implementation Standard 2210.A3 (Assurance Engagements) Adequate criteria are needed to evaluate controls. Internal auditors must ascertain the extent to which management has established adequate criteria to determine whether objectives and goals have been accomplished. If adequate, internal auditors must use such criteria in their evaluation. If inadequate, internal auditors must work with management to develop appropriate evaluation criteria.	
Implementation Standard 2210.C1 (Consulting Engagements) Consulting engagement objectives must address governance, risk management, and control processes to the extent agreed upon with the client.	
Implementation Standard 2210.C2 (Consulting Engagements) Consulting engagement objectives must be consistent with the organization's values, strategies, and objectives.	
Performance Standard 2220, "Engagement Scope" The established scope must be sufficient to satisfy the objectives of the engagement.	
Implementation Standard 2220.A1 (Assurance Engagements) The scope of the engagement must include consideration of relevant systems, records, personnel, and physical properties, including those under the control of third parties.	
Implementation Standard 2220.A2 (Assurance Engagements) If significant consulting opportunities arise during an assurance engagement, a specific written understanding as to the objectives, scope, respective responsibilities, and other expectations should be reached and the results of the consulting engagement communicated in accordance with consulting standards.	
Implementation Standard 2220.C1 (Consulting Engagements) In performing consulting engagements, internal auditors must ensure that the scope of the engagement is sufficient to address the agreed-upon objectives. If internal auditors develop reservations about the scope during the engagement, these reservations must be discussed with the client to determine whether to continue with the engagement.	
Performance Standard 2230, "Engagement Resource Allocation" Internal auditors must determine appropriate and sufficient resources to achieve engagement objectives based on an evaluation of the nature and complexity of each engagement, time constraints, and available resources.	Practice Advisory 2230-1, "Engagement Resource Allocation"

Exhibit II-1: Engagement Planning–Related *Standards* and Practice Advisories (concluded)

Standard	**Related Guidance**
Performance Standard 2240, "Engagement Work Program" Internal auditors must develop work programs that achieve the engagement objectives.	Practice Advisory 2240-1, "Engagement Work Program"
Implementation Standard 2240.A1 (Assurance Engagements) Work programs must include the procedures for identifying, analyzing, evaluating, and documenting information during the engagement. The work program must be approved prior to its implementation, and any adjustments approved promptly.	
Implementation Standard 2240.C1 (Consulting Engagements) Work programs for consulting engagements may vary in form and content depending upon the nature of the engagement.	

Topic 1: Establish Engagement Objectives/Criteria and Finalize the Scope of the Engagement (Level P)

Developing an engagement plan necessitates defining the objectives, criteria, and scope of the engagement. All should be documented. Audit engagement objectives answer the question "Why are we auditing this activity?" Audit scope answers the questions "What will we review?" and "What are the boundaries of the audit?" Audit criteria answer the question "Are the requirements being met?"

Engagement objectives

Performance Standard 2210, "Engagement Objectives," explicitly states: "Objectives must be established for each engagement." The *Standards* Glossary defines engagement objectives as "broad statements developed by internal auditors that define intended engagement accomplishments."

Practice Advisory 2210-1, "Engagement Objectives," tells us: "Internal auditors establish engagement objectives to address the risks associated with the activity under review." Additional language in Practice Advisory 2210-1 states: "For planned engagements, the objectives proceed and align to those initially identified during the risk assessment process from which the annual audit plan is derived. For unplanned engagements, the objectives are established prior to the start of the engagement and are designed to address the specific issue that prompted the engagement."

Having clear and agreed-upon engagement objectives is essential to an effective and efficient audit and to the task of supervising audit performance. The engagement objectives describe the quantity and quality of work to be performed, which in turn affect the audit work program, staffing, scheduling, and communication with clients and stakeholders.

Developing engagement objectives based on risk assessment of the area to be audited supports the fundamental risk-based focus of the internal audit activity.

Differentiating engagement objectives from operational objectives

The preliminary survey looks at the objectives of the operation—what the operation is supposed to achieve. If the internal auditor finds that the area lacks objectives, time is usually spent working with operational management to develop appropriate ones.

Engagement objectives are different from management's operational objectives. Where operational objectives specify what the client hopes to accomplish, engagement objectives deal with what the internal auditor hopes to accomplish. Engagement objectives are the internal auditor's means for determining how well operating objectives are being met. Consider the following examples of the operating and engagement objectives for different engagements.

Type of audit:	Marketing department
Operating objective:	Increase product recognition in China market.
Engagement objective:	Identify and evaluate controls in place to increase product recognition in China.

Type of audit:	Pharmaceutical research and development
Operating objective:	Bring three new drugs to market in the next five years.
Engagement objective:	Identify and evaluate controls in place to bring three new drugs to market in the next five years.

Type of audit:	Accounts payable department
Operating objective:	Pay invoices on a timely basis after verifying receipt of services or products.
Engagement objective:	Evaluate accurate and timely payment of invoices based on mitigation of risks, adequacy of controls, and compliance with financial policies and procedures.

Type of audit:	Manufacturing process
Operating objective:	Complete the manufacture of x number of products each day.
Engagement objective:	Evaluate the accuracy and efficiency of the manufacturing process to determine that the products manufactured each day are complete, accurate, and satisfactory for delivery to customers. Evaluate the accuracy and reliability of the measurement, reporting, and monitoring systems for production data.

Engagement objectives typically fall into one of the categories listed in Exhibit II-2 on the next page. These objectives are aligned with the COSO internal control framework.

At this point in the planning process, the internal audit activity may already have engagement objectives in place. For example, if the upcoming audit is part of a regular rotation, the internal auditor would have engagement objectives from prior audits. However, these internal audit objectives may very well need to be refined and/or prioritized, taking into account activity risk assessment results.

Ultimately, engagement objectives become the cornerstone for the work program and the audit fieldwork.

Engagement scope

As noted earlier, Performance Standard 2220, "Engagement Scope," states that the established scope must satisfy the objectives of the engagement. Engagement procedures help the internal auditor to accomplish engagement objectives. Collectively, engagement objectives and procedures are what define the engagement scope.

Scope establishes the boundaries of the internal audit. Essentially, it identifies what the internal auditor will do by specifying which activities will be reviewed and which activities will be excluded from the engagement.

A scope statement may include a description of the nature and extent of the audit work as well as supportive information such as the time period reviewed.

Implementation Standards 2220.A1, 2220.A2, and 2220.C1, which were described in Exhibit II-1, apply to developing scope statements and designing audit services.

Exhibit II-2: Broad Categories of Engagement Objectives

Category	Description
Effectiveness and efficiency of operations	**Measures** such as: • Profitability (maximize revenue or minimize costs). • Delivery of excellent products and services. • Reduced processing time. • Safeguarding of assets (physical, human, information). • Support of organizational mission and vision. • Support of appropriate work environment for employees. **Examples:** • Evaluate if controls installed in systems are working to maximize the accuracy and efficiency of a process. • Evaluate controls over physical access to a facility. • Evaluate controls over safeguarding of assets. • Evaluate if the right personnel have been assigned the correct job responsibilities and have received appropriate training.
Reliability of reporting	**Measures** such as: • Maintenance of accurate financial records. • Collection of useful, reliable, and timely information for decision making. **Examples:** • Evaluate controls over timely recognition of revenues. • Evaluate if the identification and reporting of risks and controls are adequate for the enterprise risk management reporting process. • Identify and evaluate if the correct reports are given to the proper managers in the organization. • Validate the accuracy of reporting by confirming the accuracy of data provided. • Evaluate if the personnel responsible for reporting are doing their jobs correctly and accurately and providing accurate reports.
Compliance	**Measures** such as: • Compliance with applicable laws and regulations. • Compliance with internal policies and procedures. **Examples:** • Evaluate if there is there a process in place to stay updated daily with legal and regulatory changes. • Evaluate how organizational objectives and procedures are communicated to all employees. • Evaluate the success of the "tone at the top" perspective of the organization as perceived in the part of the organization being audited. • Evaluate controls in place to ensure that the travel expense policy is followed.

Let's return to our previous example of the accounts payable department. Here are the objectives.

Operating objective:	Pay invoices on a timely basis after verifying receipt of services or products.
Engagement objective:	Evaluate accurate and timely payment of invoices based on mitigation of risks, adequacy of controls, and compliance with financial policies and procedures.

Based on these objectives, a scope statement should specify:

Inclusion:	What areas are within the scope (e.g., invoices, vendor management, accounts payable application, invoice processing, payments, accounting journal entries)?
Exclusion:	What are areas that a reasonable person would expect to find intentionally excluded from the scope?

A plausible scope statement example might be:

> The internal audit activity will conduct a compliance review of the accounts payable department that will take into account all payments of invoices from January 1, 20xx, to December 31, 20xx.

Scope limitations

To fulfill the internal audit activity's professional obligation to maintain independence and objectivity, any restriction placed on internal audit that thwarts it from fulfilling the intended scope should be communicated, preferably in writing, to the board, audit committee, or other appropriate governing authority.

Engagement criteria

Before an audit engagement can be performed, the internal auditor-in-charge (the lead auditor) must identify the criteria to be used during the engagement. Internal audit criteria are the benchmarks against which the subject matter of the engagement can be assessed. They are "measuring sticks" that the internal audit activity will use in drawing conclusions about performance relative to audit objectives. Meaningful assurance can be provided to the board and senior management only if the conclusions reached are made in relation to a set of suitable criteria.

What constitutes suitable criteria? Generally speaking, criteria should be consistent with audit engagement objectives and ultimately yield useful information to the client. The lack of suitable criteria may result in the internal auditor drawing inappropriate conclusions.

Examples of generally accepted suitable criteria for assurance engagements include:

- Acts and regulations.
- Policies and procedures.
- Standards or guidelines.
- Risk management.
- Control frameworks (i.e., Control Objectives for Information and Related Technology [COBIT], COSO, AS/NZS ISO 31000:2009).
- Performance information.
- Client management roles and responsibilities.
- Industry best practices.
- Guidance provided by recognized bodies of experts.
- Benchmark evidence (benchmark studies).

Using performance information as the engagement criterion in an internal audit intended to provide assurance about process efficiency is an example of generally accepted criteria. The lead internal auditor would communicate this to management and also describe what will be tested, how much time will be spent testing, what access will be necessary, and so on.

When there are no generally accepted criteria (such as the examples listed) consistent with the audit engagement objectives, the lead internal auditor will need to sit down with client management and identify the criteria suitable for the engagement.

Topic 2: Plan Engagement to Assure Identification of Key Risks and Controls (Level P)

The Definition of Internal Auditing states that a focus in internal auditing is to "add value and improve an organization's operations." During engagement planning, internal auditors need to consider how the individual engagement can support both goals. A risk-based approach in all activities is an important component in achieving these goals, as it focuses the audit on the most important areas.

The *Standards* glossary defines risk as "the possibility of an event occurring that will have an impact on the achievement of objectives." The threats to the achievement of the goals and barriers to success in the engagement are the risks.

In fact, the *Standards* specify that an analysis of the risks for the area to be audited should be a part of the planning process. The description of Performance Standard 2201, "Planning Considerations," in Exhibit II-1 earlier in this chapter, noted factors internal auditors must consider in planning an engagement, including risk exposure and control issues. According to Practice Advisory 2060-1, "Reporting to Senior Management and the Board," significant risk exposures and control issues are "those conditions that, according the CAE's judgment, could adversely affect the organization and its ability to achieve its strategic, financial reporting, operational, and compliance objectives." A key control, according to *Sawyer's*, is a control "that must operate effectively to reduce a significant risk to an acceptable level."

The implication is that internal audit should be looking at all the key areas of risk and how they are managed, and, if the internal auditor believes the organization has taken unnecessary risks or has risk exposures that are unacceptable or too high, these should be discussed and agreed-upon with management.

Risk-based approach

A risk-based approach requires internal auditors to first understand the entity and its environment in order to identify risks. An experienced auditor's skill and judgment is exercised to put focus on the specific information that should be obtained through this process.

This reduces the potential for unnecessary information or information overload, saving critical time and resources.

Understanding the entity involves documenting:

- Operational objectives or goals.
- Level of compliance with laws, policies, and procedures.
- Key processes.
- Organizational structure (e.g., reporting relationships and supervision).
- Information systems.
- Identified key risks.
- Current controls.

As mentioned previously, gathering this information can be done in many ways, including:

- Initial client meeting(s).
- Conducting a preliminary survey.
- Performing an analytical review.
- Conducting interviews.
- Observation.
- Inspection of processes and documentation.
- Benchmarking.
- Reviewing prior audit reports.

By assessing identified risks, several factors (such as the nature of the risks, relevant controls, and level of evidence) are taken into consideration. The result of a risk assessment categorizes the engagement into areas of significant risk and areas of normal risk.

Understanding internal controls

Internal auditors need to understand internal controls that are considered likely to be relevant to the engagement (not all the controls the organization employs in managing its business).

The control framework assists internal auditors to focus on gaining an understanding of relevant controls by dividing the organization's internal controls into five components:

- **The control environment.** The culture of the organization in relation to controls and their impact.

- **The risk assessment process.** How the organization identifies, assesses and responds to its own business risks.

- **Information systems relevant to the engagement.** Systems related to the capture of significant transactions, events, conditions or accounting estimates, procedures, and reporting.

- **Control activities relevant to engagement.** The policies and procedures that help ensure that management directives are carried out. Examples of control activities include those relating to authorization, performance reviews, information processing, physical controls, and segregation of duties.

- **Monitoring of control activities.** Activities the organization uses to monitor control activities as well as how it takes action to address any identified deficiencies.

Understanding internal control in this way enables the internal auditor to identify what relevant controls (if any) are in place to test, whether the absence of controls creates risk, how or when to combine controls testing with substantive testing, how to test the operating effectiveness of controls and the extent of reliance that can be placed on internal controls (thereby reducing the extent of substantive testing).

Topic 3: Complete a Detailed Risk Assessment of Each Audit Area (Level P)

We have learned that internal audit engagements are intended to provide assurance to senior management and board. Engagements are chosen largely in response to enterprise-wide risk assessment.

Assessing risk in an engagement area furthers organizational risk management by helping to ensure that:

- The engagement planning is aligned with the entity-level risk assessment.
- The engagement planning leverages information from the entity-level risk assessment.
- The engagement is focused on risk.

Additional language about risk assessment for planning purposes is found in Implementation Standards 2210.A1, 2210.A2, 2210.C1, and 2210.C2, as described in Exhibit II-1 earlier in this chapter, and in the following Practice Advisories:

- **Practice Advisory 2210-1, "Engagement Objectives."** A portion of this endorsed and strongly recommended guidance says: "Internal auditors establish engagement objectives to address the risks associated with the activity under review. For planned engagements, the objectives proceed and align to those initially identified during the risk assessment process from which the annual audit plan is derived. For unplanned engagements, the objectives are established prior to the start of the engagement and are designed to address the specific issue that prompted the engagement."

- **Practice Advisory 2210.A1-1, "Risk Assessment in Engagement Planning.** "While much of this guidance relates to the preliminary survey of the engagement area, it does include the following suggestions for internal auditors to gain sufficient confidence that relevant risks are identified for the specific engagement:

  > Internal auditors consider management's assessment of risks relevant to the activity under review. The internal auditor also considers:
  > - The reliability of management's assessment of risk.
  > - Management's process for monitoring, reporting, and resolving risk and control issues.
  > - Management's reporting of events that exceeded the limits of the organization's risk appetite and management's response to those reports.
  > - Risks in related activities relevant to the activity under review.

Use of a risk control matrix

A risk control matrix (also known as an engagement-level or audit risk assessment) is a useful tool to help ensure that internal auditors adequately account for risk at the engagement level and ensure that all significant risks identified are addressed in subsequent fieldwork. No two matrices are exactly alike. The most common features are shown in the Exhibit II-3 example on the next page. Again, keep in mind that the steps carry over from the planning phase to audit fieldwork. Flowcharts and narrative techniques are sometimes used in conjunction with a risk control matrix.

Benefits of a risk control matrix

A risk control matrix can be time-consuming to develop. But the benefits of using the tool are significant. In addition to generally helping to account for risk at the engagement level and identify all significant risks, developing a matrix during the planning phase:

- Sets the stage for a more effective and efficient audit by focusing the audit on the areas of greatest risk.
- Ties the audit together by documenting the complete thought process from risk identification to audit program development.
- "Teaches" the risk assessment thought process; area management becomes a more effective "owner" of control.
- Facilitates participatory auditing.

Many organizations use the risk control matrix as a way to develop a list of all the controls to be tested during the internal audit. By including this level of detail in the matrix (which will make the matrix a very large document), this document can also serve as the work/audit program for the engagement. Further, incorporating testing results in this document can make the risk control matrix the major work paper for each area of the engagement.

Exhibit II-3: Risk Control Matrix Features

Business Objective(s)	Risks	Likelihood/ Significance	Controls	Evaluation of Adequacy	Tests of Effectiveness	Final Evaluation

Step 1: Identify business objectives. This step considers business objectives for the unit or process, not the control objectives. This can be accomplished by asking management to discuss their goals for the activity being reviewed. If no business objectives exist, the internal audit team should work with management to develop appropriate ones.

Step 2: Identify risks to business objectives. Risks that need to be controlled or mitigated can be identified in one of two ways: 1) Ask management what events or circumstances could prevent them from achieving their goals, or 2) walk management though the organizational risks identified at the macro (entity) level and ask whether or not each of these could impact the achievement of business objectives.

Step 3: Rate each risk in terms of likelihood and significance (L/S). Risks are usually rated as high, medium, or low, depending on how likely it is that the risk will occur and how significant the impact of its occurrence would be. Some ratings combine likelihood and significance, such as high likelihood/high significance or low likelihood/low significance.

Step 4: Identify the controls. Controls identified are really the risk management techniques determined based in part on risk appetite and risk tolerance levels. Common techniques are:

- **Avoid:** Redesign the process in a way that eliminates a particular risk or give up the activity if the risk cannot be lowered to an acceptable level.
- **Share:** Transfer part of the risk to another party through an arrangement like insurance, outsourcing, or hedging or spread the risk among several investments or processes.
- **Accept:** Accept risks that are not catastrophic and would not be cost-effective to reduce.
- **Reduce:** Use techniques that reduce the likelihood or significance of a harmful event or increase the likelihood of a positive event.
- **Increase:** Increase the risk by removing constraints when this increases opportunity and the risk remains within acceptable limits.

Step 5: Evaluate the adequacy of controls. This step asks the question "Are the control processes for managing this risk well-designed?" Analytic skills and professional judgment are used to determine the answer. The internal auditor:

- Identifies and documents the controls management says are in place.
- Evaluates how well-designed the controls are—if they are effective, efficient, economical, and working the way they were designed to work.

Step 6: Test the effectiveness of controls. Controls that are deemed adequate or well-designed are tested to determine if they are in fact operating as intended.

Step 7: Arrive at the final opinion on adequacy and effectiveness of controls. Final opinions are often stated in terms of both criteria. For example, a control may be deemed adequate but ineffective due to lack of compliance with procedures. Or the design of the control may be flawed because it overcontrols insignificant risks, leading to an opinion of inadequacy.

Source: © James Roth, AuditTrends.

Topic 4: Determine Engagement Procedures and Prepare Engagement Work Program (Level P)

Engagement objectives help define an audit's deliverables—its measurable, verifiable work products. Audit deliverables document work that will be performed in the course of the engagement, for example, research activities (process mapping, walk-through, interviews), the risk assessment, the audit program, testing results, audit findings, the draft report, and the final report.

This topic first looks at the internal audit charter and audit activity plan and then focuses on the audit or work program, which designs the tasks needed to provide the level and scope of assurance specified in the engagement objectives.

Approval of the audit activity charter and plan

The internal audit activity charter

The internal audit activity operates through an audit charter, which is prepared by the chief audit executive, approved by senior management and by the board or audit committee, and communicated to engagement clients.

The standard addressing the board's approval of the audit charter is Attribute Standard 1000, "Purpose, Authority, and Responsibility": "The purpose, authority, and responsibility of the internal audit activity must be formally defined in an internal audit charter, consistent with the Definition of Internal Auditing, the Code of Ethics, and the *Standards*. The chief audit executive must periodically review the internal audit charter and present it to senior management and the board for approval." The significance of this approval is that the internal audit activity has the full authority and backing of the board in carrying out its activities, as long as it conforms to the charter.

The internal audit activity plan

The CAE presents a plan of audit engagements, usually once a year, to the board for approval. Just as the charter gives the internal auditing activity the authority to do its work without hindrance by anyone in the organization, the approval of the audit plan authorizes the specific audit engagements. We should emphasize, though, that audit plans are flexible and typically change throughout the year as new risks emerge. The CAE should inform the audit committee of these changes but does not need specific approval of a new project before carrying it out.

In addition to communicating the internal audit activity's scope of work, work schedule, staffing plan, and financial budget to the board for review and approval, updates outlining any significant changes to the plan must be presented to the board for approval, as warranted. Both the engagement plan and the interim updates should contain sufficient information to enable the board to ascertain whether the internal audit activity's objectives and plans support those of the organization and the board.

Engagement work program

All of the planning activities discussed thus far lead to the preparation of the engagement work program. The resulting document reflects the systematic and disciplined approach mentioned in the Definition of Internal Auditing as it will apply to the audit to be performed. A work program provides documentation of the planned engagement that can be used to secure management approval.

The *Standards* Glossary defines an engagement work program as "a document that lists the procedures to be followed during an engagement, designed to achieve the engagement plan." An engagement work program is also called an audit program during assurance engagements; thus, the two terms are often interchanged.

Additional language related to preparation of an engagement work program is contained in Implementation Standards 2240.A1 and 2240.C1; see Exhibit II-1 at the beginning of this chapter.

Well-crafted, an engagement work program:

- Provides an outline of work to be performed and facilitates an understanding of the audited unit.
- Furnishes evidence that the work is adequately planned.
- Provides a record for management review.
- Provides assurances that all risks have received adequate consideration.
- Assists in controlling work and assignment responsibilities.
- Gives order and coherence to the audit.

Specific time frames for activities are often included in the document. But as experience has shown, the work program often needs minor modifications at the onset of the engagement. For example, the full extent of testing required may not be known until the testing procedures are underway. Minor adjustments are to be expected during the first part of the engagement. Any major modifications should be approved by appropriate management sources.

Engagement work plan[s] should be approved in writing by the chief audit executive or designee prior to the commencement of engagement work, where practicable. Initially, approval may be obtained orally, if factors preclude obtaining written approval prior to commencing engagement work. Adjustments to engagement work plans should be approved in a timely manner.

An engagement work program becomes guidance for performing the engagement. A sample work program is shown in Exhibit II-4.

Exhibit II-4: Work Program Example (continued on next page)

Audit Objectives:

Obj. 1. To determine that a preventive maintenance schedule has been developed and adhered to so that vehicles are safe and drivable.

Obj. 2. To determine that the authorized vendor lists and contracts are current and based on company standards, so that external maintenance and repairs are performed by qualified vendors.

Obj. 3. To determine that a repair log of in-house and vendor repairs is properly prepared so that maintenance is performed and documented according to company standards.

Obj. 4. To determine that the policy governing in-house repairs is followed so that minor mechanical repairs are made in-house.

Obj. 5. To determine that vendor price lists are current, so that cars are repaired by authorized vendors at reasonable rates.

Obj. 6. To determine that supporting documentation exists and that expenses can be properly monitored and verified for reasonableness.

Obj. 7. To determine that maintenance expenses are properly recorded in the general ledger and are monitored.

Test Step	**WP Reference**	**Initial/ Date**
1. Obtain preventive maintenance schedule, a cars inventory listing at 12/31/xx, and a report of car additions and deletions for the audit period. A. Verify that all cars owned during the audit period are included on the schedule by comparing the preventive maintenance schedule to the inventory records and reports. B. Attest to the completeness of the schedule. Determine that the schedule contains the VEHNO, VIN, car description, scheduled maintenance dates, actual maintenance dates, and a description of the procedures performed. Document any exceptions and perform follow-up procedures.		
2. Select 30 cars from the preventive maintenance schedule for the audit period and test for the following attributes: A. Preventive maintenance was performed and documented on the schedule in accordance with company policy. (Belts and hoses were checked, fluids checked, brakes checked, etc.) B. Preventive maintenance was performed within established time frames or mileage parameters. C. Mechanic's record was obtained on preventive maintenance schedule repairs to be performed by outside vendors. Trace repair to repair log, vendor invoice, and canceled check. D. Mechanics initialed and dated preventive maintenance schedule. E. Evidence obtained of supervisory review.		

Exhibit II-4: Work Program Example (concluded)

Test Step	WP Reference	Initial/ Date
3. Obtain the vendor contracts. Review contract for propriety and reasonableness. Determine that contracts are current and in agreement with the authorized vendor list. 4. Obtain repair log for the audit period. A. Determine that work performed on cars is documented on the repair log and performed by approved vendors. B. Examine repair log and determine that work performed by outside vendors is in line with company policy. (Work that can be performed in-house should not be performed by outside vendors.) 5. Select 30 repairs from the repair log during the audit period and test for the following attributes: A. Proper completion of the repair log. B. Repair work performed by a vendor is adequately described. C. Mechanics initialed and dated repair log. D. Evidence of supervisory review. E. Trace repair to service request form and invoice. F. Repair work is performed by authorized vendors. Trace to the authorized vendor list. G. If repair was performed in-house, ascertain that current policy authorizes repair to be performed in-house. 6. Obtain current price lists for vendor repairs. Compare to an industry auto parts and service guide to determine reasonableness of prices. **Note:** An actual work program would contain additional steps to achieve the audit objectives.		

Source: "Auditing Techniques" course, The Institute of Internal Auditors, 2006.

Keep in mind that each work program will be unique depending on the scope of the engagement. In larger organizations a work program is typically very large. Work programs are less complex in small organizations and for internal audits being done by one person or when the amount of time is relatively short.

Engagement procedures are the means to attain engagement objectives. As in other areas of engagement planning, the internal auditor's judgment is key in determining the specific procedures to be employed and the level of evaluation necessary. Similar logic applies to determining which procedures apply to which engagement objectives.

Engagement procedures must be relevant to the selected objectives. A procedure may be applicable to the internal audit as a whole, but if it is erroneously applied to an objective, the result will be irrelevant. A simple example of this is designating interviewing in lieu of testing in a scenario that clearly necessitates actual testing. The interview results might be interesting, but they will be irrelevant in providing assurance.

There is no definitive list of internal audit procedures or a road map for matching procedures to engagement objectives. The internal auditor needs to discriminate between procedures that may be relevant and those that are unimportant.

One approach is to ensure that procedures are designed to test that controls achieve key attributes. For example, in an audit of a purchasing area, an engagement objective may be to assure that purchase transactions are authorized. In this case, engagement procedures should include verifying that the documentation received by purchasing agents contains signed approvals. Tasks such as the review of receiving memos and vendor invoices would provide no relevant information. "Authorized" is the attribute deemed to be important in this function.

Other attributes include accurate, reliable, timely, safe, secure, consistent, appropriate, actual, reasonable, compliant, and complete. For example, it's more likely that an auditor would look for "reasonable" processes than for "accurate" processes, because budgets are only estimates. However, the budget should also be "complete," including input from all departments within the organization.

Data collection

The *Standards* are very clear on the need for gathering the right facts to support audit objectives.

- Standard 2300, "Performing the Engagement": Internal auditors must identify, analyze, evaluate, and document sufficient information to achieve the engagement's objectives.
- Standard 2310, "Identifying Information": Internal auditors must identify sufficient, reliable, relevant, and useful information to achieve the engagement's objectives.

Sources of evidence

The information gathered to support the conclusions and recommendations in a final audit report—audit evidence—bears a resemblance to legal evidence, but they are not the same.

Audit evidence

Audit evidence—facts used to support audit opinions, conclusions, and recommendations—can derive from the following:

- **People.** This might include management of the area being audited, other personnel, individuals in other areas that interact with the audited area, and external individuals or groups (e.g., vendors). Representations or testimonial evidence include statements or written responses to inquiries or interviews, questionnaires, etc. They should have documentary support, such as system flowcharts or written policies and procedures.

- **Physical evidence.** Physical evidence generally is considered more reliable than the testimony of a person. It includes statements of observers, photographs, charts, maps, graphs, pictures, or videos of an act or condition.

- **Documentation.** Documentation is the most common source of audit evidence. It can be recorded in other media than paper and includes, among other examples, letters, memos, e-mails, invoices (external documents) and accounting records, program listings, activity and control logs, and systems development documentation. A caution is that documents can be forged.

- **Operations.** This includes activities, systems, work processes, and functions.

- **Measurements.** Measurements may be made by the auditor or the audit client. They can include measurements made on nominal, ordinal, linear, or ratio scales.

- **Software and electronic databases.** This includes operating and control software, applications, and data storage.

The source of evidence can add to, or detract from, its persuasiveness. Corroborative audit evidence from an independent third party can be more reliable than audit evidence from the organization being audited. Third-party evidence may be called external evidence to distinguish it from internal evidence provided by the audit customer.

The strength or weakness of the evidence depends on how persuasive it is. Audit evidence is persuasive if it enables the internal auditor to formulate well-founded conclusions and advice confidently. Recall the characteristics of information identified in Standard 2310: sufficient, reliable, relevant, and useful. Interpretation helps us define these terms:

> ***Sufficient*** *information is factual, adequate, and convincing so that a prudent, informed person would reach the same conclusions as the auditor.*
>
> ***Reliable*** *information is the best attainable information through the use of appropriate engagement techniques.*
>
> ***Relevant*** *information supports engagement observations and recommendations and is consistent with the objectives for the engagement.*
>
> ***Useful*** *information helps the organization meet its goals.*

Sufficient means that there should be enough evidence and different but related pieces of evidence should corroborate each other.

Reliable implies that the evidence comes from a credible source. This considers whether or not the internal auditor directly obtained the evidence.

Evidence may be reliable in itself but of no use if not relevant to the matter at hand. Relying on evidence that has little or no pertinence increases audit risk—the risk of reaching invalid conclusions and providing faulty advice.

The usefulness of information is a function of whether the information is germane to the organization.

There are no hard and fast rules regarding sufficiency, reliability, relevance, and usefulness of evidence. For example, while evidence obtained from independent (external) third parties is more reliable than evidence from internal personnel and corroborated evidence is more sufficient than uncorroborated or contradictory evidence, it is rare that the internal auditor would go directly to external sources without first investigating internal evidence.

The auditor must also consider when the evidence is needed and the methods used to collect the evidence in determining which engagement procedures will be performed. Management culture and operating style may impact evidence-gathering techniques. The internal auditor should consider what types of evidence will be most persuasive to those managers who will be making decisions concerning corrective actions.

Legal evidence
Internal auditors need not be expert in gathering evidence for use in court, but they may be called upon to gather data for use by a lawyer. If this happens, the auditor needs to be familiar with the major types of legal evidence:

- **Best evidence** is also called primary evidence and is generally physical or documentary. Original writing is required when available.
- **Secondary evidence** is inferior to primary evidence (best evidence) in reliability and may be a copy of a document or oral evidence of the document's contents. Oral testimony and written summaries are generally considered to be inferior to copies.
- **Direct evidence** proves a fact without requiring presumptions or interference. Testimony of an eyewitness to a fraud, for example, is direct evidence.
- **Conclusive evidence** leads to only one conclusion.
- **Circumstantial evidence** proves an intermediate fact from which a primary fact can be logically inferred.
- **Corroborative evidence** supplements evidence already given and tends to support it.
- **Opinions** are generally not considered allowable testimony in court unless offered by experts. Auditors should follow a similar guideline when they gather data, relying on opinion only if 1) the subject is outside their own knowledge and 2) the opinion is rendered by an unbiased expert.
- **Hearsay** is secondhand evidence and is generally ruled inadmissible in court. The auditor should not simply ignore the secondhand testimony, however, but should follow up with further inquiries to see if firsthand evidence exists.

Other concerns

The type of evidence is not always the auditor's sole concern when deciding the best way to support conclusions and recommendations. The auditor also needs to consider matters of timing and availability.

Availability of audit evidence

The internal auditor should consider the time during which evidence will be available for testing. This applies especially when the evidence is electronically stored. Audit evidence processed by electronic data interchange (EDI), document image processing (DIP), and dynamic systems such as spreadsheets may not be retrievable after a specified period of time if files are revised without being controlled or backed up.

Confidentiality of evidence

The internal auditor should always bear in mind the mandatory injunction, in the Code of Ethics, to honor the confidentiality requirements of the owners of audited data as well as regulatory requirements that may apply to certain types of evidence.

Access to necessary evidence

The other side of the coin of confidentiality of data is access to data. According to Standard 1110.A1, "The internal audit activity must be free from interference in determining the scope of internal auditing, performing work, and communicating results."

Audit tests

Audit tests are a means to obtain the data or evidence described above. Tests should be chosen according to the type of information that is required. Typical audit tests include:

- **Physical examination of objects.** For example, an audit test might entail verifying that a safety device is attached to a piece of equipment, checking an inventory against items in an office or warehouse, or confirming that cash or securities are presented as indicated.

- **Documentation tests.** These tests involve scrutiny of documents used in the organization. For example, the auditor might test that a business continuity plan has been revised and distributed as specified in policy. Entrance logs may be checked to test security controls. Contracts may be examined for proper signatures. Documents may be traced backward (vouching) or forward (tracing).

- **Inquiries.** These are appropriate when the auditor is seeking evidence from people, such as confirmation that employees have received necessary training to perform certain tasks.

- **Observations.** These may be necessary to assure that work processes or tasks are being performed according to defined procedures. For example, the auditor may observe a business process to test whether quality controls are working. Controls may be reperformed and observed to assure that they are performing accurately and as designed.

- **Computations and analysis.** These can gather evidence of errors and possibly fraud.

- **Comparisons.** These can reveal evidence of procedures that are not being followed, variances between specifications and actual performance that indicate lapses in quality controls, or improbable trends or relationships that can indicate fraud. For example, an increase in materials purchased can be compared to sales and inventory to test fraud controls.

Topic 5: Determine the Level of Staff and Resources Needed for the Engagement (Level P)

As noted earlier, Performance Standard 2230, "Engagement Resource Allocation," states: "Internal auditors must determine appropriate and sufficient resources to achieve engagement objectives based on an evaluation of the nature and complexity of each engagement, time constraints, and available resources."

The nature and complexity of the engagement can be assessed by evaluating the results of the enterprise-wide risk assessment and the preliminary survey and risk assessment of the engagement area under review.

The following additional guidance dealing with how to determine the appropriate level of staff and resources is contained in Practice Advisory 2230-1, "Engagement Resource Allocation":

> Internal auditors consider the following when determining the appropriateness and sufficiency of resources:
> - The number and experience level of the internal audit staff.
> - Knowledge, skills, and other competencies of the internal audit staff when selecting internal auditors for the engagement.
> - Availability of external resources where additional knowledge and competencies are required.
> - Training needs of internal auditors as each engagement assignment serves as a basis for meeting the internal audit activity's developmental needs.

In determining the level of audit staff for an engagement, the audit leader should consider:

- **The objectives of the audit and their implications in terms of necessary skills and knowledge.** Team leaders should consider the need for "soft" skills as well, especially in audits of sensitive areas, such as governance. Well-known and respected staff members may be needed to staff these audits.

- **The availability of staff with the necessary knowledge and skills.** If staff have experience in the audit area, the audit time may be shortened. If less-experienced auditors are used, more time may have to be allotted to review their work. (At the same time, providing experience to these auditors is an essential part of developing the human resources of the internal audit activity.)

- **The nature of the audit's deadline.** This may be a concern if a report is needed for compliance reasons or due diligence. It may be necessary to complete this audit in order to proceed to a related audit area.

- **The activity's priorities and resources.** Some resources may be necessary for audits considered to have a higher priority in the audit plan.

A decision may be made that additional knowledge, skills, and competencies are needed to perform the engagement. External services may need to be obtained to support or complement the internal audit team. Information technology is an example of an area that often requires external expertise.

Budget considerations

Setting a budget is an important consideration in engagement planning. It is often the principal control over the audit engagement.

The success of an engagement is often judged by:
- Achievement to the level of standards.
- Fulfillment of engagement objectives.
- Completion within budget.

Engagement budgets include statements of the time allowed, as time is the key factor in an internal audit activity. Budgeted hours (or time budgets) must be realistic and achievable. Some internal audit activities use deadlines to manage their budgets. They are often based on the level of associated risk.

The work accomplished in the time scheduled largely reflects the collective skills and expertise of the internal audit team. Logistics (such as client availability, site locations, complexity of operations to be examined, security clearances, and travel time) are additional factors that can impact a time budget. Setting intermediate target dates or milestones can help teams stay on target toward a final deadline. If target dates are missed, the root cause for the delay can be analyzed and possibly fixed by adding resources. If delays cannot be avoided, adjusting the time budget accordingly at least allows the audit manager to redeploy resources that are not yet needed to other engagements.

There are different schools of thought about the execution of time budgets:

- Adhere to the defined number of hours and move from the work once the time is expired.
- Perform engagement responsibilities to the fullest extent, even if this means budgeted hours are exceeded.
- If necessary, add staff and possibly money to perform the work within the scheduled time.

Completing an engagement on time and within budget is the ideal scenario. But no two engagements are exactly the same. Should mitigating circumstances arise, there is no universal correct position. It is always best that time budgets be sufficiently flexible to cover unanticipated demands on the internal audit activity.

Topic 6: Construct an Audit Staff Schedule for Effective Use of Time (Level P)

A staff schedule is an important tool in using the activity's resources efficiently. Engagement schedules are built on six basic blocks of time:

- Initial planning (e.g., interviews with the audit client, research into risks)
- Creation of the audit program, including audit objectives and tests
- Fieldwork (e.g., interviews, observations, process mapping, analyses)
- Internal audit manager review
- Report writing, which also includes review and editing
- Client review and discussions

Time required for each of these stages will vary, depending on the type of engagement and the complexity of the engagement's objectives. Staff required at each stage is indicated. It may be possible to allocate resources at certain points in the schedule and then transfer resources to another engagement.

Events must also be sequenced with an eye toward dependent tasks, tasks that must be completed first before another dependent activity can be begun. Efficiencies in scheduling can be achieved by finding tasks that can be completed concurrently.

Gantt chart

The Gantt chart (also known as a horizontal bar chart, a milestone chart, or an activity chart) is a project scheduling technique that divides each project into sequential activities with estimated start and completion times. It allows the decision maker to visually review a schematic presentation of the project time budget and allows for subsequent comparison with actual times. It can be a useful tool in identifying dependencies and concurrent activities and in scheduling audit team members.

To create a Gantt chart, the project manager plots the steps of the project and their sequence and duration. The list includes the earliest start date for each task, the estimated length of time it will take, and whether it is parallel or sequential. This forms the basis of the scheduling chart shown in Exhibit II-5. A Gantt chart's simplicity allows for easy schedule modifications.

Exhibit II-5: Gantt Chart

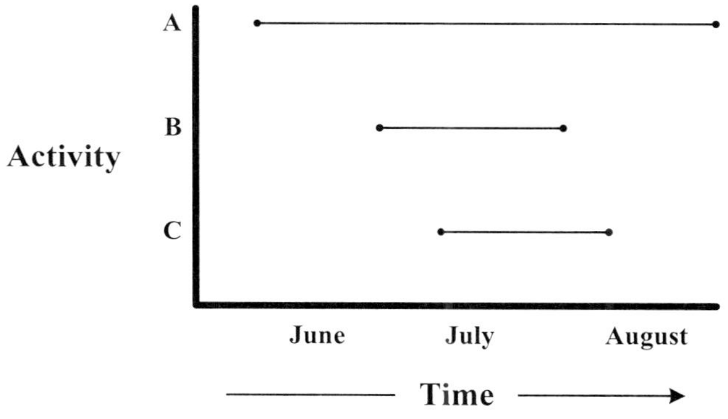

A Gantt chart:

- Helps plan tasks that need to be completed.
- Provides a basis for scheduling when tasks will be executed.

- Helps plan the allocation of resources necessary to complete the project.
- Helps determine the critical path for a project that needs to be completed by a specific date.
- Is appropriate for internal audit scheduling because the audit process does not often require sequence revisions.

Chapter B: Supervise Engagements

Chapter Introduction

To ensure that the internal audit function fulfills its charter, meets its key performance indicators, and continually improves the quality of its work, the chief audit executive or designee must maintain oversight of the activity's individual engagements. This chapter describes what is involved in the process of supervision, motivating internal audit team members, coordinating work for greater efficiency and effectiveness, and ensuring quality results and continuous improvement.

Because communication—within the team and with engagement clients—is such a critical component of effective supervision, communication merits its own discussion, in the next chapter, "Engagement Communication as a Process."

Topic 1: Direct/Supervise Individual Engagements (Level P)

Performance Standard 2340, "Engagement Supervision," states: "Engagements must be properly supervised to ensure objectives are achieved, quality is assured, and staff is developed." Interpretation tells us: *"The extent of supervision required will depend on the proficiency and experience of internal auditors and the complexity of the engagement. The chief audit executive has overall responsibility for supervising the engagement, whether performed by or for the internal audit activity, but may designate appropriately experienced members of the internal audit activity to perform the review. Appropriate evidence of supervision is documented and retained."*

Practice Advisory 2340-1, "Engagement Supervision," elaborates on how supervision is accounted for during engagement planning, emphasizing the chief audit executive's role in facilitating staff work, reviewing or ensuring review of work papers and reports, and resolving differences in professional judgment.

The Practice Advisory tells us:

> The chief audit executive (CAE) or designee provides appropriate engagement supervision. Supervision is a process that begins with planning and continues throughout the engagement. The process includes:
> - Ensuring designated auditors collectively possess the required knowledge, skills, and other competencies to perform the engagement.
> - Providing appropriate instructions during the planning of the engagement and approving the engagement program.
> - Ensuring the approved engagement program is completed unless changes are justified and authorized.
> - Determining engagement working papers adequately support engagement observations, conclusions and recommendations.
> - Ensuring engagement communications are accurate, objective, clear, concise, constructive, and timely.
> - Ensuring engagement objectives are met.
> - Providing opportunities for developing internal auditors' knowledge, skills, and other competencies.

Supervision focuses on progress toward achieving the engagement objectives. The audit manager can use an audit plan checklist to gauge this progress. A sample checklist is shown in Exhibit II-6 on the next page.

The audit manager must also monitor the engagement's progress against time budgets and schedules. Time records submitted periodically by audit staff can be aggregated and compared to budgets for the different phases of the audit. Milestone deliverables or accomplishments can be compared against the audit schedule to determine if the audit is on track to meet its completion date.

On a tactical level, planning and supervision involve considerations such as (but certainly not limited to) the following items:

- **Travel arrangements.** Are travel authorizations (e.g., passports, visas) or other arrangements required for the internal auditors to go to and from the client location?

- **On-site logistics.** On-site logistics encompasses whatever is required for the internal auditors to perform their work. Meeting rooms, office space, access to necessary locations, access to required equipment such as computers or telephones, and interpreters (if the client's and the auditor's native languages differ and require translation) are all examples.

Exhibit II-6: Sample Audit Work Plan Checklist

Audit title: ____________________ Targeted start date: __________

Audit budget: ____________________ Targeted completion date: __________

	W/P Ref.	Done By:
1. Review the annual plan risk assessments, the prior audit report, and post-audit review form to determine/document follow-up steps required.		
2. Review the audit time summary from the prior audit versus the findings and conclusions actually reported. Document your observations regarding scope adjustments, if any, driven by past audit results.		
3. Document your current assessment of risks and highlight areas of concern.		
4. Contact the independent accountants to determine if they have any specific concerns about this audit or any specific audit tests they want internal auditing to perform.		
5. Summarize the audit objectives in writing to focus efforts toward meeting objectives and to later facilitate evaluation of whether or not the audit accomplished the purpose intended. As a guide, audit objectives can generally be summarized regarding the evaluation of: • Reliability and integrity of information or recorded transactions. • Compliance with policies, directives, procedures, plans, laws, regulations. • Safeguarding of assets. • Economic and efficient uses of resources. • Accomplishment of established goals and objectives for programs or operations.		
6. Develop a staffing plan for the audit, appropriately matching skills and competencies to the identified needs and objectives and ensuring adequate objectivity.		
7. Prepare a project time record .		
8. Develop a detailed audit program and obtain internal audit management approval before fieldwork begins.		
9. Prepare and mail an audit notice advising all who need to know about the audit, its timing, and the audit objectives.		
10. Document the rationale for selecting audit entrance- and exit-level management to make sure that the management level selected has the authority to implement the agreed corrective actions.		
11. At the entrance conference, communicate the audit objectives to management audit customers. Obtain and document their comments and suggestions on how to facilitate positive audit results.		
12. Based on the entrance conference and an on-site survey, prepare a detailed audit program, if appropriate, to reflect the results of communications with management and the on-site survey.		
13. Document the detailed audit program changes, if any, and obtain the audit manager's approval of the revised audit program.		
14. Prepare a budget revision form, if necessary, to document the revised budget.		

Source: Archie R. Thomas, *Essentials: An Internal Audit Operations Manual*, 2008

- **Assignments.** In an engagement requiring multiple internal auditors, will individuals work independently, in teams, or in paired assignments (e.g., pairing an experienced practitioner with a novice)?

- **Team coordination and supervision.** What level of team communication is necessary before the engagement starts? Will the lead auditor hold regular meetings during the engagement? Planning should address how engagement work papers will be reviewed during the internal audit activity to ensure that they properly support the engagement communications and that all necessary audit procedures have been performed. It should also be determined if the internal auditors will have a team meeting to close the engagement.

- **Team development.** Consideration should be given to how staff training and development, employee performance evaluation, time and expense control, and similar administrative items will be handled.

An engagement that is properly planned, including provisions for supervision, provides a smooth transition to on-site performance and helps to ensure that engagement objectives are fulfilled. Planning and supervision also support appropriate assessment of risks, controls, and governance processes associated with the activities under review.

Topic 2: Nurture Instrumental Relations, Build Bonds, and Work with Others toward Shared Goals (Level P)

Part of the supervisory responsibility is to tend to the human factors in an auditing project. This includes fostering cooperative relationships between the audit team and individuals in the audited area—both managerial and nonmanagerial—as well as with individuals in other areas of the organization or outside the organization who may be involved in gathering evidence.

These individuals can support the work aimed at meeting the engagement's objectives, or they can obstruct it. They can restrict access to people who should be interviewed. They can delay providing evidence because they are "too busy." The absence of good working relationships makes the audit less effective and less efficient. In a consulting engagement, the quality of relationships created during the audit can affect internal auditing's ability to secure repeat and similar engagements in other areas of the organization. The problem and challenges of relationship building can grow in relation to the physical distance between auditor and audit client.

The types of working relationships implied in the title of this topic are usually based on mutual interest and honest, respectful behavior.

During initial contact with audit clients, the audit manager should discuss what each side—auditor and audit client—needs to succeed and how the audit can help serve the needs of each. Managers must understand how they can benefit from this event—that the auditor is there not to find fault and assign blame but to apply objectivity to finding the answers to problems the manager is probably already aware of and to identifying issues that may have escaped the manager's attention. The outcome of the audit may be ways in which operations can be more efficient and profitable, support in avoiding time-consuming and expensive disputes with regulators, or finding the root causes of problems with quality.

Honest, respectful behavior entails:

- Accurately estimating how much time and trouble a task will require from the manager and nonmanagerial staff.
- Listening and showing interest in the business of the area.
- Keeping promises and following up on questions and concerns.
- Avoiding accusations and assumptions. Ask open-ended questions with follow-up clarifying questions.
- Using clear and common language. Auditor jargon may make audit clients feel confused and threatened. A shared language underscores shared perspectives and goals.

Audit managers should monitor the performance of staff in this area. The audit manager can ask audit clients informally about their reactions to the audit process and the auditors themselves. Client surveys can include this dimension. Post-audit and annual performance discussions can focus on ways to develop relationship building skills.

Topic 3: Coordinate Work Assignments among Audit Team Members when Serving as the Auditor-in-Charge of a Project (Level P)

During initial planning meetings, the auditor-in-charge should communicate specific area assignments and audit tests to audit team members to ensure that all aspects of the work program are covered and that work is not duplicated. Dependent tasks should be clearly identified and acknowledged, and close communication and coordination between affected team members should be encouraged. A primary contact or liaison with the audit client should be assigned.

Coordination can be a particular challenge in a large and/or complex audit in which many auditors with different expertise are working independently on different parts of the audit. The challenge increases when engagements involve multiple audit sites, some remote. It increases further when the audit is occurring within a global organization where business practices and cultural practices may vary.

The auditor-in-charge may consider using periodic meetings, in addition to a kickoff meeting, to support communication among audit team members. This can help avoid duplicating effort and can foster sharing of knowledge and experience in solving problems that have arisen. Meetings can be conducted virtually, either in Web-assisted meetings or teleconferences.

The auditor-in-charge should examine ways to encourage the right amount of communication among the right team members. While it is desirable to share information, team members can find themselves wasting time on e-mails that have little to do with their areas. Part of the initial team meeting should be devoted to defining what should be communicated to whom, within what time frame, and in what manner. Some issues may merit an e-mail sent to the entire team, while others should be more focused in distribution. Legal restrictions on communication should also be reviewed so that the team understands what communications must be retained and when it may be better to communicate in person or over the phone.

Secure pages on internal auditing Web sites can be created so that team members can easily and quickly view each other's work or pose questions. Resources (e.g., previous audit reports, guidelines, templates) can also be placed on the Web site.

The auditor-in-charge or delegate may issue regular progress memos or team meeting minutes. These memos can document assignments, agreements on procedures and approaches, commitments, and open issues that require follow-up. By revisiting minutes at a subsequent meeting, the auditor-in-charge can confirm that open issues have been resolved.

Topic 4: Review Work Papers (Level P)

Proper supervision of engagements includes reviewing and approving work papers. Work papers are the primary documentation for the audit tests that have been conducted and the evidence that has been compiled. They support the conclusions reached and the recommendations made to the audit client.

Beyond assuring that the engagement has been carried out in accordance with high quality standards, work paper review also allows the CAE, or the delegated supervisor, to evaluate each internal auditor's current skills and future development requirements.

Practice Advisory 2340-1 specifies that the reviewer can provide acceptable evidence of work paper review in one of several ways: "Evidence of supervisory review consists of the reviewer initialing and dating each working paper after it is reviewed. Other techniques that provide evidence of supervisory review include completing an engagement working paper review checklist; preparing a memorandum specifying the nature, extent, and results of the review; or evaluating and accepting reviews within the working paper software."

If the reviewer has questions about the work papers, he or she may make a written record—"review notes"—for the auditor to consider. The work papers should then include evidence that these questions have been resolved. As for the notes themselves, the Practice Advisory specifies that:

> Alternatives with respect to disposition of review notes are as follows:
>
> - Retain the review notes as a record of the reviewer's questions raised, the steps taken in their resolution, and the results of those steps.
> - Discard the review notes after the questions raised are resolved and the appropriate engagement working papers are amended to provide the information requested.

Topic 5: Conduct Exit Conferences (Level P)

The final act of an audit engagement is communicating its results—the findings and recommendations. The discussion here focuses on written audit reports, but the communication may be in other formats: verbal, Web-based, or a PowerPoint presentation.

Success in this phase is crucial, since audit reports are not meant to be filed with other seldom-read reference works but are intended instead to stimulate activity—or at the very least receive serious consideration. The chief audit executive bears responsibility for seeing that the final report is skillfully prepared, adroitly presented, brought to the attention of the client's decision makers, and kept out of the hands of those who are not authorized to receive it. Chances for a favorable reception of the audit report can be improved if client managers have been consulted about the findings and recommendations before communication of the final draft. It helps to have key people on your side when you deliver the recommendations.

After creation of a rough draft of the final report, there should be a meeting between the process owners (the audit clients) and the internal auditing team. This is generally called the exit conference, exit interview, or post-engagement meeting. People attending the exit conference are often the same participants who attended the entrance conference, including:

- People familiar with operations details.
- People who can authorize the implementation of corrective actions.

The objectives of the exit conference include:

- Discussing conclusions and recommendations.
- Resolving any misunderstandings or misinterpretations of fact by allowing the client to ask for clarification of specific items and to express views on observations, conclusions, and recommendations.
- Reaching agreement on possible solutions to problems identified in the report. This can help management of the area to formulate its response to the audit findings, which may require requesting budget or policy making/changing by senior management.
- Expressing appreciation for participation in the performance of the internal audit and providing required information.

The IIA seminar "Tools and Techniques for the Beginning Auditor" recommends the following best practices for the logistics of exit conferences:

- Ensure that the right people attend.
- Provide the necessary documents (i.e., the draft report) in advance.
- Set the agenda and manage the meeting.
- Explore and resolve as many issues as possible.
- Provide clear messages, even about difficult issues.
- Thank the audit customer for cooperation, both at the beginning and end of the conference, thanking the key contacts by name and acknowledging that audits can be disruptive to normal activities.
- Hold a post-meeting debriefing with the audit team.

Topic 6: Complete Performance Appraisals of Engagement Staff (Level P)

One very important part of any quality program is the continuous improvement of the people at all levels of an organization. We learned in Section I that interpretation of Standard 1300, "Quality Assurance and Improvement Program," specifies that a quality assurance and improvement program *"assesses the efficiency and effectiveness of the internal audit activity and identifies opportunities for improvement."* Standard 1311 specifies that internal assessments should include both ongoing and periodic reviews of the internal audit activity.

Performance assessment focuses on several levels of performance:

- The entire internal audit activity is assessed on the basis of the annual audit plan and aggregated accomplishments.
- An audit team for a specific engagement can be assessed by both the audit client and the auditor-in-charge.
- Individual auditors can be assessed on the basis of their performance on a specific audit. The post-audit appraisal can be delivered and discussed immediately following the audit. It can also be aggregated into the basis for discussion at the auditor's annual performance review meeting.

The post-audit appraisals can enhance the quality of the audit activity by helping auditors learn more effective techniques for carrying out their work. The organization itself, through managers and supervisors, can assist in staff development in a number of ways, such as off-site and on-the-job training, job enhancement, continually more challenging assignments, opportunities for promotion, and, central to all these efforts, periodic performance reviews.

Gathering evidence of audit performance quality

Evidence of audit staff performance can be gathered from the audit client and from direct observation and review of an auditor's performance during an audit.

An audit effectiveness survey, like the one shown in Exhibit II-7 on the next page, can be distributed to audit clients at exit meetings.

Audit managers/supervisors should also note and record during audits specific examples of the level of work delivered by individual staff members. These notes can be used during post-audit and annual appraisals.

Examples of performance may involve observed behaviors (e.g., the ability to conduct an effective interview or meeting, knowledge of the audit area's business, acuity in developing appropriate audit tests) and reviews of work papers.

Exhibit II-7: Sample Audit Effectiveness Questionnaire

Customer: ______________________________

Location/function audit: ______________________________

Audit team members: ______________________________

Please evaluate the internal audit recently completed at your location by circling or highlighting the number corresponding to your rating of each performance factor listed below. If you are unable to rate a particular performance factor, simply draw a line through or delete the factor.

	Excellent	Good	Fair	Poor*
SCOPE OF WORK				
1. Timely and clear notification to you of audit purpose and scope	4	3	2	1
2. Inclusion of your concerns and/or suggestions in the audit coverage	4	3	2	1
3. Adequacy of audit coverage on key functions and/or areas	4	3	2	1
PERFORMANCE OF AUDIT WORK				
4. Minimal disruption of normal activities	4	3	2	1
5. Timely communication of audit findings	4	3	2	1
6. Reasonableness and value-added effectiveness of recommendations	4	3	2	1
7. Clarity and objectivity of audit reports	4	3	2	1
8. Consistency of verbal review and written report	4	3	2	1
9. Overall usefulness of the audit to your organization	4	3	2	1

Was there anything about the audit you especially liked or disliked?

____

____

* Please provide explanations for any performance factors rated "poor."

____

____

How could we have improved the effectiveness of the audit?

____

____

Please provide any suggestions for future audits:

____

____

Additional comments:

____

____

Signature: ______________________ Date: ____________

Please send completed survey to John Doe, Chief Auditing Executive, XYZ, Inc.

Performance review scheduling

The performance review provides the internal auditor with the opportunity to define his or her professional objectives, cooperate with the manager in designing a program to achieve those objectives, and periodically discuss progress and problems related to that program. This aspect of quality is captured in Standard 1230, "Continuous Professional Development": "Internal auditors must enhance their knowledge, skills, and other competencies through continuing professional development."

Performance reviews should take place on a dual schedule. The first track consists of the annual review by the chief audit executive. The second track consists of reviews that take place after each audit in which the internal auditor participates. These reviews are conducted by the auditor-in-charge for that engagement.

Annual review

The annual review should consider job competencies—the behaviors, abilities, and attributes that can link individuals or teams to enhanced performance and the critical success factors needed to perform the internal auditing role in an organization.

Competencies are more than basic job knowledge, skills, and abilities. Job competencies are behaviors that are usually developed over time and represent the compilation of multiple abilities, traits, and knowledge required for success. Competencies are personal to the employee and are something the employee can take from one audit engagement and project to another, from one position to another, and even from employer to employer.

Specific job competencies vary from organization to organization. But many organizations are focusing on the competencies that individuals or audit departments need to perform jobs rather than on specific tasks, duties, knowledge, skills, and responsibilities.

A task force composed of IIA volunteers, national institute education officers, and former CFIA (Competency Framework for Internal Auditors, 1999) authors have developed a global competency framework for the internal audit professional.

Four competency categories have been associated with specific staff levels and their designated competency levels for specific areas. The categories include:

- Interpersonal skills.
- Tools and techniques.
- Internal audit standards, theory, and methodology.
- Knowledge areas.

Within these buckets are pertinent competencies, each with an assigned proficiency level rating of:
1 = Awareness only.
2 = Basic competence and knowledge with support from others.
3 = Independently competent in routine situations.
4 = Independently competent in unique and complex situations.

The details are documented in the competency framework, available at na.theiia.org/standards-guidance/Public%20Documents/IA%20Standards,%20Theory,%20and%20Methodology-IPPF%20Aligned.pdf.

The annual review with the CAE should include consideration of all the reviews performed for the internal auditor during the year (See the discussion of the post-audit review below.). The CAE can then provide a more unified viewpoint on the auditor's overall performance, creating continuity in the longer-term program of professional development for that auditor.

Post-audit review

The post-audit review has both strong and weak points:

- On the plus side, the post-audit performance review takes place immediately after the assignment, when the auditor's performance is relatively fresh in the mind of the auditor and the reviewer.
- On the negative side, post-audit reviews tend to exhibit wide variability because engagements may be very different from one another and so may the reviewers. Five reports on one auditor may seem to be referring to five different people.

Since audit engagements can be so different from one another, the auditor-in-charge may have to develop a unique rating form for each audit—or at least may have to adapt standard forms used in the audit activity. Certain factors would seem to be fairly constant from audit to audit, however:

- The quantity of work completed and ability to stay on schedule
- The quality of the work, including such measures as:
  - Computational accuracy
  - Selection of appropriate tests—and the right number of tests
  - Thoroughness in completing all necessary fieldwork tasks
  - Clarity, conciseness, logical organization, professional appearance, and usefulness of work papers in supporting the final report
  - Quality of written documents and spoken presentations
- General grasp of audit procedures and specific understanding of the requirements of the particular engagement

- "People skills," demonstrated in interviews with the audit client's staff and management—and with the audit supervisor
- Special technical skills demonstrated on the job, such as ability to perform statistical tests, work with computer-assisted audit programs, create graphic illustrations in a spreadsheet, etc.
- General business knowledge evidenced in understanding of the particular challenges faced by the audit client

Post-audit appraisals should focus separately on job performance issues on the one hand and "traits" on the other. "Traits" indicate qualities, such as attention to detail, creativity in problem solving, resilience, leadership, judgment, logical thinking, self-confidence, and ability to form and maintain relationships.

The face-to-face meeting

In addition to documenting the review on a rating form provided to the internal auditor and the CAE, the auditor-in-charge should schedule a face-to-face conference to discuss the ratings with the internal auditor. While these conferences can be approached in different ways, some tactics seem to be generally effective and some seem almost universally ill-advised. The following are some guidelines.

- Schedule the review in advance—don't sneak up on the auditor—and be specific about the time it will take and the agenda.

- Open the review in a manner suited to the personalities and relationship of both parties. If a question or two about the auditor's family or hobbies is appropriate, for example, that may provide a comfortable start. (It also may turn out to be highly inappropriate if the reviewer and the auditor have no previous personal connection. Fitting the introduction to the personalities of both parties requires skill and practice.)

- Preface the review with a brief outline of what will be covered, including some indication of the overall ratings: "You did a very professional job on the whole and there are a few areas in which I think I can suggest ways you can enhance your performance." Unfortunately, the performance of the auditor doesn't always lend itself to such a positive beginning. Negative news should be delivered in as objective a manner as possible—without an accusatory or scolding tone of voice. This, too, is a skill that auditors with supervisory responsibilities should work to develop. Always begin with a positive statement, assuming there is one.

- Some supervisors ask the person being reviewed to start the conversation with a self-assessment. This should not be done without advance warning.

An easy way to provide that warning is to give the auditor a copy of the ratings sheet to fill out before the conference. In essence, then, reviewer and auditor compare notes during the meeting.

- Be straightforward during the discussion, whatever the format. The only thing more unfair for the auditor than an hour of humiliating condemnation is a falsely flattering review. The task of the reviewer is to help the auditor develop, and that cannot happen unless reviewer and auditor discuss areas of weakness honestly. There is no kindness in allowing a person to keep doing inferior work until he or she is unexpectedly fired.
- Summarize the review at the end—the positives and the negatives—and gain a commitment from the auditor to take whatever actions have been agreed upon.

Chapter C: Engagement Communications as a Process

Chapter Introduction

Effective communication during an engagement—written and verbal, formal and informal—has many dimensions and many benefits:

- **Within the audit team.** Good communication is needed among audit team members to ensure that all aspects of the audit work program are covered and not duplicated. Helpful information must be exchanged as it is learned to improve the quality and efficiency of audit work.
- **With the engagement client.** The audit team and the client must share expectations about the outcomes of the audit and the processes that will be used. Communication can be used to build strong and cooperative relationships with clients and to improve the overall efficiency of the audit.

This chapter focuses on the role of communication throughout the engagement process: from initial meetings with clients to interim or status meetings to the development and distribution of recommendations and reports.

Topic 1: Initiate Preliminary Communication with Engagement Clients (Level P)

Communication is a critical aspect in engagement planning. Once the internal auditor has a draft of the engagement plan, pertinent management parties should be briefed about the upcoming audit.

Practice Advisory 2200-1, "Engagement Planning," states:

> The internal auditor informs those in management who need to know about the engagement, conducts meetings with management responsible for the activity under review, summarizes and distributes the discussions and any conclusions reached from the meetings, and retains the documentation in the engagement working papers. Topics of discussion may include:
>
> - Planned engagement objectives and scope of work.
> - The resources and timing of engagement work.
> - Key factors affecting business conditions and operations of the areas being reviewed, including recent changes in internal and external environment.
> - Concerns or requests from management.
>
> The CAE determines how, when, and to whom engagement results will be communicated. The internal auditor documents this and communicates it to management, to the extent deemed appropriate, during the planning phase of the engagement. The internal auditor communicates to management subsequent changes that affect the timing or reporting of engagement results.

Initial client meeting

During the initial client meeting (also referred to commonly as the kickoff meeting), practical considerations that may impact the engagement should be addressed. A variety of logistics should be discussed and/or confirmed.

Items to cover include (but are not necessarily limited to):

- Identification of key contacts and their availability.
- Preferred communication methods (means and frequency).
- Documents and records needed.
- Complexity of operations to be examined.
- Access to necessary facilities and site locations (may require personal protective equipment or safety certifications).
- Security clearances.
- Distance between site locations and travel time.
- Escorts.
- Tours.
- Vacation schedules.

If international travel is required, allowances for passports and/or visas may need consideration. Language/translation issues should all be allowed for as well.

The initial client meeting is a good time to consider these logistics, as any downtime will need to be factored into the engagement schedule.

A significant point about the first meeting is that it often sets the tone for the upcoming audit. If it is conducted well, it can mark the start of a productive and cooperative relationship. Handled professionally, the preliminary client contact can encourage positive, open communications for the duration of the engagement. The internal auditor needs to manage the expectations of the audit team and personnel in the area being audited in order to reduce potential conflicts.

Typically, meeting arrangements should be made in advance. Unannounced visits should be avoided unless warranted by the nature of the audit (e.g., cash audits, security audits, or fraud investigation). While the formality and duration of the initial meeting will be dictated by factors such as the purpose of the audit, the audit scope, and internal auditor and client participants, an agenda outlining the matters to be discussed is recommended.

In addition to discussing the purpose and approach of the audit, the initial meeting with the client provides an opportunity for the internal auditor to gain insights about management in the area being audited. The meeting may also serve as a forum for other tasks. The internal auditor may request specific assistance desired from the client and/or discuss the role of internal auditing in the organization.

Topic 2: Communicate Interim Progress (Level P)

Some years ago a major European manufacturer of luxury automobiles aired a commercial about certain safety innovations it had made and, for altruistic reasons, had not patented. The concluding line of the spot was, "Some things are too important not to share." Those words accurately identify a major reason for having interim progress reports during an audit engagement. Some audit information is too important not to share immediately rather than in the final report.

According to Practice Advisory 2410-1, "Communication Criteria": "Interim reports may be written or oral and may be transmitted formally or informally. Interim reports may be used to communicate information that requires immediate attention, to communicate a change in engagement scope for the activity under review, or to keep management informed of engagement progress when engagements extend over a long period."

This type of interim progress can be reported through a status meeting, report, or e-mail. The point is that ongoing communication should be maintained throughout the audit engagement.

Sawyer adds another reason: to inform management of significant matters not related to the engagement.

Sawyer notes that communicating observations on an interim basis has advantages:

- The engagement process becomes more efficient, as auditors have the opportunity to clarify issues before unnecessary work is performed. Clients can save auditors time by suggesting possible causes for problems uncovered. Important issues can be uncovered and addressed early, reducing impact on schedules.
- The engagement process is more effective since interim informal meetings help ensure that relevant information is uncovered and understood before evaluations are made and recommendations formulated. Clients also have more time to develop responsive action plans.
- Auditor-client relationships are strengthened. Informal meetings can increase client involvement in the audit process.

Practice Advisory 2410-1 advises internal auditors that the use of interim reports "does not diminish or eliminate the need for a final report." Sawyer recommends interim written reports as a path to higher-quality final reports and more client buy-in to observations and recommendations. They may increase the amount of detail in reports since experience will be fresher in the writers' memories, and they may shorten the time required to create a draft final report, since many sections will have already been reviewed by internal auditing management and the audit client. Sawyer adds a qualifier to the effect that the findings in the interim report may be excluded from the final report if they have been properly resolved and are no longer of importance to the client's operations.

One especially significant piece of news too important not to share is a strong suspicion that fraud has occurred. The chief audit executive is charged with reporting such unpleasant discoveries immediately to senior management and the board. "Immediately" means as soon as an investigation has established with reasonable certainty that the fraud has occurred. In this report, the CAE should state whether or not the internal auditor recommends a full fraud investigation. The report should also summarize observations and recommendations leading to the decision that an investigation is warranted.

Topic 3: Develop Recommendations when Appropriate (Level P)

If audit findings, as Sawyer characterizes them, are an answer to the question "So what?" and if audit conclusions answer the question "What do you think about our operation?" then recommendations answer the question "How should we fix this problem?" Recommendations should address the condition as well as the cause.

What's in a recommendation?

Practice Advisory 2410-1.9 offers some specific guidance about recommendations:

- Recommendations are based on the internal auditor's observations and conclusions.
- They call for action to correct existing conditions or improve operations and may suggest approaches to correcting or enhancing performance as a guide for management in achieving desired results.
- Recommendations can be general or specific. For example, under some circumstances, the internal auditor may recommend a general course of action and specific suggestions for implementation. In other circumstances, the internal auditor may suggest further investigation or study.

In practice, recommendations should adhere to the SMART principle shown in Exhibit II-8.

Exhibit II-8: The SMART Model for Composing Recommendations

S	Specific
M	Measurable
A	Action-oriented
R	Relevant
T	Time-based

- **Specific** recommendations outline exactly what the organization should aim to accomplish.
- **Measurable** recommendations can be evaluated to determine whether they have been accomplished.
- **Action-oriented** recommendations specify the actions that the organization will be able to take.
- **Relevant** recommendations relate to the nature of the organization, and they are attainable.
- **Time-based** recommendations specify the time frame for accomplishing the recommendations.

The internal auditor should go through a logical, thorough process and analyze the recommendations before issuing a report.

Basic considerations include (but are not limited to) the following:

- Will the recommendations address the root cause?
- Are the costs realistic in terms of the expected benefits?

Practice Advisory 2410-1.12 acknowledges, implicitly, that the audit client's management won't always agree with, or want to act upon, the auditor's recommendations: "As part of the internal auditor's discussions with the engagement client, the internal auditor obtains agreement on the results of the engagement and on any necessary plan of action to improve operations. If the internal auditor and engagement client disagree about the engagement results, the engagement communications state both positions and the reasons for the disagreement. The engagement client's written comments may be included as an appendix to the engagement report, in the body of the report, or in a cover letter."

When making recommendations, the auditor should disclose any conflicts of interest, such as previous work with the client.

Audit, don't manage

One of the difficulties involved in making recommendations is that doing so threatens encroachment on territory that belongs to management, not to the internal audit activity. Indeed, the internal auditor is specifically enjoined not to take on responsibilities that rightly belong to management, because doing so threatens the auditor's objectivity. This is particularly true in consulting engagements, since the auditor may have been called specifically to give advice based on research into a particular problem, such as whether or not to accept a particular contract, how to develop a new software system, whether or not a particular company is a good takeover target, and so on.

Once a consulting auditor feels some sense of responsibility for the actions based upon audit recommendations, the auditor's objectivity for any future assurance audit comes into doubt. Internal auditors should maintain their objectivity when drawing conclusions and offering advice to management. Any impairments that exist before an engagement or that develop during it should be disclosed to management immediately.

Give managers credit for managing

Sawyer notes that recommendations are not commands, merely options, and the auditor should not deliver a recommendation as if it were the only possible course of action, because the manager generally has a broader view of the possible consequences of acting upon a recommendation than the auditor. It's a good idea to bring recommendations to the manager for discussion before the end of the audit. Working jointly with the manager to come to agreement about a corrective course of action improves the relationship. The manager will look better to superiors if the audit report states that recommendations were developed after discussion with the manager.

The internal auditor, in Sawyer's view, should consider the relationship between the cost of a recommended action and the benefit to the organization. Some actions must be taken regardless of cost to bring the organization into compliance with a law or regulation, but otherwise there should be a balance between cost and risk.

Topic 4: Prepare a Report or Other Communication (Level P)

The final presentation to the client no longer requires a written document. Many auditors present their conclusions and recommendations in a PowerPoint presentation.

Report components

According to Practice Advisory 2410-1, the format and content of the engagement's final conclusions may vary with the type of organization and engagement but nevertheless should include at least sections describing the purpose, scope, and results of the engagement.

- **Purpose of the engagement.** A precise statement of the purpose (or objective) of the engagement can provide coherence to the rest of the report and make it easier to read and discuss. Presentation of the audit findings should always be related to the audit's objective.

- **Scope of the engagement.** The scope statement may be combined with the objective. It identifies the activities audited. It may also specify activities excluded from the audit, if the title of the audit would naturally lead readers to expect to find coverage of those activities.

- **Audit methods.** This may or may not be a separate section. A separate section is often merited if new methodologies or technology are being used or if the work of other bodies (internal or external) provides a substantial basis for the work. In place of a separate section, the report may include a section on relevant methodology in the discussion of each observation.

- **Results.** The results section should include observations, conclusions, opinions, recommendations, and action plans. Some complex reports may be preceded by an observations summary, perhaps in a table format that identifies and describes specific observations that will be discussed in the body of the report. Minor observations may be put in a separate section.

- **Recommendations.** This may be a separate section if recommendations are general and not tied to specific observations.

Final communications may also include other, optional, sections:

- **Background information.** Background information may describe the organization and the activities to be reviewed along with the results and status of previous audits of the same activities.

- **Summaries.** A summary can be a useful memorandum accompanying the full report when it is provided to an executive in the organization. Executives may want to know the overall results of each audit in their area of concern but not have time to read full reports.

- **Client accomplishments.** The final communication may include descriptions of improvements the client has made in response to a previous audit.

- **Client views.** The report may include the client's views on the engagement's conclusions and recommendations. Disagreements between the client and the internal audit activity may require intervention from an executive. The client's written comments may be included in an appendix or cover letter.

The report must be signed by the internal auditor authorized by the CAE (Practice Advisory 2410-1.15). A signed version of the report must be kept on file by the internal audit activity.

Produce a quality report

Standard 2420, "Quality of Communications," states that communications must be accurate, objective, clear, concise, constructive, complete, and timely. According to interpretation:

> *Accurate communications are free from errors and distortions and are faithful to the underlying facts. Objective communications are fair, impartial, and unbiased and are the result of a fair-minded and balanced assessment of all relevant facts and circumstances. Clear communications are easily understood and logical, avoiding unnecessary technical language and providing all significant and relevant information. Concise communications are to the point and avoid unnecessary elaboration, superfluous detail, redundancy, and wordiness. Constructive communications are helpful to the engagement client and the organization and lead to improvements where needed. Complete communications lack nothing that is essential to the target audience and include all significant and relevant information and observations to support recommendations and conclusions. Timely communications are opportune and expedient, depending on the significance of the issue, allowing management to take appropriate corrective action.*

This interpretation emphasizes the characteristics of an effective report:

- Organization that is easily understood and followed
- Clarity
- Conciseness
- Constructive tone
- Good mechanics (e.g., spelling, punctuation, grammar, word choice)

Organization

The IIA seminar "Effective Writing for Auditors" lists five common logical patterns that are used to organize complex content:

- **Chronological.** Observations are described in the order in which they were recorded.
- **Topical.** Similar observations are grouped under headings—e.g., personnel training, contracting terms and conditions.
- **Comparative.** Observations are compared to specific policies, such as a requirement for management signatures on certain financial transactions.
- **Cause and effect.** Observations are grouped by similar causes or effects. For example, lapses in physical security could be discussed with other observations caused by a lack of management control over policies and procedures.
- **Spatial.** This can reflect both geography and organizational structure. In an audit covering multiple locations, observations can be grouped by unit or office. Problems affecting only certain groups may merit their own sections—such as subcontractor behavior or warehouse issues.

Organizational tools—such as headings, topic sentences, and bulleted lists—can all help the reader understand the content more quickly and easily.

Clarity

The reading ability of the audience in the language of the report should be considered as well as their familiarity with the business processes being described. A reader's ability to understand the "message" of the report could be affected by:

- Sentence length and grammatical complexity.
- Word choice. Common terms are preferable to jargon or specialized language (and acronyms and abbreviations) that can be understood only by experts in the field.

Conciseness

Summaries should be used as necessary, providing an understanding of the main point first and then allowing the reader to pursue more details in the following text. A more formatted organization, such as a table with consistent headings, can be used to avoid repeating similar information.

Constructive tone

The tone of the report should be objective—not overwhelmingly positive or negative but balanced, not alarmist but focused on responses, not assigning blame but focused on solutions. Tone is a hard thing to master, as witnessed by the many misunderstandings and conflicts fueled by e-mails that were not reread for tone before being sent. Some writers are good self-editors, but most writers benefit from having someone else review and comment on matters such as tone.

Good mechanics

Auditors are experts in auditing, not necessarily in the mechanics of writing. It is desirable for auditors to improve their writing skills, and this can be part of a personal development program. Until this happens, however, an auditor assigned with writing a report should find someone in the activity who can fulfill this role and ask them to review report drafts before they are shared outside the activity. The credibility of a good report can be undermined by poor mechanics that may convey to a reader a certain carelessness and lack of attention and value for detail.

Auditors can also look to numerous Web sites that provide rules about grammar and the use of punctuation.

Avoid an adversarial tone

Whatever the format of the presentation, however, its chances of success can be enhanced by taking care to avoid creating an adversarial atmosphere. A few "soft skill" suggestions in that regard are:

- Assume that auditor and client are on the same side as partners looking for the best ways to achieve the organization's objectives (or the objectives established in a consulting contract). History is not necessarily on your side; the traditional relationship of auditor and client has not always been a happy one. Break with tradition.
- Always begin at a general level rather than launching immediately into detailed findings. Show that you've grasped the nature of the operation, its overall mission, and its special challenges.
- Put the most positive findings first.
- Insofar as possible, present negative findings as opportunities for improvement, but don't overdo it. Nothing is less persuasive than a falsely positive presentation.
- Be sure to emphasize the "effects" aspect of findings—what consequences loom down the road if changes aren't made.
- Don't simply stop talking; conclude. Summarize the results briefly with an emphasis on action steps the client can take. End on a positive note, just as you began on one.

Topic 5: Approve the Engagement Report (Level P)

The chief audit executive or a designee should review and approve the final engagement communication before it is issued and should decide who should receive it.

The auditor-in-charge, supervisor, or lead auditor may be considered as the proper person to sign on behalf of the CAE. In large, international organizations, requiring the CAE's signature on all final communications might cause delays.

However, Performance Standard 2440, "Disseminating Results," states that the chief audit executive maintains responsibility for communicating the final results of an engagement. Although it is not required in the standard, in many organizations the CAE signs the final report before distribution, as a sign of commitment to the quality of audit work.

Topic 6: Determine Distribution of the Report (Level P)

The CAE bears responsibility for communicating final results to individuals who can ensure that the results are given due consideration. The report should go to those in a position to take corrective action—for example, management of the audited area or operation, senior management, or associated functions that may be affected by or can support recommended action plans.

Communications may also go to external auditors, the board, and others who are affected by or interested in the results.

If substantive corrections must be made to a report after it has been distributed, the CAE should issue a new report that highlights the changes and see that is distributed to all recipients of the original report.

Topic 7: Obtain Management Response to the Report (Level P)

Having gone to the trouble of researching and assembling the findings and recommendations, the audit activity would naturally like to see them acted upon. Guidance on getting the findings reviewed and taken seriously is spelled out in Practice Advisory 2440-1: "Disseminating Results." It specifies, among other things, appropriate times for discussion of the results as well as appropriate recipients.

For example, the Practice Advisory suggests that "internal auditors discuss conclusions and recommendations with appropriate levels of management before the chief audit executive (CAE) issues the final engagement communications." Why? Because once the report has been completed and distributed, the chance for serious dialogue on the findings may have passed.

As the Practice Advisory notes, "This is usually accomplished during the course of the engagement and/or at post-engagement meetings (i.e., exit meetings)."

The Practice Advisory also suggests that management of the audit client may be engaged in discussions of draft versions of observations and recommendations. At this stage, the client can clear up misunderstandings and react to the findings while there is time to collaborate on revisions.

The participants in these discussions will generally be "individuals who are knowledgeable of detailed operations and those who can authorize the implementation of corrective action."

In other words, if you can get early agreement on the recommendations from the people who can effect changes in the client's operations, you have a much better chance of getting the final report acted upon.

Topic 8: Report Outcomes to Appropriate Parties (Level P)

Performance Standard 2440 directs the CAE to "communicate results to the appropriate parties." The CAE should ensure that appropriate parties receive the type of information appropriate to their interests and, for external parties, a level and scope of information that protects the organization's proprietary interests and well-being.

Reports of improper or illegal actions should be made separately to senior management and the board—or to the board alone if the actions involve senior management. Practice Advisory 2400-1, "Legal Considerations in Communicating Results," encourages the internal auditor to "consult legal counsel in matters involving legal issues." The report may be considered privileged information under local law. For example, in the US, work performed at the direction of an attorney is protected as "work product."

Before releasing reports to parties outside the organization, the CAE should assess potential risks to the organization and obtain approval of senior management, legal counsel, or both. The CAE is responsible for controlling the distribution of the report.

Release of consulting reports should be consistent with the organization's established practices. Because of the nature of the activities that internal auditing helps to evaluate, many organizations allow only limited distribution of consulting reports.

The CAE may customize the distribution of reports. For example, with their agreement, the CAE may distribute only the general summary of the report to senior management and the board, who may not be as interested in audit methodology as in the audit results. Related functions may receive only those portions of the report that affect their relationship with the audited area.

Sawyer notes that senior management and boards are often well served by receiving multi-report summaries. Multi-report summaries include the results of multiple engagements that have focused on similar observations or trends, such as a decrease in coordination of units in a business process or a cross-functional deterioration in the effectiveness of quality controls. These reports do not describe all the work done by the internal audit team, but only the results of audit work.

Chapter D: Monitor Engagement Outcomes

Chapter Introduction

Internal auditing assurance or consulting engagements are discrete projects that use project management approaches during planning and execution. A risk of project-based work is that no one will follow up on management action plans documented in the final audit report because the team members have moved on to the next project and have other responsibilities, deadlines, and time constraints. However, if this natural tendency is allowed to occur or persist, it can create a more significant risk for the internal audit activity: The activity could be perceived as irrelevant and not value-added because no real changes are being made and no improvements in results are therefore being realized. The entire internal control framework could be jeopardized if management falls into a routine of ignoring audit recommendations and fails to properly execute its control monitoring responsibilities. Therefore, monitoring of engagement outcomes is not just a minor afterthought but a critical control step that needs to be championed to the board, senior management, and process owners, included in the annual audit plan and personnel schedules, and assigned to specific personnel who are held responsible and accountable.

We learned in the previous chapter that at the end of the internal auditing engagement, the internal audit team and chief audit executive prepare a report that assesses conditions found against the criteria defined at the beginning of the audit. This report identifies gaps in performance or potential risks and prioritizes their correction according to a variety of factors, including their financial effects (e.g., inefficiency, waste, damage or loss claims, and fraud) and ethical or legal impacts (e.g., violation of organizational codes of ethics, laws, or regulations). The report also describes (if necessary) criteria to correct shortcomings—an action plan that management of the area being audited agrees to accomplish along with a timeline for implementation. This decision can be to implement all or some of the recommendations or to accept the risk and do nothing. The decision should have been arrived at in collaboration with internal auditing, so the CAE should be in support of the method used. If not, the CAE should escalate the issue to the board or senior management.

This chapter starts by outlining various methods to monitor engagement outcomes. Internal auditors will typically decide on the most appropriate monitoring method in consultation with the manager responsible for implementing the action plan. Internal auditors document the process to be used in the final engagement report; therefore, the first topic of this chapter is a step that should occur before issuing the final report. The remainder of the chapter shows how to execute this follow-up process and report adequate or inadequate actions to the board or management depending on their significance.

Topic 1: Identify Appropriate Method to Monitor Engagement Outcomes (Level P)

The responsibility for follow-up is stated in the following standards:

- Performance Standard 2500, "Monitoring Progress": The chief audit executive must establish and maintain a system to monitor the disposition of results communicated to management.
- Standard 2500.A1: The chief audit executive must establish a follow-up process to monitor and ensure that management actions have been effectively implemented or that senior management has accepted the risk of not taking action.
- Standard 2500.C1: The internal audit activity must monitor the disposition of results of consulting engagements to the extent agreed upon with the client.

The right of the internal audit activity to perform these activities should be specifically expressed in the internal audit activity's written charter.

Practice Advisory 2500.A1-1, "Follow-Up Process," tells us, "Internal auditors determine whether management has taken action or implemented the recommendation. The internal auditor determines whether the desired results were achieved or if senior management or the board has assumed the risk of not taking action or implementing the recommendation."

The method used to monitor management response and ensure that it is addressing the identified risk (or opportunity) will vary according to the change being implemented. Scheduling of follow-up should be based on the risk and exposure involved as well as the difficulty and significance of timing in implementing the corrective action.

Planning

As with the initial engagement project, planning is the key to success in monitoring outcomes of engagements. The monitoring plan will depend on factors like the significance of the recommendation and its complexity. Basic issues of planning include:

- **Who will monitor the outcomes of the recommendations.** Specific internal auditing personnel are assigned to monitoring responsibilities. If the cooperation or support of other areas is required, those areas are contacted and efforts are coordinated. For example, if a recommendation involves the physical redesign of an area to improve employee safety, it may be necessary to secure the services of an ergonomic workplace designer and to work with management of the physical operations area to schedule remodeling.
- **What will be monitored.** The objectives of the recommendation must be translated into measurable and observable criteria. For example, a recommendation that the accounting department adopt new accounting methods may require only acquisition of training and necessary materials (e.g., computer applications) and adoption by a certain date. A recommendation that all existing and future vendors demonstrate compliance with tax and other regulatory requirements will require proof of compliance. Assigned internal auditors will need to review all or a sample of vendor documents to witness the presence of a vendor agreement.

  It is important that management be aware of and agree with what internal audit needs to conduct monitoring and verify achievement of the recommendations so management actions will be accepted by internal audit.

- **How the monitoring will be accomplished.** Monitoring can be conducted on an ongoing basis. For example, internal auditing may recommend that transactions above a certain amount be conducted only by personnel with certain privileges. Internal auditing might access the computer system remotely a certain number of times to confirm that the new practice is in place and is being followed.

  For an especially significant recommendation—e.g., to correct irregularities in preparing a financial statement—internal auditing may schedule a complete follow-up engagement. For less critical recommendations—e.g., improvement of physical security measures in an office—a follow-up questionnaire or conversation may be adequate. Internal auditing should specify in what manner management should confirm their response to the recommendation—in writing, by e-mail, or verbally.

- **When or how often monitoring will be conducted.** Management is informed of the time frame in which its response is expected and of the fact that follow-up will occur after that date. As discussed, the time frame for follow-up depends on the significance of the recommendation. An urgent matter should be resolved immediately. If a recommendation has involved a particularly complex solution, internal auditing may decide to schedule a series of follow-up activities keyed to specific stages in the solutions. For example, internal auditing may review a proposal by an information systems vendor who will create the recommended application. Later, internal auditing may check to see if the project is on schedule. Auditing may be involved in a beta test of the system and in analysis of the test results. Auditing may decide to confirm final results after full implementation of the new system.

Important procedures to develop during planning include:

- Developing an issues tracking system
- Developing specific monitoring procedures

Developing an issues tracking system

Since monitoring of engagement outcomes is a process that will occur sporadically throughout each year for various engagements, an important step is to develop a system for tracking issues and resolution status of action plans. To ensure that follow-up is conducted on the agreed-upon schedule, the CAE may use scheduling software to record follow-up periods for each engagement, which may be a particular date or set of milestones, on a regular basis such as monthly, quarterly, or annually, or only as the lead-up to the next audit of the area such as in four years. An automated system with automatic schedule reminders for specific internal auditors can help reduce the risks that these tasks will be overlooked. If process owners have committed to following up themselves, these individuals should also be provided with automated schedule reminders.

Developing specific monitoring procedures

Internal audit activities can develop specific monitoring procedures and predetermine a threshold for deciding whether a control weakness or other audit recommendation has been resolved or not. The purpose of such procedures is to give internal auditors clear decision criteria on how to evaluate data collected during monitoring.

Monitoring procedures should be based on a monitoring framework. According to COSO's *Internal Control—Integrated Framework* and a 2009 supplemental COSO document, *Guidance on Monitoring Internal Control Systems,* the monitoring component of this framework is developed by establishing a monitoring foundation and designing monitoring procedures. The framework guides execution and assessment of results, prioritization of observations, reporting results at the appropriate level, and following up on corrective action. COSO makes monitoring the responsibility of management; however, the internal auditing function enables management to fulfill these responsibilities and so should adopt or develop a monitoring framework for the internal audit function.

While some monitoring may require specialized or customized methods and thresholds for acceptance, others can be standardized. A common area for setting predetermined methods and acceptance thresholds is sampling. For example, the procedure may be to use judgmental sampling for certain transaction controls and may require testing of, say, 50 items. The procedure could be as follows:

- If five or fewer fail, then pass the control.
- If more than five items fail, then test another sample of 50 items, and if five or fewer fail, still pass the control.
- If more than five items fail in the first or second pass, fail the control.

A control that requires more reliability could set the allowed failure rate to fewer noncompliant transactions, for example, just one failed item.

Topic 2: Monitor Engagement Outcomes and Determine Appropriate Follow-Up by the Internal Audit Activity (Level P)

Responsibility of the CAE to monitor engagement outcomes

According to Practice Advisory 2500-1, "Monitoring Progress," if the audit report produces recommendations to management, it is the responsibility of the CAE to establish procedures that ensure that management responds to those recommendations:

> To effectively monitor the disposition of results, the chief audit executive (CAE) establishes procedures to include:
> - The timeframe within which management's response to the engagement observations and recommendations is required.
> - An evaluation of management's response.
> - Verification of the response (if appropriate).
> - Performance of a follow-up engagement (if appropriate).
> - A communications process that escalates unsatisfactory responses/actions, including the assumption of risk, to the appropriate levels of senior management or the board.

Follow-up by internal audit is defined as a process by which the internal auditors determine the adequacy, effectiveness, and timeliness of actions taken by management on reported engagement observations and recommendations, including those made by external auditors and others. The follow-up process is described in Practice Advisory 2500.A1-1: "Follow-Up Process."

Achieving an adequate response from management will be more likely if internal audit ensures that its recommendations are made to individuals who have the authority and the ability to make the changes that will address the problems. Management may respond to auditing's recommendations orally or in written form. Management should be informed about the level of detail that internal auditing needs in order to evaluate the appropriateness of management's response and determine the most appropriate follow-up. An adequate management response should demonstrate a complete and accurate understanding of the risks that have been identified and should establish clear objectives for the control that is being implemented.

Types of follow-up procedures

The audit charter may specify that a particular type of follow-up must be used, or it may allow the CAE to determine the nature, timing, and extent of follow-up. The latter method allows internal auditors to employ different follow-up procedures depending on the significance of the recommendations or other factors discussed later.

Types of follow-up procedures include the following:

- Process owner is responsible for following up.
- Auditor conducts a targeted follow-up review.
- Auditor conducts a follow-up audit.

Process owner is responsible for following up

Making the process owner responsible for following up minimizes the required schedule time and involvement of the internal auditor; it also provides the weakest form of audit evidence of the three methods because the process owner may not be objective or could be reporting results that were not actually accomplished. However, this method can be structured by specifying a reporting frequency and by requiring written documentation on each action item with KPIs that can be verified. This method can also help with relationship building as it empowers the process owner and reinforces that the process owner is responsible for changes. The drawback of empowerment is that the process owner could unilaterally change the action plan or do nothing as the situation changes, believing (perhaps incorrectly) that the new events justify the changes. The auditor can decide whether he or she is satisfied with the responses or if additional clarification or follow-up is needed.

Auditor conducts a targeted follow-up review

The internal auditor can decide to be directly involved in follow-up but only target action items of high priority related to significant risks to objectives. While the level of involvement may be less overall, checking on resolution of these significant risks may still require multiple follow-ups on a regular basis. The review may take the form of observation and discussions, selected audit tests, or some balance between the two. There should be clear criteria for success, and internal auditors must determine the level of reliance that is given to each type of evidence. Determining what is significant enough to follow up on and an appropriate follow-up frequency are also important. Formal and informal communication procedures and a method of addressing when plans need to change should also be determined. This type of audit can appear less bureaucratic than a full-scale follow-up audit because it is clearly linked to risk-based methodology. Auditor check-ins can help keep actions moving, but process owners could come to rely on regular reminders rather than being proactive. This method can produce risk-based, objective, and verifiable results.

Auditor conducts a follow-up audit

Scheduling a follow-up audit after allowing sufficient time for correction is the most involved type of follow-up, and it provides the strongest evidence of whether or not all changes have been implemented correctly. Scheduling the follow-up can be difficult as it needs to give sufficient time for process owners to finish changes while not giving so much time that critical changes could be delayed unnecessarily. Even so, some changes may still be incomplete when the audit begins. The level of reliance on various types of tests should be determined during follow-up audit planning as well as a process for formal or informal reporting.

It is important for internal auditors to determine whether changing business conditions created any changes in action plan implementation. The process owner may not have consulted with the internal auditors prior to making such changes, and the changes could fail to address significant risks. An advantage of this method is that the internal auditor may be in a position to determine not only that the plans were implemented but also measure the effect the new methods have on the related risks or intended results. This evidence could influence internal auditors' recommendations for future audit areas. While this type of follow-up can be risk-based, it may still involve spending more time than needed on some less-critical items. Process owners could also view the process as being bureaucratic.

Determining appropriate follow-up

The CAE's decision on the type of follow-up procedure to use and on its specific scope may be affected by the following considerations:

- **Significance of the reported observation or recommendation.** Significant engagement observations are those conditions that, in the judgment of the CAE, could adversely affect the organization in achieving its objectives. Significant engagement observations may include conditions dealing with irregularities, illegal acts, errors, inefficiency, waste, ineffectiveness, conflicts of interest, and control weaknesses.

  For example, consider the internal audit activity in a pharmaceutical company that uncovers a pattern of payments to investigators (usually physicians responsible for independently gathering data that will be used to obtain approval for new drug products). This is a serious violation of federal law. It may have extremely serious repercussions for the company, from heavy fines to denial of product approval. It is reasonable for internal audit to anticipate that management will promptly implement measures to mitigate the potential risk associated with these improper actions. Internal audit will also want to ensure the effectiveness of management's response through periodic monitoring of accounting records.

In contrast, the internal audit department may find fairly minor instances of inadequate documentation of travel expenses by the company's marketing executives. This audit result requires management's response to mitigate the risk, but follow-up may require only a notation in the internal auditor's records to recheck this item during the next audit.

- **Degree of effort and cost needed to correct the reported condition.** Will the cost of repair—in terms of both money and lost productivity—compare favorably with its benefits? For example, internal auditing in a manufacturing company could find that there may be risk of injury to employees from a specific traffic pattern of equipment and workers. After discussing the situation, internal audit and manufacturing management agree that redesigning the physical layout of the facilities would be extremely costly and would decrease productivity by making access to materials more difficult. In addition, while risk exists, it is fairly remote, as shown by an absence of accidents in the past two years. Auditing and management might agree to explore alternative, more cost-effective solutions.

- **Impact that may result should the corrective action fail.** The CAE must consider whether management's response is likely to succeed in correcting the problem and what an inadequate response will mean to the organization. For example, say that local regulations require that data sheets on all hazardous materials used in a workplace be placed in a binder located in a specific place. Internal auditing discovers that the required documentation is, in some cases, missing or outdated. Management agrees to revise the data sheets to reflect the situation after the coming peak work season. The CAE considers the fact that the employees are thoroughly trained in the materials and that warning signs are posted wherever the materials are used and decides that, for now, there is probably little cost associated with any potential tardiness by management in adding the necessary data sheets. The CAE accepts the time frame offered by management.

  Consider a contrasting example. An internal auditor uncovers evidence that suggests an unusual level of familiarity between an employee and certain vendors but is not able to identify specific acts of fraud. Internal audit includes this potential risk in its report to management of the area. Management responds by saying that, in the absence of specific evidence of wrongdoing, it will not transfer this individual but will instead "keep an eye on the situation." The CAE may determine that management's response is inadequate because of the size of the theft that could occur.

- **Time period involved.** Sawyer recommends that the CAE assign different time frames to management's response to audit findings. Significant findings of risk—as measured by "frequency, magnitude, and exposure"—should elicit an immediate response from management. Ideally, when a finding involves a significant level of risk or loss, management should begin to respond during the audit itself, so that the problem is at least partially corrected by the time the audit report is released. For example, the CAE might expect that a security gap in data exchange between the organization's intranet and external users (e.g., customers) that could result in compromising the security of both the organization's and its customers' financial data should be corrected as soon as possible and at least within 60 days.

  Less significant findings may allow a longer time frame for response, such as 120 days. For example, internal auditing may recommend that, for economic and social reasons, the lighting in the organization's offices should be changed to more energy-efficient fixtures that produce less hazardous waste upon disposal. It will be reasonable for management to implement the recommendation over time, completing areas on a schedule over the next four months.

  Other findings may not call for a specific time frame of response, either because they are so critical that they have been implemented immediately (e.g., the disciplining or discharge of an employee who is harassing other employees) or so minor that they do not require specific follow-up (e.g., a recommendation regarding off-site archiving of documentation to save office space). Minor recommendations usually become items in the next regularly scheduled engagement.

  The CAE should ask management to identify a time frame for corrective action and a target date for completion of the implementation. There should be an agreement from management to report progress on a weekly or monthly basis until the target date has been reached. At times, this communication may require discussions between internal audit and management as to the correctness of the activity to address the audit finding and recommendations. This progress helps to assure that the right activity is being done and that the risks identified will be mitigated by the controls and changes to the process. Depending on the significance of the findings, internal audit may want to do an evaluation of the success of the new process implementation when it is completed, or in some instances an additional audit may be performed.

Securing action

In 1991 the US General Accounting Office (now the US Government Accountability Office, or GAO) released a white paper that focused entirely on the issue of audit follow-up, "How to Get Action on Audit Recommendations." The GAO report recommends considering the following six questions:

- **Is the recommendation still valid?** Conditions may have changed that have removed or lessened the risk or significantly changed the solution requirements. For example, internal audit may report that few purchasing employees in a multinational corporation are trained in local regulations and pose a risk to compliance with local laws. The corporation decides that instead of training the employees, it will rely on local independent companies to accomplish purchasing. Since local purchasing is no longer the responsibility of this department, the recommendation, as it stands, is no longer relevant.

- **Were the recommendations' objectives met by an alternative approach?** For example, auditing may have recommended a physical log to record access to a secure area. Management decides instead to install a video surveillance camera system. The objective for increased security has been achieved although the specific recommendation has not been followed.

- **Is there anything else that can be done to change management's mind about implementing the recommendation?** Getting the desired response from management may benefit from helping management more fully understand the costs of the risk and the full benefits of addressing the risk. It may help to provide management with a more comprehensive analysis of the financial costs associated with not implementing the recommendation or the ancillary benefits of the recommendation (e.g., increased flexibility in using employee time).

- **Should implementation of the recommendation be delayed?** For example, a CAE may know that a company needs a better transportation tracking system, but the need may be more apparent after a pending acquisition is completed. With a larger market and transportation fleet, the need for greater coordination, risk management, and efficiency will be more obvious.

- **Is the recommendation key to resolving issues of control in this area?** This is an issue of deciding priorities. A CAE may decide that, ultimately, one recommendation may be sacrificed in the interest of gaining management agreement to implementing a more critical recommendation.

- **Can the recommendations be revised in any way to make them more achievable and therefore more palatable to management?** For example, an area that feels understaffed and overworked may not welcome a recommendation for a new and additional process. Could management accomplish the recommendation by purchasing a service from a vendor?

The GAO's suggestions underscore the need for thorough communication and possibly negotiation between the CAE and management. Solutions imposed by senior management without management's understanding and support may face a more challenging future than solutions mutually agreed upon.

Topic 3: Conduct Follow-Up and Report on Management's Response to Internal Audit Recommendations (Level P)

During the follow-up activity, internal auditing will gather data to confirm the status of its recommendations to management. Monitoring may directly involve internal audit in the form of a follow-up engagement, but it may also include receiving periodic progress reports from management or other organizational units assigned responsibility for procedures of a follow-up or corrective nature. As with the initial engagement, internal auditors in a follow-up engagement should cultivate a cooperative, positive relationship with the area. The engagement may involve data collection and analysis, review of documents, observation of job performance, and interviews with management and personnel. Both data collection and monitoring observations may be enhanced through the use of computer tools.

Internal audit's goal during the conduct of follow-up is to determine:

- Whether the recommendation has been acted on and accomplished, or whether a response to the recommendation is in progress.
- If the change has focused on the root cause, which will prevent a future occurrence or recurrence of the observed problem.
- What benefits are accruing to the area and to the organization as a whole from implementation of the recommendation.
- Whether the measured benefits and savings match those anticipated in the recommendation and, if not, why. (Defining benefits in follow-up reports will help establish the validity of recommendations and the value of the internal auditing function.)

If progress is being made, it must be documented in some relevant fashion—e.g., through auditing of documents or data, testing, or direct observation.

If progress is not being made, internal auditing must uncover and document reasons for this:

- Is management resisting implementation of the recommendation?
- Has it encountered unforeseen problems?
- Have conditions changed in such a way that the recommendation is no longer necessary?
- Has implementation of the recommendation been delayed due to the pressures of daily operations and crises?
- Is the recommendation itself inadequate? In what ways?

It may be possible to resume progress on the recommendation by talking through issues with management and personnel in the area and, if necessary, developing alternative approaches for implementing the recommendation.

If progress is not being made, additional follow-up monitoring must be scheduled.

The nature of internal audit's communication of the monitoring plan and results depends on whether the CAE has determined that management's response has been adequate or inadequate. The following discusses adequate management response; the next topic discusses inadequate response.

Reporting adequate management response

Performance Standard 2060, "Reporting to Senior Management and the Board," directs the CAE to report "on the internal audit activity's purpose, authority, responsibility, and performance relative to its plan. Reporting must also include significant risk exposures and control issues, including fraud risks, governance issues, and other matters needed or requested by senior management and the board."

As part of this charge, the CAE submits periodic activity reports, including quarterly reports of ongoing projects. These reports should reflect newly initiated auditing engagements as well as the results of the monitoring activities conducted to follow up on and confirm completed engagements. In many organizations, this reporting process involves the CAE performing this reporting in person at senior management meetings and board (audit committee) quarterly meetings.

When monitoring may stop

Reports may highlight the need to continue monitoring (because of recommendations that have not been fully implemented or implemented incorrectly or because the recommendation failed to resolve the observed problem) or the ability to cease monitoring and declare the issue resolved.

Monitoring may stop when a recommendation is successfully implemented (or its objectives achieved in some other way) or when the problem has disappeared. For example, a market change may eliminate a specific business risk, or an unexpected benefit of a new technology may be that it has addressed a control issue. It is critical to remove monitoring engagement items from internal audit's list of ongoing projects when appropriate.

Reporting monitoring results

The report should document the monitoring plan's results specifically—ideally using the criteria set out in the original recommendations—and emphasize the benefits that have accrued to the organization because of implementation of the recommendations. Results may be qualitative ("Customer satisfaction with order delivery has improved") or quantitative ("Time from order placement to customer receipt has decreased from an average of 8.5 days to 6 days"). The report should be brief—a one-page summary of objectives, monitoring activity, and results with supporting evidence listed in appendices as needed. However, if other issues have arisen that have interfered with achieving the recommendations, necessitated changes in the recommendations, or suggested new and related issues of risk or control, these matters should be discussed fully in the report.

Topic 4: Escalate Issues if Auditor-in-Charge Believes Management Is Accepting Too Much Risk (Level P)

Inadequate management response

Management response to internal audit recommendations may at times be considered inadequate by internal audit for benign reasons. For example, a reorganization could bring a change of managers and the new manager may not be aware of audit's recommendations. However, an internal audit observation that represents a significant risk to the organization requires a prompt and effective management response. If the CAE believes that management is not responding or is responding inadequately to the observed risk and is unwilling to control the risk, then the CAE is professionally obliged to escalate the matter to the next level of attention—to senior management, if necessary, and to the board if senior management fails to respond.

Performance Standard 2600, "Communicating the Acceptance of Risks," states: "When the chief audit executive concludes that management has accepted a level of risk that may be unacceptable to the organization, the chief audit executive must discuss the matter with senior management. If the chief audit executive determines that the matter has not been resolved, the chief audit executive must communicate the matter to the board."

Interpretation of Standard 2600 states: *"The identification of risk accepted by management may be observed through an assurance or consulting engagement, monitoring progress on actions taken by management as a result of prior engagements, or other means. It is not the responsibility of the chief audit executive to resolve the risk."*

Topic 5: Report Significant Audit Issues Periodically to Senior Management and the Board (Level P)

Practice Advisory 2060-1, "Reporting to Senior Management and the Board," explains that:

> The purpose of reporting is to provide assurance to senior management and the board regarding governance processes (Standard 2110), risk management (Standard 2120), and control (Standard 2130). Standard 1111 states: "The chief audit executive must communicate and interact directly with the board."

Practice Advisory 2060-1 goes on to direct internal auditors on the necessary timing and scope of these periodic communications, noting that exception communications should relate to significant differences between the most recent audit plan or other type of plan and actual changes or results:

> The chief audit executive (CAE) should agree with the board about the frequency and nature of reporting on the internal audit activity's charter (e.g., purpose, authority, responsibility) and performance. Performance reporting should be relative to the most recently approved plan to inform senior management and the board of significant deviations from the approved audit plan, staffing plans, and financial budgets; reasons for the deviations; and action needed or taken. Standard 1320 states: "The chief audit executive must communicate the results of the quality assurance and improvement program to senior management and the board."
>
> Significant risk exposures and control issues are those conditions that, according to the CAE's judgment, could adversely affect the organization and its ability to achieve strategic, financial reporting, operational, and compliance objectives. Significant issues may carry unacceptable exposure to internal and external risks, including conditions related to control weaknesses, fraud, irregularities, illegal acts, errors, inefficiency, waste, ineffectiveness, conflicts of interest, and financial viability.

The last parts of Practice Advisory 2060-1 help CAEs decide when a management decision to avoid or delay addressing a risk or control issue should be considered significant enough to require reporting the discrepancy to the board and possibly with external auditors if related to financial reporting. It also describes a best practice for presenting unresolved issues in a joint meeting that includes management, the CAE, and the board so that all perspectives can be fairly represented:

> Senior management and the board make decisions on the appropriate action to be taken regarding significant issues. They may decide to assume the risk of not correcting the reported condition because of cost or other considerations. Senior management should inform the board of decisions about all significant issues raised by internal auditing.
>
> When the CAE believes that senior management has accepted a level of risk that the organization considers unacceptable, the CAE must discuss the matter with senior management as stated in Standard 2600. The CAE should understand management's basis for the decision, identify the cause of any disagreement, and determine whether management has the authority to accept the risk. Disagreements may relate to risk likelihood and potential exposure, understanding of risk appetite, cost, and level of control. Preferably, the CAE should resolve the disagreement with senior management
>
> If the CAE and senior management cannot reach an agreement, Standard 2600 directs the CAE to inform the board. If possible, the CAE and management should make a joint presentation about the conflicting positions. For financial reporting matters, CAEs should consider discussing these issues with the external auditors in a timely manner.

Next Steps

You have completed Part 2, Section II, of The IIA's CIA Learning System®. Next, check your understanding by completing the online section-specific test(s) to help you identify any content that needs additional study.

Once you have completed the section-specific test(s) and feel confident that you have mastered the information, you can advance to studying Section III.

Section III: Fraud Risks and Controls

This section is designed to help you:

- *Define fraud and the conditions that must exist for fraud to occur.*
- *Identify common types of fraud associated with the engagement area during the engagement planning process.*
- *Consider the potential for fraud risks in the engagement area during the engagement planning process.*
- *Determine if fraud risks require special consideration when conducting an engagement.*
- *Determine if any suspected fraud merits investigation.*
- *Demonstrate an understanding of fraud investigations.*
- *Ensure that the organization and internal audit learn from fraud investigations.*
- *Complete a process review to improve controls to prevent fraud and recommend changes.*
- *Provide examples of fraud risk management controls.*
- *Employ audit tests to detect fraud.*
- *Use computer data analysis to detect fraud, including continuous online monitoring.*
- *Support a culture of fraud awareness, and encourage the reporting of improprieties.*
- *Describe the features of an effective whistleblower hotline.*
- *Demonstrate an understanding of fraud interrogation/investigative techniques.*
- *Demonstrate an understanding of forensic auditing techniques.*

The Certified Internal Auditor (CIA) exam questions based on content from this section make up approximately 5% to 15% of the total number of questions for Part 2. Some topics are covered at the "A—Awareness" level, meaning that you are responsible for comprehension and recall of information. However, most topics are covered at the "P—Proficiency" level, meaning that you are responsible not only for comprehension and recall of information but also for higher-level mastery, including application, analysis, synthesis, and evaluation.

Section Introduction

In its 2012 "Report to the Nations on Occupational Fraud and Abuse," the Association of Certified Fraud Examiners reported that the average organization lost 5% of its revenues to fraud, or an estimated global total of US $3.5 trillion in losses to fraud. A large portion of those incidents—20%—represented losses of over US $1,000,000. As disturbing as the size of the loss is the fact that reported fraudulent activities usually continued for a median of 18 months before they were uncovered, most often after a tip from an employee within the organization. Only 3% of reported incidents were uncovered by external audits.

These facts suggest that fraud represents a serious risk for most organizations around the world. The internal auditing function can play a major role in managing the organization's fraud risk by assuring the effectiveness of the organization's fraud risk management framework and by considering the potential for fraud and the effectiveness of controls during specific assurance engagements.

The chapters in this section address the areas of knowledge concerning fraud and fraud audits:

- The types of fraud and fraud risks an internal auditor might encounter in different engagements
- Assessing fraud risks when conducting an engagement
- Determining the need for initiating a fraud investigation
- Analyzing processes to improve fraud controls
- Tools to detect fraud
- Creating a culture of fraud awareness
- Interrogation/investigative tools for fraud investigations
- Forensic auditing to compile legal evidence

Relevant *Standards*

The supporting role of the internal auditor in detecting fraud is reflected in Attribute Standard 1210.A2, which reads: "Internal auditors must have sufficient knowledge to evaluate the risk of fraud and the manner in which it is managed by the organization, but are not expected to have the expertise of a person whose primary responsibility is detecting and investigating fraud." The ability of the internal auditor to detect fraud and assess controls is a necessary component of other standards as well:

- Attribute Standard 1220, "Due Professional Care," requires internal auditors to exercise prudence and competence. Attribute Standard 1220.A1 applies to preparing for engagements by considering the probability of fraud and Attribute Standard 1220.A2 to using technology and data analysis tools to detect fraud.
- Performance Standard 2120, "Risk Management," requires internal auditors to "evaluate the effectiveness and contribute to the improvement of risk management processes." Standard 2120.A2 states: "The internal audit activity must evaluate the potential for the occurrence of fraud and how the organization manages fraud risk."
- Performance Standard 2210, "Engagement Objectives," requires internal auditors to set objectives for each engagement and, in Standard 2210.A2, to "consider the probability of significant errors, fraud, noncompliance, and other exposures when developing the engagement objectives."

Chapter A: Common Types of Fraud and Fraud Risks per Engagement Area

Chapter Introduction

This chapter focuses on providing a general understanding of fraud itself: what it is in general and how it may appear in different types of auditing engagements, why it occurs, and how an auditor can consider fraud potential during the engagement preparation process. Fraud risk awareness is discussed in more detail in Part 1, Section II.

The IIA also provides educational materials to help the auditor fulfill the requirement to become, and remain, proficient at the level required by the *Standards*. These materials include related Practice Advisories, Practice Guides and Position Papers, seminars, publications, and links to additional resources.

Being sufficiently knowledgeable to notice fraud opportunities and indicators of fraud requires:

- Knowing the definition of fraud as it appears in The IIA Glossary or in other authoritative professional or legal sources.
- Being able to identify the types of fraud most likely to occur in a specific audit client and being able to assess the client's level of vulnerability (fraud risk).
- Knowing the symptoms of fraud (red flags).

The topics in this chapter focus on these knowledge areas.

Topic 1: Define and Introduce Fraud (Level A)

Definition of fraud

The *Standards* Glossary defines fraud as "any illegal act characterized by deceit, concealment, or violation of trust. These acts are not dependent upon the application of threat of violence or of physical force. Frauds are perpetrated by parties and organizations to obtain money, property, or services; to avoid payment or loss of services; or to secure personal or business advantage."

In 2008, The IIA, in conjunction with the American Institute of Certified Public Accountants (AICPA) and the Association of Certified Fraud Examiners (ACFE) published "Managing the Business Risk of Fraud, A Practical Guide." It defines fraud as "any intentional act or omission designed to deceive others, resulting in the victim suffering a loss and/or the perpetrator achieving a gain."

The specific legal definition of fraud may vary by jurisdiction.

Why does fraud occur?

Three conditions must exist for fraud to occur—motive, opportunity, and rationalization. Together, these conditions are referred to as the "fraud triangle."

- **Motive.** Pressure or incentive represents a need that an individual attempts to satisfy by committing fraud. Often, pressure comes from a significant financial need or problem. This may include the need to keep one's job or earn a bonus. In publicly traded companies, there may be pressure to meet or beat analysts' estimates. For example, a large bonus or other financial award can be earned based on meeting certain performance goals. The fraudster has a desire to maintain his or her position in the organization and to retain a certain standard of living to compete with perceived peers.

- **Opportunity.** Opportunity is the ability to commit fraud and not be detected. Since fraudsters do not want to be caught in their actions, they must believe that their activities will not be detected. Opportunity is created by weak internal controls, poor management, or lack of board oversight and/or through the use of one's position and authority to override controls. Failure to establish adequate procedures to detect fraudulent activity also increases the opportunities for fraud to occur. A process may be designed properly for typical conditions; however, a window of opportunity may arise creating circumstances for the control to fail. Persons in positions of authority may be able to create opportunities to override existing controls because subordinates or weak controls allow them to circumvent the controls.

- **Rationalization.** Rationalization is the ability for a person to justify a fraud, a crucial component in most frauds. It involves a person reconciling his/her behavior (e.g., stealing) with the commonly accepted notions of decency and trust. For example, the fraudster places himself or herself as the priority (self-centered) rather than the well-being of the organization or society as a whole. The person may believe that committing fraud is justified in the context of saving a family member or loved one so he/she can pay for high medical bills. Other times, the person simply labels the theft as "borrowing" and intends to pay the stolen money back at a later time. Some people will do things that are defined as unacceptable behavior by the organization yet are commonplace in their culture or were accepted by previous employers. As a result, they can rationalize their behavior by thinking that the rules don't apply to them.

Special considerations for detecting and investigating fraud

Fraud is an area where the services of outside experts are often retained. The internal auditor's responsibilities for detecting fraud during engagements include:

- Considering fraud risks in the assessment of control design and determination of audit steps to perform.
- Have sufficient knowledge of fraud to identify red flags indicating that fraud may have been committed.
- Being alert to opportunities that could allow fraud, such as control weaknesses.
- Evaluating the indicators of fraud and deciding whether any further action is necessary or whether an investigation should be recommended.
- Notifying the appropriate authorities within the organization if a determination is made that fraud has occurred to recommend an investigation.

Topic 2: Identify Common Types of Fraud Associated with the Engagement Area During the Engagement Planning Process (Level P)

It is not the intent of this discussion to list the myriad types of fraud and red flags for fraud. The IIA publication *Effective Fraud Detection and Prevention Techniques Practice Set* by Hubert D. Glover and James C. Flag provides many specific examples of both. There is additional information on The IIA's Web site, and more information is available through other resources that can help internal auditors understand common types of fraud and potential red flags.

Ultimately, the specific nature of the engagement and the less tangible but equally important judgment skills of the internal auditor help to identify the relevant types of fraud and red flags for inquiry. Let's consider an example of a routine internal audit of the purchasing function that Glover and Flag describe in *Effective Fraud Detection and Prevention Techniques Practice Set* for an overview of fraud applied to a specific engagement.

Background and risks

Purchasing represents an activity where liabilities and commitments to expend cash are incurred. Fraud risks include unauthorized expenditures, illegal or corrupt procurement activities, and inefficient operations.

Engagement objectives

In considering these risks, the audit objectives are to:

- Authorize vendors in accordance with management's criteria.
- Determine if purchases eligible for competitive bids are reviewed and authorized.

- Ensure that goods received are properly reflected in purchasing and shipping records and receiving reports are independently verified.
- Verify that liabilities incurred are properly recorded and updated upon cash disbursement and purchasing-related adjustment.

Audit scope

The audit of the purchasing function will primarily focus on the duties performed by the purchasing function. However, the internal auditor will have to interface with other functions such as receiving or accounts payable as deemed appropriate to verify the existence of controls.

Red flags

Fraud red flags in this case could include the following:

- Turnover among purchasing department buyers that significantly exceeds attrition rates in other areas of the organization
- Purchasing order proficiency rates that fluctuate significantly among buyers with comparable workloads
- Dramatic increases in purchase volumes per certain vendors that are not justified by competitive bidding or changes in production specifications
- Unaccounted purchase order numbers or physical loss of purchase orders
- Rise in the cost of routine purchases that exceed the inflation rate
- Unusual purchases not consistent with the categories identified by prior trends or operating budget

Topic 3: Consider the Potential for Fraud Risks in the Engagement Area During the Engagement Planning Process (Level P)

Be knowledgeable of the risk factors and red flags of fraud

Consideration must be given during the planning phase to the potential for fraud in the proposed area of inquiry. While internal auditors are not expected to be experts in fraud, they are expected to understand enough about internal controls to identify opportunities for fraud. They should also understand fraud schemes and scenarios as well as be aware of the signs that point to fraud and how to prevent them.

Internal auditors may gain this knowledge through training, certification programs, experience, and self-study. One source of information concerning risk factors and red flags is "Managing the Business Risk of Fraud, A Practical Guide," mentioned earlier. The IIA book store also contains many reference publications on the subject.

Fraud risk

All organizations are exposed to a degree of fraud risk in any process where human input is required. The degree to which an organization is exposed relates to the fraud risks inherent in the business, the extent to which effective internal controls are present either to prevent or detect fraud, and the honesty and integrity of those involved in the process.

Fraud risk is the probability that fraud will occur and the potential severity or consequences to the organization when it occurs. The probability of a fraudulent activity is based, typically, on how easy it is to commit fraud, the motivational factors leading to fraud, and the company's fraud history.

Fraud triangle

The fraud triangle, discussed in the first topic of this chapter, can help internal auditors gauge the potential for fraud in a specific engagement area:

- **Motive.** Could employees in the area be motivated to commit fraud? For example, are morale problems well known? Are employees underpaid relative to the local market or industry? Are employees under unusual stress to perform—for example, to meet certain cost parameters?
- **Opportunity.** Do employees have opportunity to commit fraud? For example, do processes include reasonable controls against fraud? Is management supervision adequate? Is there high turnover that might make detection more difficult? Are processes so complex or highly automated that detection would be challenging?
- **Rationalization.** Does the culture in the organization or in the engagement area encourage a certain amount of ethical laxity?

Fraud red flags

An internal auditor also needs to understand fraud indicators—signs that indicate both the inadequacy of controls in place to deter fraud and the possibility that some perpetrator has already overcome these weak or absent controls to commit fraud. Such indicators are referred to as red flags. Fraud red flags may surface at any stage of the internal audit. Red flags are only warning signs; they are not proof that fraud has been committed. However, they serve an important function during planning to direct the internal auditor's attention to questionable areas and/or activities. Identification of red flags directs the scope of current and subsequent audit steps until sufficient evidence is gathered to form an objective conclusion regarding the existence of fraud. The occurrence of red flags combined with other corroborating audit evidence provides an effective detection technique.

There are several general tenets that apply in fraud detection. Consider these examples.

- A good system of internal controls is likely to expose irregularities perpetrated by a single individual without the aid of others.
- A group has a better chance of perpetrating fraud than does a single individual.
- Management can often override controls, singularly or in groups.

Design appropriate engagement steps to address significant risk of fraud

When planning the audit, the auditor should determine the most likely fraud risks associated with the audit customer's mission, markets, culture, operations, staff, and management. After identifying these, the auditor can design appropriate engagement steps to determine whether controls are in place to prevent the fraud occurrence or whether those types of frauds are occurring. Effectively identifying fraud risks specific to a particular client requires thinking like a criminal—asking yourself, "If I were managing or working in this organization, what sorts of fraud might I be tempted to commit on behalf of the organization or to its detriment (and my gain)? And if I decided to commit that fraud, how would I carry it out with greatest likelihood of success?"

When assessing the fraud risk in an audit client, the internal auditor should use the organization's own model for risk management, such as the COSO model.

The internal auditor should also factor cost and benefit considerations into account. No organization can be 100% free of fraud risk. Controls should be designed to reduce fraud risk to a reasonably small amount in relation to the investment required and the consequences they prevent. A million-dollar program to reduce pencil theft is unlikely to pass the cost-benefit test.

Design steps appropriate to conditions

In planning the audit, the auditor should consider the specific environment of the engagement and its vulnerabilities to fraud. For example, managers will have different temptations from staff and will also have access to different opportunities. People working as mortgage lenders in a bank will be tempted in different ways from computer programmers in the same organization—and will likely have access to different methods of carrying out their kind of fraud. Employees in a retail establishment will have different temptations and options than employees in pharmaceutical research organizations.

Different types of processes also present different opportunities for fraud and red flags. For example, the types of activities the internal auditor should watch for when auditing an e-commerce operation include:

- Unauthorized movement of money (e.g., transfers to jurisdictions where the recovery of funds would be difficult).
- Duplication of payments.
- Denial of orders placed or received, goods received, or payments made.
- Exception reports and procedures and effectiveness of the follow-up.
- Digital signatures. (Are they used for all transactions? Who authorizes them? Who has access to them?)
- Protections against viruses and hacking activities (history file, use of tools).
- Access rights. (Are they reviewed regularly? Are they promptly revised when staff members are changed?)
- History of interception of transactions by unauthorized persons.

Seek authority to take the necessary engagement steps

While the *Standards* mandate that the internal auditor should carry out engagements with proficiency and due professional care, they also recognize that management, too, bears responsibilities in this regard. (The Sarbanes-Oxley Act also assigns to senior management personal responsibility for establishing controls to prevent fraud and for reporting any that comes to their attention.) According to Sawyer, et al., management is not only responsible for creating a moral atmosphere in the organization ("tone at the top") and for developing adequate controls but must also grant the auditor certain authorities, without which the auditor cannot be held responsible for detecting signs of fraud. Specifically, the internal auditor must have authority to:

- Review and comment on annual reports.
- Audit all consulting arrangements. (Contract work is especially prone to generating overcharges. Contracts should include a right-to-audit clause.)
- Analyze the organization's procedures.
- Review transactions approved by executives.
- Have access to the board of director's actions.
- Review transactions with subsidiaries and associated organizations.
- Test documentation supporting financial reports.
- Monitor compliance with the organization's record retention policies.
- Ask managers about political contributions, etc.
- Review expense accounts.
- Monitor the conflict-of-interest policy.

Chapter B: Assessing Response to Engagement Area Fraud Risks

Chapter Introduction

This chapter applies the enterprise risk management model to planning the audit engagement. The auditor considers the potential for fraud in the audited process or area, weighs its priority against the organization's objectives and the engagement's budget, and plans the audit accordingly.

Topic 1: Determine if Fraud Risks Require Special Consideration When Conducting an Engagement (Level P)

To assess fraud risk, internal auditors should use the organization's enterprise risk management model, if one is available. Otherwise, auditors should try to understand the specific fraud schemes that could threaten the organization.

A risk model maps and assesses the organization's vulnerability to fraud schemes, covering all inherent risks to the organization. The model should use consistent categories (i.e., there should be no overlap between risk areas) and should be detailed enough to identify and cover anticipated high-risk areas.

COSO's enterprise risk management framework provides a useful model that includes sections on:

- **Event identification,** such as brainstorming activities, interviews, focus groups, surveys, industry research, and event inventories.
- **Risk assessments,** including probabilities and consequences.
- **Risk response strategies,** such as treating, transferring, tolerating, or terminating risk.
- **Control activities,** such as linking risks to existing anti-fraud programs and control activities and validating their effectiveness.
- **Monitoring,** including audit plans and programs that consider residual fraud and risk due to misconduct.

The evaluation should consider whether fraud could be committed by an individual or requires collusion. Considerations also should be made regarding the negative effects of unjustly suspecting employees or giving the appearance that employees are not trusted.

Fraud risk assessment

Risk assessment (also known as risk analysis) is the identification and measurement of risk and the process of prioritizing risk. COSO tells us that specific to fraud, a risk assessment evaluates management's fraud risk assessment, in particular their process for identifying, assessing, and testing potential fraud misconduct schemes and scenarios that could involve suppliers, contractors, and other parties.

The fraud risk assessment process is a critical activity in establishing a basis to design and implement anti-fraud programs and risk control activities. *Internal Auditing: Assurance and Consulting Services* lists the following characteristics of effective fraud risk assessment:

- Performed on a systematic and recurring basis
- Considers possible fraud schemes and scenarios, including consideration of internal and external factors
- Assesses risk at a company-wide, significant business unit, and significant account level
- Evaluates the likelihood, significance, and pervasiveness of each risk
- Assesses exposure arising from each category of fraud risk by identifying mitigating control activities and considering their effectiveness
- Is performed with the involvement of appropriate personnel
- Considers management override of controls (i.e., nonroutine transactions and journal entries or temporary suspension of controls)
- Is updated when special circumstances arise (i.e., mergers and acquisitions and new systems)

Judgment skills

The final determination of whether or not the risk of fraud warrants special consideration when conducting the engagement involves the internal auditor's judgment skills. This mental attitude or judgment is a combination of the internal auditor's analytical skills and all information related to the organization to determine if internal control weaknesses exist and signal the potential for fraud activity. Armed with this information, the internal auditor can respond accordingly in planning the engagement.

Chapter C: Determining Need for Fraud Investigation

Chapter Introduction

It is the task of the internal auditor to be one of the "early warning systems" of the organization—to detect the indicators of fraud. However, a complete fraud examination is a serious and potentially costly undertaking, since it may culminate in legal proceedings and may require the assembly of a full fraud investigation team to identify evidence that can meet demanding legal criteria. Any fraud case also carries the potential of legal liability for the organization if the charges cannot be proven.

Although the internal auditor is not expected to have the level of expertise required to perform fraud investigations, internal auditors do play an important role in these investigations. The internal auditor assists members of the organization in the effective discharge of their responsibilities by furnishing them with analyses, appraisals, recommendations, counsel, and information concerning the activities reviewed. To be better prepared to support fraud investigations, internal auditors should be aware of how investigations are conducted.

Topic 1: Determine if Any Suspected Fraud Merits Investigation (Level P)

Organizations investigate possible fraud when there is a concern or suspicion of wrongdoing within the organization. Suspicion can result from a formal complaint process, an informal complaint process such as a tip, or an audit, including an audit designed to test for fraud. Investigating a fraud is not the same as auditing for fraud, which is an audit designed to proactively detect indications of fraud in those processes or transactions where analysis indicates the risk of fraud to be significant.

If significant control weaknesses are detected, additional tests conducted by internal auditors should be directed at identifying other fraud indicators. The internal auditor should:

- Recognize that the presence of more than one indicator at any one time increases the probability that fraud has occurred.
- Evaluate the indicators of fraud and decide whether any further action is necessary or whether an investigation should be recommended.
- Notify the appropriate authorities within the organization if a determination is made that fraud has occurred to recommend an investigation.

In addition, it is the responsibility of the internal auditor to support further investigation by providing sound data and by ensuring that the suspected perpetrators are not alerted prematurely to the investigation.

Maintaining continuity

When fraud is suspected, the internal auditor will, in most cases, refer the case to the chief audit executive, who will secure appropriate resources for further investigation—for example, a certified fraud examiner or an IT security specialist. The internal auditor plays an important role in transitioning to a fraud investigation. The succeeding auditor/investigator should be briefed on fraud risks in the engagement, red flags noticed, fraud tests implemented to date, and preliminary findings.

Internal auditors assigned to an engagement should be similarly prepared to discuss specific concerns about suspected fraud with a successor in the event that the audit must be handed off to a colleague before definite conclusions can be reached. The potential impact of fraud is too great to risk losing critical focus during staffing transitions.

Topic 2: Demonstrate an Understanding of Fraud Investigations (Level A)

A fraud investigation consists of gathering sufficient information about specific details and performing the procedures necessary to determine whether fraud has occurred, the loss or exposures associated with the fraud, who was involved, and how it happened. An important outcome of investigations is that innocent persons are cleared of suspicion.

Investigations attempt to discover the full nature and extent of the fraudulent activity, not just the event that may have initiated the investigation. Investigation work includes preparing, documenting, and preserving evidence sufficient for potential legal proceedings.

Internal auditors, lawyers, investigators, security personnel, and other specialists from inside or outside the organization usually conduct or participate in fraud investigations.

Investigations and the related resolution activities need to be carefully managed in accordance with laws. Local laws may direct how and where investigations are conducted, disciplinary and recovery practices, and investigative communications. It is in the best interest of the company, both professionally and legally, to work effectively with the organization's legal counsel and to become familiar with the relevant laws in the country in which the fraud investigation occurs.

According to *Sawyer's Internal Auditing,* the objectives of a fraud investigation are:

- First and foremost, to protect the innocent, establish the facts, resolve the matter, and clear the air.
- To determine the basic circumstances quickly to stop the loss as soon as possible.
- To establish the essential elements of the crime to support a successful prosecution.
- To identify, gather, and protect evidence.
- To identify and interview witnesses.
- To identify patterns of actions and behavior.
- To determine probable motives that often will identify potential suspects.
- To provide accurate and objective facts upon which judgments concerning discipline, termination, or prosecution may be based.
- To account for and recover assets.
- To identify weaknesses in control and counter them by revising existing procedures or recommending new ones and by applying security equipment when justified.

Investigation process

Management is responsible for developing controls for the investigation process, including policies and procedures for effective investigations, preserving evidence, handling the results of investigations, reporting, and communications. Such standards are often documented in a fraud policy; internal auditors may assist in the evaluation of the policy. Such policies and procedures need to consider the rights of individuals, the qualifications of those authorized to conduct investigations, and the relevant laws where the frauds occurred. The policies should also consider the extent to which management will discipline employees, suppliers, or customers, including taking legal measures to recover losses and civil or criminal prosecution. It is important for management to clearly define the authority and responsibilities of those involved in the investigation, especially the relationship between the investigator and legal counsel. It is also important for management to design and comply with procedures that minimize internal communications about an ongoing investigation, especially in the initial phases.

The policy needs to specify the investigator's role in determining whether a fraud has been committed. Either the investigator or management will decide if fraud has occurred, and management will decide whether the organization will notify outside authorities. A judgment that fraud has occurred may in some jurisdictions be made only by law enforcement or judicial authorities. The investigation may simply result in a conclusion that organization policy was violated or that fraud is likely to have occurred.

The role of internal audit

The role of the internal audit activity in investigations needs to be defined in the internal audit charter as well as in the fraud policies and procedures. For example, internal auditing may have the primary responsibility for fraud investigations or may act as a resource for investigations. Internal auditing may also refrain from involvement in investigations because they are responsible for assessing the effectiveness of investigations or they lack the appropriate resources. Any of these roles can be acceptable as long as their impact on internal auditing's independence is recognized and handled appropriately.

To maintain proficiency, fraud investigation teams have a responsibility to obtain sufficient knowledge of fraudulent schemes, investigation techniques, and applicable laws. There are national and international programs that provide training and certification for investigators and forensic specialists.

If the internal audit activity is responsible for the investigation, it may conduct an investigation using in-house staff, out-sourcing, or a combination of both. In some cases, internal audit may also use non-audit employees of the organization to assist. It is often important to assemble the investigation team without delay. If the organization is likely to need external experts, the CAE may prequalify the service provider(s) so external resources are quickly available when needed.

In organizations where primary responsibility for the investigation function is not assigned to the internal audit activity, the internal audit activity may still be asked to help gather information and make recommendations for internal control improvements, such as:

- Monitoring the investigation process to help the organization follow relevant policies and procedures and applicable laws and statutes.
- Locating and/or securing misappropriated or related assets.
- Supporting the organization's legal proceedings, insurance claims, or other recovery actions.
- Evaluating and monitoring the organization's internal and external post-investigation reporting and communication plans and practices.
- Monitoring the implementation of recommended control enhancement.

Conducting the investigation

An investigation plan is developed for each investigation, following the organization's investigation procedures or protocols. The lead investigator determines the knowledge, skills, and other competencies needed to carry out the investigation effectively and assigns competent, appropriate people to the team. This process includes obtaining assurance that there is no potential conflict of interest with those being investigated or with any of the employees in the organization.

The plan should consider the following investigative activities:

- Gathering evidence through surveillance, interviews, or written statements
- Documenting and preserving evidence, considering legal rules of evidence and the business uses of the evidence
- Determining the extent of the fraud
- Determining the techniques used to perpetrate the fraud
- Evaluating the cause of the fraud
- Identifying the perpetrators

At any point during this process, the investigator may conclude that the complaint or suspicion was unfounded. The investigator then follows the organization's process to close the case.

Obtaining evidence

The collection and preparation of evidence is critical to understanding the fraud or misconduct, and it is needed to support the conclusions reached by the investigation team. The investigation team may use computer forensic procedures or computer-assisted data analysis based on the nature of the allegations, the results of the procedures performed, and the goals of the investigation. All reports, documents, and evidence obtained should be recorded chronologically in an inventory or log. Some examples of evidence include:

- Letters, memos, and correspondence, both in hard copy or electronic form (such as e-mails or information stored on personal computers).
- Computer files, general ledger postings, or other financial or electronic records.
- IT or system access records.
- Security and time-keeping logs, such as security camera videos or access badge records.
- Internal phone records.
- Customer or vendor information, both in the public domain and maintained by the organization, such as contracts, invoices, and payment information.
- Public records, such as business registrations with government agencies or property records.
- News articles and internal and external Web sites such as social networking sites.

Interviewing and interrogating

The investigator will interview individuals such as witnesses and facilitating personnel with the goal of gathering evidence to support a suspicion that fraud may be occurring and/or establish the scope of fraud activity and the degree of complicity in the fraud. Many investigators prefer to approach the accused with sufficient evidence that will support the goal to secure a confession.

Generally the accused is interrogated by two people: 1) an experienced investigator and 2) another individual who takes notes during the interrogation and later functions as a witness if needed. In addition, it is essential that all information obtained from the interrogation is rendered correctly.

The differences between interviews and interrogations and the techniques appropriate to each are discussed in Chapter G later in this section.

Investigative activities need to be coordinated with management, legal counsel, and other specialists such as human resources and insurance risk management as appropriate throughout the investigation.

Investigators need to be knowledgeable and cognizant of the rights of persons within the scope of the investigation and the reputation of the organization itself. The investigator has the responsibility to ensure that the investigation process is handled in a consistent and prudent manner.

The level and extent of complicity in the fraud throughout the organization needs to be assessed. This assessment can be critical to not destroy or taint crucial evidence and to avoid obtaining misleading information from persons who may be involved.

The investigation needs to adequately secure evidence collected, maintaining chain-of-custody procedures appropriate for the situation.

Reporting investigation results

Reporting fraud investigations consists of the various oral, written, interim, or final communications to senior management and/or the board regarding the status and results of fraud investigations. Reports can be preliminary and ongoing throughout the investigation.

A written report or other formal communication may be issued at the conclusion of the investigation phase. It may include the reason for beginning the investigation, time frames, observations, conclusions, resolution, and corrective action taken (or recommendations) to improve controls. Depending on how the investigation was resolved, the report may need to be written in a manner that provides confidentiality for some of the people involved. In writing the report, the investigator should consider the needs of the board and management while complying with legal requirements and restrictions and the organization's policies and procedures.

Some additional considerations concerning fraud reporting are:

- Submitting a draft of the proposed final communications to legal counsel for review. In cases where the organization is able to invoke attorney-client privilege and has chosen to do so, the report is addressed to legal counsel.
- Notifying senior management and the board in a timely manner when significant fraud or erosion of trust occurs.
- Considering the effect on financial statements. The results of a fraud investigation may indicate that fraud had a previously undiscovered adverse effect on the organization's financial position and its operational results for one or more years for which financial statements have already been issued. Senior management and the board need to be informed of such a discovery so they can decide on the appropriate reporting, usually after consulting with the external auditors.

If the internal audit activity conducts the investigation, Standard 2400, "Communicating Results," provides information applicable to necessary engagement communications. As specified in this standard, distribution of investigation results should be appropriately limited and information should be treated in a confidential manner. Practice Advisory 2440-2 notes that information regarding fraud comes under the category of "matters that may adversely impact the organization's reputation, image, competitiveness, success, viability, market values, investments and intangible assets, or earnings."

In addition, communication of results should take care to protect internal whistleblowers. This will help create an atmosphere in which future whistleblowers feel less vulnerable to pressures and repercussions from within the organization. Without these protections, whistleblowers may feel that it is safer to take sensitive information to outside bodies first. This hinders the organization's ability to conduct its own investigations and take corrective actions.

In the case of fraud, local laws may accelerate communication of investigation reports to the board and may require reporting to local authorities as well.

Resolution of fraud incidents

Resolution consists of determining what actions will be taken by the organization once a fraud scheme and perpetrator(s) have been fully investigated and evidence has been reviewed. Management and the board are responsible for resolving fraud incidents, not the internal audit activity or the investigator.

An important decision at this stage is whether to prosecute the wrongdoer. This decision is made by management and the board, usually based on the input of legal counsel. While internal auditors do not make these decisions, they may indicate to management and the board that prosecutions discourage future fraud by reinforcing the repercussions of fraudulent behavior and thus serve as a fraud deterrent.

Resolution may include all or some of the following:

- Providing closure to persons who were initially under suspicion but were found to be innocent
- Providing closure to those who reported a concern
- Disciplining an employee in accordance with the organization's policies, employment legislation, or employment contracts
- Requesting voluntary financial restitution from an employee, customer, or supplier
- Terminating contracts with suppliers
- Reporting the incident to law enforcement, regulatory bodies, or similar authorities; encouraging them to prosecute the fraudster; cooperating with their investigation and prosecution
- Entering into civil litigation or similar legal processes to recover the amount taken
- Filing an insurance claim
- Filing a complaint with the perpetrator's professional association
- Recommending control enhancements

Communication by the board and senior management

Management or the board determines whether to inform entities outside the organization after consultation with individuals such as legal counsel, human resources personnel, and the CAE. The organization may have a responsibility to notify government agencies of certain types of fraudulent acts. These agencies include law enforcement, regulatory agencies, or oversight bodies. Additionally, the organization may be required to notify the organization's insurers, bankers, and external auditors of instances of fraud. Any comments made by management to the press, law enforcement, or other external parties are best coordinated through legal counsel.

Typically, only authorized spokespersons make external announcements and comments.

Internal communications are a strategic tool used by management to reinforce its position relating to integrity, to demonstrate that it takes appropriate action (including prosecution, if appropriate) when organizational policy is violated, and to show why internal controls are important. Such communications may take the form of a newsletter article or a memo from management, or the situation may be used as an example in the organization's fraud training program. These communications generally take place after the case has been resolved internally, and they do not specify the names of perpetrators or other specific investigation details that are not necessary for the message or that contravene laws. An investigation and its results may cause significant stress or morale issues that may disrupt the organization, especially when the fraud becomes public. Management may plan employee sessions and/or team-building strategies to rebuild trust and camaraderie among employees.

Lessons learned

After the fraud has been investigated and communicated, it is important for management and the internal audit activity to step back and consider the lessons learned. For example:

- How did the fraud occur?
- What controls failed?
- What controls were overridden?
- Why wasn't the fraud detected earlier?
- What red flags were missed by management?
- What red flags did internal audit miss?
- How can future frauds be prevented or more easily detected?
- What controls need strengthening?
- What internal audit plans and audit steps need to be enhanced?
- What additional training is needed?

The dynamic feedback within these sessions needs to stress the importance of acquiring up-to-date information on fraudsters and fraud schemes that can help internal auditors and the anti-fraud community engage in best practices to prevent losses.

Internal auditors typically assess the facts of investigations and advise management relating to remediation of control weaknesses that lead to the fraud. Internal auditors may design steps in audit programs or develop "auditing for fraud" programs to help disclose the existence of similar frauds in the future.

Chapter D: Process Review for Fraud Controls Improvement

Chapter Introduction

The goal of the process review is to ensure that the existing controls are achieving their objectives—that all risks have been identified and controlled to the level required by the organization's risk attitude—and to identify opportunities for improving fraud controls.

Topic 1: Complete a Process Review to Improve Controls to Prevent Fraud and Recommend Changes (Level P)

The process review may occur as the focus of one engagement within the audit plan—an individual engagement within the annual audit plan designed to review, analyze, and improve the current fraud risk management framework. It may also be included as one objective of an individual engagement, if the audited area or process is considered vulnerable to some manner of fraud.

Applied to the area of auditing for fraud controls, process review implies that, in the course of an assurance engagement, the internal auditor will:

- Review the risk assessment to identify risks that have not been identified.
- Assess whether controls are in place—according to an analysis of the degree of likelihood and impact of a fraud scenario and according to the organization's risk attitude—to prevent or mitigate fraud.
- Gather evidence to establish whether fraud controls are operating as defined.
- Propose ways to improve fraud controls in the program, audited area, or process.

For example, an internal auditor may note that it is possible for some cash transactions to go unrecorded in a retail environment, such as small rental fees for equipment or space at a sports facility. There may be no controls in place or only very weak controls. After assessing the potential for loss by fraud, the internal auditor may recommend various controls, ranging from policy ("Cash transactions must be documented in a manner that will allow reconciliation") to procedure (implementation of rental logs and numbered customer receipts) to collection of benchmarking data (typical levels of equipment/space rentals and resulting income).

Auditing the fraud risk management program

The audit plan may include an engagement to audit the risk management, internal control, and governance activities in regard to fraud—the fraud risk management program. The components of a fraud risk management program are described in "Managing the Business Risk of Fraud, A Practical Guide," which states:

> Only through diligent and ongoing effort can an organization protect itself against significant acts of fraud. Key principles for proactively establishing an environment to effectively manage an organization's fraud risk include:
>
> Principle 1: As part of an organization's governance structure, a fraud risk management program should be in place, including a written policy (or policies) to convey the expectations of the board of directors and senior management regarding managing fraud risk.
>
> Principle 2: Fraud risk exposure should be assessed periodically by the organization to identify specific potential schemes and events that the organization needs to mitigate.
>
> Principle 3: Prevention techniques to avoid potential key fraud risk events should be established, where feasible, to mitigate possible impacts on the organization.
>
> Principle 4: Detection techniques should be established to uncover fraud events when preventive measures fail or unmitigated risks are realized.
>
> Principle 5: A reporting process should be in place to solicit input on potential fraud, and a coordinated approach to investigation and corrective action should be used to help ensure potential fraud is addressed appropriately and timely.

Internal auditors usually consider fraud risks and controls during audit engagements, covering issues in Principles 2, 3 and 4. An audit of the organization's fraud risk management program takes a macro approach and ensures coverage of activities named in Principles 1 through 5.

Additional areas to evaluate may include:

- Board roles, responsibilities, and oversight activities.
- Fraud statistics and performance measures.
- The ethics culture and opinions of stakeholders.
- Compliance reporting functions.
- The effectiveness of corrective action (recovery of losses, disciplinary action, identification and improvement of control weaknesses).

Fraud risk management framework controls

Fraud prevention and mitigation encompasses those actions taken to discourage fraud and limit fraud exposure when it occurs. Strong safeguarding controls and an anti-fraud program are proven fraud deterrents. As with other internal controls, management has the primary responsibility for establishing and maintaining the fraud controls.

The AICPA, in its publication "Management Antifraud Programs and Controls," tell us that organizations need to take three fundamental actions:

- Create a culture of honesty and high ethics.
- Evaluate anti-fraud processes and controls.
- Develop an appropriate oversight process.

Creating a culture of fraud awareness is discussed later in this section, in Chapter F.

In addition to cultural controls, specific controls can be designed to meet the fraud risks in different types of functions and processes. Exhibit III-1 applies the five COSO control components to the task of fraud risk management.

Exhibit III-1: COSO Fraud Prevention and Control and the Internal Audit Activity (continued on next page)

Control Elements	Internal Auditing Responsibilities
Control environment	
Companies must establish an appropriate control environment that includes: • A code of conduct, ethics policy, or fraud policy to set the appropriate "tone at the top." • Ethics and whistleblower hotline programs to report concerns. • Hiring and promotion guidelines and practices. • Oversight by the audit committee, board, or other oversight body. • Investigation of reported issues and remediation of confirmed violations.	• Assess aspects of the control environment. • Conduct proactive fraud audits and investigations. • Communicate results of fraud audits. • Provide support for remediation efforts. • May own the whistleblower hotline.
Fraud risk assessment	
• Organizations should identify and assess fraud-related risks, including assessing the potential for fraudulent financial reporting, asset misappropriations, improper receipts and expenditures, or financial misconduct by management and others. • Companies also should assess whether adequate segregation of duties exists.	Evaluate management's fraud risk assessment, in particular their processes for identifying, assessing, and testing potential fraud and misconduct schemes and scenarios, including those that could involve suppliers, contractors, and other parties.

Exhibit III-1: COSO Fraud Prevention and Control and the Internal Audit Activity (concluded)

Control Elements	Internal Auditing Responsibilities
Control activities	
• Companies should establish and implement effective control practices, including actions taken by management to identify, prevent, and mitigate fraudulent financial reporting or misuse of the organization's assets as well as prevent override of controls by management. • Companies should establish an affirmation or certification process to confirm that employees have read and understood corporate policies and are in compliance with them.	• Assess the design and operating effectiveness of fraud-related controls. • Ensure that audit plans and programs address fraud risk. • Evaluate the design of facilities from a fraud or theft perspective. • Review proposed changes to laws, regulations, or systems and their impacts on controls.
Information and communication	
Companies must establish effective fraud-related information and communication practices, including: • Documentation and dissemination of policies, guidance, and results. • Opportunities to discuss ethical dilemmas. • Communication channels. • Training for personnel. • Considerations of the impact and use of technology for fraud deterrence, such as the use of continuous monitoring software.	Assess the operating effectiveness of information and communication systems and practices as well as provide support to fraud-related training initiatives.
Monitoring	
Organizations should conduct ongoing and periodic performance assessments and identify the impact and use of computer technology for fraud deterrence.	• Assess monitoring activities and related computer software. • Conduct investigations. • Support the audit committee's oversight related to control and fraud matters. • Support the development of fraud indicators. • Hire and train employees so they can have the appropriate fraud audit or investigative experience.

Whether an organization uses the COSO control framework or another framework, the key components in creating a culture of fraud awareness are setting a tone of honesty and integrity, developing a strong code of conduct and ethics policy, and clearly communicating it to all employees. Then the risks must be identified and quantified according to the probability of occurrence and their potential impact. With these elements in place, internal auditors can examine and evaluate the adequacy and effectiveness of their internal controls system commensurate with the extent of a potential exposure within the organization.

Chapter E: Detecting Fraud

Chapter Introduction

A program to detect fraud results from the realization that, in most cases, fraud cannot be entirely prevented. Fraud detection controls aim at uncovering actions or events that could be symptomatic of fraud, such as reconciling vendor payments with purchase orders, invoices, vendor information (e.g., address on file), and employee personal national identification number (e.g., a Social Security number in the US or a resident identity card in China). Detection controls can be passive or active. A passive fraud detection example would be a whistleblower program that facilitates reporting of fraud by employees, while an active detection control would be an analytic test performed during an audit. They can be performed periodically, during an assurance audit engagement, or applied continually, which may provide a much shorter time frame for detection. As stated earlier, in the 2012 “Report to the Nations,” the ACFE reported that the median length of time for a fraudulent activity was 18 months. For significant fraud risks, detecting fraud can be especially important.

This chapter focuses on different ways to detect fraud.

Topic 1: Employ Audit Tests to Detect Fraud (Level P)

When the internal auditor discovers an indication that fraud might have occurred or that control systems are weak in some particular area, the auditor should design further tests to uncover other indicators of fraud. Analytical procedures used to detect fraud include trend analysis and proportional analysis. (Using computer-based data analysis is discussed in the next topic.)

Trend and proportional analysis require that the internal auditor have an adequate understanding of the business being audited, both in terms of activity levels and in the relationships between activities.

Trend analysis

Reasoning that related activities will show consistent trends unless some factor disrupts the relationship, an auditor may analyze trend data to see if any such disruptions have occurred. After finding such a disruption, the auditor will do further research to identify a cause. Sometimes the cause of a breakdown in trends turns out to be fraud. For example, a study of trends in sales and freight costs could reveal a much faster rate of increase in freight costs than in sales. Since the costs of shipping materials and goods should be directly related to the amount of goods produced and sold, the auditor initiates an investigation, uncovering a pattern of recording false shipments and pocketing the resulting expenditures.

Proportional analysis

Proportional analysis is another way of comparing related pieces of data. Instead of tracking the data's trends, however, the auditor using proportional analysis determines the ratio of one to the other to see if it is reasonable and matches expectations. For example, instead of doing a trend analysis of data over the long term, the auditor in the previous analysis might (perhaps more simply) determine the ratio of the number of shipments based upon sales and the number of shipments based upon freight costs. If the organization is paying for more shipments than is necessary to get product to buyers, then the ratio would be unreasonable.

Another example demonstrates the application of proportional analysis. An auditor conducting an engagement at a brewery compares the cost of hops against the annual output of beer and discovers that the brewery is paying for twice the amount of hops required by its output. Investigation determines that the treasurer is diverting the excess hops to another brewery in which he is an investor.

Topic 2: Use Computer Data Analysis to Detect Fraud (Level P)

The use of computers in auditing has given the internal auditor greater power to verify large numbers of transactions. The computer can compare transactions with the events they effect to highlight unusual conditions, which can then be studied to determine whether they are tied to fraud or some other, perhaps more benign, explanation.

Consider the following comparisons:

- Sales of manufactured products to labor and materials costs (Run in one direction, this comparison might highlight nonexistent sales; run backward, it might indicate fraudulent materials or labor costs.)
- Purchases with increases in inventories or sales
- Payroll costs with employee payroll tax reports

These analytical tests do not prove fraud—or another causal mechanism. They simply identify anomalies worth investigating to find an explanation; one explanation could be fraud.

Audit departments should consider these various techniques when applying technology to fraud detection:

- Calculation of statistical parameters (e.g., averages, standard deviations, highest and lowest values)—to identify outlying transactions that could be indicative of fraudulent activity
- Classification—to find patterns and associations among groups of data elements
- Stratification of numeric values—to identify unusual (i.e., excessively high or low) values
- Digital analysis using Benford's Law—to identify statistically unlikely occurrences of specific digits in randomly occurring data sets (Benford's Law is covered later in this topic.)
- Joining different data sources—to identify inappropriately matching values such as names, addresses, and account numbers in disparate systems
- Duplicate testing—to identify simple and/or complex duplications of business transactions such as payments, payroll, claims, or expense report line items
- Gap testing—to identify missing numbers in sequential data
- Summing of numeric values—to check control totals that may have been falsified
- Validating data entry dates—to identify postings or data entry times that are inappropriate or suspicious

According to a 2008 white paper by ACL Services Ltd., to maximize the effectiveness of data analysis in fraud detection, the technology employed should enable auditors to:

- Compare data and transactions from multiple IT systems (and address control gaps that often exist within and between systems).
- Work with a comprehensive set of fraud indicators.
- Analyze all transactions within the target area.
- Perform the fraud detection tests on a scheduled basis and provide timely notification of trends, patterns, and exceptions.

Critical to the analysis of data is the establishment of normal values for comparative purposes. The first step in preparing to detect fraudulent deviations is defining a baseline. For example, having a five-year history of inventory or sales levels will help internal auditors identify unusual increases in inventory that may indicate theft of company property or year-end increases in sales that could be channel stuffing. (Channel stuffing is the practice of inflating sales figures by forcing more products through a distribution channel than the channel can actually sell. The excess goods are returned in a later financial reporting period.) Benchmarks may be created from internal data or may be purchased from industry research organizations.

We will describe here two types of analysis—numerical analysis and regression analysis—and two auditing tools for information systems.

Numerical analysis

Most auditing programs performing numerical analysis are based on Benford's Law, a probability principle using observations about the frequency of occurrence of the leading digit in a series of numbers. In the 1920s physicist Frank Benford noticed that the first few pages of his book of logarithm tables were much more worn from use than the last pages. He went on to observe geographical, scientific, and demographic data and deduced that, in sets of numbers, the number one will appear as the leading digit about 60% of the time. The numbers must be describing size of similar phenomena (e.g., number of transactions or sizes of payments), must not be assigned according to some set of rules (like ZIP codes or payment codes), and must not have an inherent minimum or maximum value (e.g., legally specified amounts, like minimum wage). Larger numbers appear in the leading digit position in indirect proportion to their size, so that the number nine appears in the leading position only 5% of the time.

Since most people believe that numbers occur randomly, it is possible that an employee committing fraud by, for example, writing checks to a fictitious vendor would choose amounts that violated Benford's Law. The amounts of the checks may begin an inordinate number of times with more improbable higher numbers.

Benford's Law has been extended to describe probabilities for second numbers and for two- and three-digit sets of numbers.

It may also be coupled with other forms of numerical analysis to identify irregularities, such as:

- **Relative size factor,** which determines when the largest number in a group is out of line with the rest of the items.
- **Same, same, different tests,** which search for improbable matches of two of three variables.
- **Same, same, same tests,** which search for identical entries.

Regression analysis

Computer programs may also be developed using regression analysis—a statistical modeling tool used to find relationships between a dependent variable (e.g., an unauthorized payment) and one or more independent variables (e.g., the number of checks issued, vendors paid, vendors paid at the same address as an employee address, payments made below a certain threshold). A program might correlate expense claims with events associated with travel or with a calendar to spot unreasonably frequent travel or travel that could not be associated with the stated purpose.

Enterprise auditing

Some software tools have been developed to build data analysis models and then apply them across an integrated enterprise management system. These enterprise management systems are useful in large organizations. They provide the means to coordinate various areas of control, analysis, and information storage throughout what is often a physically decentralized organization, like a multinational company or a vertically organized company with multiple manufacturing divisions, marketing, sales, research and development, shipping, customer service, and so on. Data mining refers to the capability of sifting through and analyzing large volumes of data to find certain patterns or associations. Enterprise data mining can be helpful, first, in defining what constitutes a suspicious pattern and, then, in detecting suspicious transactions, like fraudulent wire transfers.

Continuous online auditing

Continuous auditing (or continuous monitoring) uses computerized techniques to perpetually audit the processing of business transactions. Continuous online auditing programs edit transactions as or shortly after they occur, looking for transaction details that do not fall within preset parameters or, alternatively, transactions that match the patterns in fraudulent activity. Auditing reports can be generated at time intervals set according to need. An example of an online auditing system is a program that monitors payments being received at a data center. The online auditing program checks to see that each step of the required process for receiving payments is followed.

Continuous auditing might be used to compare payment addresses for each payment mailed with a database of employee addresses. This might detect payments to fictitious entities or duplicate payments.

Another example is cited in *Changing Internal Audit Practices in the New Paradigm: The Sarbanes-Oxley Environment* by Glen L. Gray. Gray describes the use of data mining to collect and compare data from a nationwide chain of retail outlets. Automated comparisons of "clear sale" or "no sale" or cash transactions with national averages identified problematic stores in which employees were stealing cash.

Continuous auditing provides an effective way of maximizing audit coverage and allowing the internal audit function to focus on exceptions and obtain greater coverage of high-risk areas. In addition, fraud can be detected on a timelier basis.

Gray makes the point that while continuous auditing of an entire database provides total assurance and the capture of even small errors and deviations, it offers two other benefits as well. Analysis of the entire database provides legal coverage against charges that sampling might have been discriminatory or misrepresentative. It also improves the ethical environment of the workplace. If employees think there is a greater chance that they will be caught, there are fewer attempts to commit fraud and a more positive workplace atmosphere.

Various publications on the topic and the results of related research projects are available through the IIA, including the following:

- *Continuous Auditing Potential for Internal Auditors* by J. Donald Warren, Jr., and Xenia Ley Parker (2003)
- *Proactively Detecting Occupational Fraud Using Computer Audit Reports* by Richard B. Lanza (2004)
- *Continuous Auditing: An Operational Model for Auditors* by Sally F. Culter (2005)
- GTAG 3: "Continuous Auditing: Implications for Assurance, Monitoring, and Risk Assessment" (2005)

Building comprehensive software systems of this nature requires thorough business, system, and analytical techniques. Continuous auditing has been most successful in industries with large volumes of transactions, such as the financial services and retail industries. Although most organizations want to develop continuous monitoring systems, doing so requires the right skill set along with a commitment to implement the program for long-term success. Smaller internal audit functions have to rely on the IT group or draw from other resources outside the internal audit function in order to be successful in implementing continuous auditing.

Chapter F: Culture of Fraud Awareness

Chapter Introduction

The five fraud risk management principles discussed earlier in this section stress the importance of fraud risk assessment, the establishment of prevention and detection controls, and periodic auditing of fraud risk controls. These principles also emphasize actions that support the creation of a culture of fraud awareness. This soft control—created through clearly communicated and enforced policies, employee training in fraud awareness, and a reporting mechanism for suspected fraud—is continually in place to prevent acts of fraud and to ensure a more rapid detection when fraud is committed.

The ACFE's "Report to the Nations" states that over 43% of occupational frauds were initially detected as the result of a tip—usually by another employee but also by customers, vendors, and others. Management review, internal audit, and monitoring systems are simply not as efficient or effective in detecting fraud as ensuring that employees know what fraud looks and feels like, know what to do when they become aware of fraud, and can easily report fraud without fear of retaliation. The topic in this chapter focuses on the role of whistleblowing in managing fraud risk.

Topic 1: Support a Culture of Fraud Awareness and Encourage the Reporting of Improprieties (Level P)

Individuals who report fraud and abuse are commonly referred to as whistleblowers. A whistleblower is typically an employee, but a former employee or someone outside of an organization may also report fraud or other misconduct. Legitimate whistleblowers who have proof of fraud must have confidence that they will be protected from retaliation.

Whistleblower hotlines are the most common mechanism for reporting fraud. Compared to organizations without formal whistleblower hotlines, organizations with hotlines are more likely to detect fraud by receiving tips and are less dependent on accident and external audit to uncover fraud.

An effective hotline includes the following features:

- **Confidentiality or anonymity.** Confidentiality and anonymity are not the same thing, and it must be made clear to all concerned whether the information received will be confidential or anonymous. Confidentiality implies that the caller's name and identity will be communicated only to those with an essential or authorized need to know (e.g., the legal department, human resources, or an investigative unit) and not openly disclosed. Confidentiality can be promised only within the limits allowed by law, and callers should know who might learn their identity. Anonymity provides both secrecy and nondisclosure of the caller's identity. With full anonymity, the caller's gender and any other identifying information are also withheld. Promises of anonymity must be kept, and safeguards should be put in place to ensure that the caller's identity is not disclosed.

- **Accessibility.** A whistleblower hotline must be easily accessible. For telephone hotlines, a toll-free number or an international number that accepts collect calls is best. The hotline number should be available 24 hours a day, seven days a week. There should also be provisions for reporting by e-mail, letter, and fax. Employees should have as many mechanisms as possible for reporting fraud or abuse.

- **Staffing.** Hotlines must be staffed by "real" people (not voice-recorded messaging) who are thoroughly screened and trained. If the hotline is international, skilled translators must be available.

- **Use of third-party vendors.** Although administering a hotline in-house may be adequate, using the services of an independent third-party vendor helps to ensure both the perception and reality that tips will remain confidential or anonymous.

- **Naming the hotline.** Some corporations choose to keep the term "hotline" in the title for their reporting tool (e.g., "Risk Hotline" or "Ethics Hotline"). Other schools of thought recommend using another term for hotline (e.g., "Business Conduct Line"). Whatever name is chosen, it should clearly signify the intent of a quick and direct telephone line.

- **Communicate the existence.** A hotline and fraud reporting system will fail unless all employees and people outside the organization are aware of it. Prominently displaying information about the hotline on the organization's Web site, the company intranet, and internal postings in public places (e.g., break rooms and cafeterias) are a few ways to publicize the hotline.

- **Organizational responses to hotline reports.** Quick responses are paramount. They build confidence with potential reporters of fraud and abuse that the organization is committed to ethical behavior and a culture of compliance.

The Sarbanes-Oxley Act, the US Federal Sentencing Guidelines for Organizations, and other regulations and laws require accountability and oversight. But embedding fraud awareness within the internal control framework makes even better business sense by promoting zero tolerance for fraud.

Chapter G: Interrogation/Investigative Techniques

Chapter Introduction

As mentioned previously, internal auditors are expected to be familiar with, but not experts in, fraud investigative techniques. If a specialist in fraud investigations is not available in-house, the CAE may contract with external service providers to perform fraud investigations. This may be particularly necessary when fraud schemes involve multiple perpetrators, computers, security, or complex financial transactions.

Attribute Standard 1210.A1 states that: "The CAE must obtain competent advice and assistance if the internal auditors lack the knowledge, skills, or other competencies needed to perform all or part of the engagement." Practice Advisory 1210.A1-1 advises the CAE to consider the service provider's professional certifications, memberships in professional associations, reputation, experience, and familiarity with the organization's industry or business. In addition, the CAE must ensure the independence and objectivity of the service provider.

This chapter focuses on the particular investigative skill of interrogation. While internal auditors are not expected to conduct interrogations—these are usually conducted by security/loss prevention and law enforcement professionals—internal auditors should be aware of the unique nature of interrogations.

Topic 1: Demonstrate an Understanding of Fraud Interrogation/ Investigative Techniques (Level A)

Interviewing and interrogating

Although the terms "interviewing" and "interrogation" are often used interchangeably, these two activities generally occur in different contexts. They have different goals and, thus, different techniques are used for achieving those goals. Put simply, in an interview, the interviewer doesn't know the answer to most of the questions he or she is asking. In an interrogation, the interviewer probably already knows the answers to many of the questions that will be asked. The interviewer is seeking an admission of those answers by the perpetrator and any accomplices or evidence of lying and the methods used for committing the fraud.

Key distinctions between interviewing and interrogation are summarized in Exhibit III-2.

Exhibit III-2: Comparison of Key Features of Interviewing and Interrogation

	Interviewing	**Interrogation**
Goals	To uncover information.	To secure confession or obtain evidence.
Interviewees	Could include suspected perpetrator; potential witnesses and victims; those who may have aided the perpetrator; those who can provide background information about the area, activity, or perpetrator.	Will probably focus on suspected perpetrators and accomplices.
Questioning strategy	• Establish comfort level to encourage conversation. • Convey a clear sense of what is being sought without using the word "fraud." • Ask questions in a logical and sequential manner.	• Question repeatedly to detect changes in explanations. • May change direction suddenly to elicit an unguarded response.
Atmosphere	• Cooperative, open tone. • Usually at the interviewee's place of work. • Private and seeking to maintain low visibility of interview to others, especially suspected perpetrators.	• Confrontational at times. • Neutral ground, free of distractions (no windows, decorations, minimal furniture). • Presence of security.

Because their role is to detect signs of fraud and establish grounds for further investigation, internal auditors are usually interviewing, rather than interrogating, individuals. Their responsibility is not to seek confessions or establish evidence that can be used in court, unless they are acting in the role of investigator rather than auditor. The task of the internal auditor is to learn enough about the suspicious activity or individual to confirm or eliminate suspicion and then make a recommendation to the auditing department. It is therefore in the best interest of the internal auditor to use discovery techniques that will encourage communication.

Interview behaviors that may be red flags

Many writers have described specific behaviors during interviews that may become fraud indicators or red flags or at least signs that the interviewee is lying or withholding information. These interview red flags might include:

- Restlessness (frequent shifting of position, standing up, pacing).
- Posture (angling the body away from the interviewer).
- Reluctance to make eye contact. (Auditors should remember, however, that eye contact is often a culturally determined behavior. In these cases, failure to make eye contact may simply be a sign of courtesy rather than concealment.)
- Inappropriate attitudes (ranging from an unusual and immediate level of candor and friendliness to unfounded hostility or sarcasm).
- Signs of anxiety like sighing, perspiring, dry mouth, rubbing hands or face, or rapid and high-pitched speech.
- Sudden change in attitude about answering questions.
- Changes in answers given to questions during the interview.

Auditors should remember that these are only indicators of a potential problem, not proof or evidence that fraud has been committed. They may, however, influence the internal auditor's recommendation for a follow-up fraud audit.

Interviewing model

There are various steps internal auditors should follow when conducting interviews in the course of any type of audit. These steps are condensed into the following four phases.

- **Prepare.** This may involve defining the purpose and goals of the interview, gathering background information about the interview subject that may help in establishing rapport and forming questions, preparing specific questions and strategies, and securing an acceptable time and place for the interview.

- **Conduct the interview.** The interviewer should try to follow the plan and not be distracted from the goals that have been set. Additional areas of questioning may develop in the course of the interview, but the auditor should try to accomplish the interview in the time allotted. The auditor should ensure that interviewee statements are clearly understood to be either factual or hearsay (based on another's experience or on rumor). There should be adequate notes on the content of the interview to produce an accurate, complete report.

- **Gain agreement with the interview subject.** In concluding the interview, the auditor should summarize key points to gain the subject's confirmation or to correct misunderstandings.

- **Document the interview.** As soon as possible, the interviewer should complete a report of the interview. This is not a transcript but a summary of areas in which questions were asked, key information was received, and information is still lacking. Interview subject attitude should also be described. The report may suggest the next step in the interviewing or investigative process.

We have presented a simplified overview of interviewing skills. A fraud-related interrogation will usually be conducted by someone familiar with many more strategies for establishing rapport and comfort that can be used for a range of purposes, from simply assessing truthfulness to gaining evidence or a confession.

What is most critical for an internal auditor to know is the difference between interviews and interrogations and the impact that confusing the two can have on an organization. An interview treated inappropriately as interrogation can result in legal action against the company. Interview subjects may feel as if they have been libeled or coerced. Equally important to the legal implications, however, are the practical effects on the information-gathering goals of the interview.

Chapter H: Forensic Auditing

Chapter Introduction

The term "forensic" means "used in or suitable for use in court." In other words, forensic auditing is the application of auditing skills to gather evidence that may be used in a court of law for a criminal or civil matter.

Topic 1: Demonstrate an Understanding of Forensic Auditing Techniques (Level A)

When an internal audit uncovers reasonable and sufficient evidence that fraud has been committed, the internal auditor summarizes this evidence in a report for the chief audit executive. The executive will determine if the evidence and the scope of the fraud merit further investigation for possible criminal or civil prosecution. The internal auditing activity will then assemble an appropriate fraud audit team whose members include specialists in forensic auditing.

Fraud audit team

As suggested by Standard 1210.A2, while the internal auditor must be able to identify the indicators of fraud, he or she is not expected to have the special skills required to gather evidence and establish facts that will be admitted into court and will be effective in securing convictions or favorable judgments. This expertise belongs to a group of individuals who comprise the fraud audit team. A fraud team may include a ACFE-certified fraud examiner, security investigators, human resources personnel, legal counsel, and outside consultants (e.g., surveillance or computer experts). Depending on whether senior management is suspected of involvement in the fraud, the team may or may not include members of senior management.

If external service providers are used, the CAE should ensure that a work agreement clearly describes the scope of work, expectations and limitations, and deliverables.

Required skills and expertise

By necessity, forensic auditing requires not only understanding of accounting standards and practices but also familiarity with the practices and policies in the business activity being audited and expertise in investigative techniques and the rules and standards of legal proceedings. Forensic auditors must be able to both gather evidence and present it in court in a convincing manner. The evidence they present must follow the rules of evidence established for the court in which the case is presented—whether it is at a federal/national or local level, whether it is a civil or criminal proceeding. They must be able to ensure that evidence is not lost or destroyed by the perpetrator or mishandled in some way so that it will no longer be considered reliable in court.

As with any area of specialization, the more experience professionals gather while doing their jobs, the more adept and intuitive they become. Their intuition is based on a personal mental database of examples of fraud indicators and cover-up techniques they have seen before. They are especially skilled in piecing together the story of a fraud—from establishing motivation and opportunity to describing how the fraud was perpetrated and tracking each step of the fraudulent activity to its final outcome. Organizing this detailed and often technical data into a well-supported story that is easy to follow will be essential in court. Forensic auditors are thus skilled in identifying the gaps in their stories and following trails to find the missing information.

In addition to their investigative and legal responsibilities, forensic auditors may also be used by corporations proactively as consultants. Their experience equips them to identify potential weaknesses in controls that can be exploited by perpetrators of fraud.

Computers as sources of evidence

It is perhaps obvious that an organization's information system or computers can provide much valuable data that may be analyzed independently or compared with other types of information, which could include paper-based receipts, logs, invoices, or work orders; information from interviews; and information gathered through observation of the area or function.

It will be important for the auditor to remember the less obvious sources of information on a computer or information system, such as:

- Word-processed documents (e.g., correspondence that can corroborate an action like writing off an uncollected debt or lost shipment).
- Customer lists. (These might be useful in identifying fictional or inactive accounts that are being used to conceal theft.)
- E-mail logs. (These might reveal, for example, extensive communication with a customer that is uncharacteristic of the work situation.)
- Financial records. (These will yield data that can be further analyzed for irregularities.)
- Scheduling systems or logs. (These can be used to identify irregular contacts or activities or to demonstrate false claims for expense or time reimbursements.)
- Operations logs. (For example, pilfering of waste or diversion of company property might be identified by comparing expected levels of waste or use with actual data.)
- Personnel records. (Personnel records can point to various red flags. For example, employees may not have been screened completely or properly. An employee's employment record may reveal a history of brief tenures at jobs that afforded opportunity for fraud.)
- Computer-stored voice mail. (These records may suggest instances of theft of intellectual property.)
- Internet history reports. (These may provide evidence related to activities such as harassment or hate crimes.)

It will be critical for auditors to be aware of applicable data privacy practices, policies, and restrictions before reviewing correspondence and items on personal computers. Organizations should also be aware of the rules of evidence in the countries in which they operate. These rules may require the retention of data for specified periods and the ability to search stored data. They may also dictate how evidence may be handled and what is admissible in court.

Computer forensics is an investigative discipline that includes the preservation, identification, extraction, and documentation of computer hardware and data for evidentiary purposes and root cause analysis. Computer forensic technology and software packages are available to assist in the investigation of fraud—where computers are used to facilitate the fraud—or to identify red flags of potential fraud.

Examples of computer forensic activities include:

- Recovering deleted e-mails.
- Monitoring e-mails for indicators of potential fraud.
- Performing investigations after terminations of employment.
- Recovering evidence after formatting a hard drive.

The challenge of using computers as a source of evidence is maintaining the integrity of the evidence while, at the same time, investigating what is on the computer in question. Since accessing anything on a computer may inadvertently change significant access dates in files, investigators generally begin by isolating the computer under investigation and making a digital copy of the computer's hard drive. The original is stored in a secure location to maintain the pristine, untouched condition that is required of evidence—termed the "chain of evidence." Investigation and analysis is conducted on the copy, including searching hidden folders and unallocated disk space for deleted, encrypted, or damaged files.

Computer forensic activities help establish and maintain a continuing chain of custody, which is critical in determining admissibility of evidence in courts. Although the CAE and internal auditors are not expected to be experts in this area, the CAE should have a general understanding of the benefits this technology provides so that he or she may engage appropriate experts, as necessary, for assisting with a fraud investigation.

Next Steps

You have completed Part 2, Section III, of The IIA's CIA Learning System®. Next, check your understanding by completing the online section-specific test(s) to help you identify any content that needs additional study.

Once you have completed the section-specific test(s) and feel confident that you have mastered the information, complete the Part 2 online post-test.

Bibliography

The following references were used in the development of The IIA's CIA Learning System. Please note that all Web site references were valid as of March 2013.

American Institute of Certified Public Accountants. "Management Antifraud Programs and Controls." New York: American Institute of Certified Public Accountants, Inc., 2002.

"Analyze Every Transaction in the Fight Against Fraud: Using Technology for Effective Fraud Detection." ACL Services Ltd., 2008, www.adfor.it/DOWNLOAD/whitepaper/index.asp.

Apostolou, Barbara. *Sampling: A Guide for Internal Auditors.* Altamonte Springs, Florida: The Institute of Internal Auditors, 2004.

"AS (Australian Standard) 3806—2006 Compliance Program, infostore.saiglobal.com/store/details.aspx?ProductID=304437.

"AS/NZS ISO 31000:2009, "Risk Management—Principles and Guidelines." Standards Australia/Standards New Zealand, sherq.org/31000.pdf.

"Assessing the Adequacy of Risk Management Using ISO 31000" (IPPF Practice Guide). Altamonte Springs, Florida: The Institute of Internal Auditors, 2010.

Audit Committee Effectiveness—What Works Best, third edition. Altamonte Springs, Florida: The Institute of Internal Auditors, 2005.

"The Audit Committee: Purpose, Process, Professionalism." The Institute of Internal Auditors, www.theiia.org/download.cfm?file=6676.

"Auditing External Business Relationships" (IPPF Practice Guide). Altamonte Springs, Florida: The Institute of Internal Auditors, 2009.

"Auditing Privacy Risks" (IPPF Practice Guide). Altamonte Springs, Florida: The Institute of Internal Auditors, 2012.

"Auditing Techniques" course. Altamonte Springs, Florida: The Institute of Internal Auditors.

"Auditing the Control Environment" (IPPF Practice Guide). Altamonte Springs, Florida: The Institute of Internal Auditors, 2011.

Baker, Sunny. *The Complete Idiot's Guide to Business Statistics.* Indianapolis, Indiana: Alpha, 2002.

Baxter, Ralph. "The Role of Spreadsheets in Today's Corporate Climate." *ITAudit,* Vol. 9, December 2006.

Bluman, Allan G. *Probability Demystified.* New York: McGraw-Hill, 2005.

Bologna, G. Jack, et al. *The Accountant's Handbook of Fraud and Commercial Crime.* New York: John Wiley and Sons, 1993.

Breon, Michael A. and Randall F. Stellwag. "Soft Skills to Improve Internal Audit Results." www.theiia.org/chapters/pubdocs/88/InternalAuditSoftSkills.pdf.

"Building a Strategic Internal Audit Function." PricewaterhouseCoopers, 2009, www.pwc.be/en/systems-process-assurance/pwc-strategic-internal-audit.pdf.

Coenen, Tracy L. "The Fraud Files: The True Cost of Fraud." *Wisconsin Law Journal*, May 24, 2006.

Committee of Sponsoring Organizations of the Treadway Commission (COSO), www.coso.org.

Committee of Sponsoring Organizations of the Treadway Commission. *Enterprise Risk Management—Integrated Framework.* Jersey City, New Jersey: American Institute of Certified Public Accountants, 2004.

Committee of Sponsoring Organizations of the Treadway Commission. *Guidance on Monitoring Internal Control Systems.* Jersey City, New Jersey: American Institute of Certified Public Accountants, 2009.

Committee of Sponsoring Organizations of the Treadway Commission. *Internal Control—Integrated Framework.* Jersey City, New Jersey: American Institute of Certified Public Accountants, 1994.

Committee of Sponsoring Organizations of the Treadway Commission. *Internal Control Over Financial Reporting—Guidance for Smaller Public Companies.* Jersey City, New Jersey: American Institute of Certified Public Accountants, 2006.

"Coordinating Risk Management and Assurance" (IPPF Practice Guide). Altamonte Springs, Florida: The Institute of Internal Auditors, 2012.

"Corporate Governance: A Practical Guide." London Stock Exchange, 2004, www.ecgi.org/codes/code.php?code_id=118.

Corporate Governance and the Board—What Works Best. Altamonte Springs, Florida: The Institute of Internal Auditors, 2000.

"Corporate Governance Principles and Recommendations with 2010 Amendments." ASX Corporate Governance Council, www.asxgroup.com.au/media/PDFs/cg_principles_recommendation s_ with_2010_amendments.pdf.

Culter, Sally F. *Continuous Auditing: An Operational Model for Auditors.* Altamonte Springs, Florida: The Institute of Internal Auditors, 2005.

Dalal, Chetan. "Foiled by Nanoscience." *ITAudit,* April 1, 2005.

"Developing the Internal Audit Strategic Plan" (IPPF Practice Guide). Altamonte Springs, Florida: The Institute of Internal Auditors, 2012.

Directory of Software Products for Internal Auditors. Altamonte Springs, Florida: The Institute of Internal Auditors, 2010.

"Effective Writing for Auditors." Altamonte Springs, Florida: The Institute of Internal Auditors.

"Enhancing Board Oversight." COSO, March 2012, www.coso.org/ documents/COSO-EnhancingBoardOversight_r8_Web-ready%20(2).pdf.

"Formulating and Expressing Internal Audit Opinions" (IPPF Practice Guide). Altamonte Springs, Florida: The Institute of Internal Auditors, 2009.

Fraud Examiners Manual, 2003 edition. Austin, Texas: Association of Certified Fraud Examiners, 2003.

Frigo, Mark L. *A Balanced Scorecard Framework for Internal Auditing Departments.* Altamonte Springs, Florida: The Institute of Internal Auditors Research Foundation, 2002.

Galloway, David. *Internal Auditing: A Guide for the New Auditor,* second edition. Altamonte Springs, Florida: The Institute of Internal Auditors, 2002.

Global Technology Audit Guides (GTAG). Altamonte Springs, Florida: The Institute of Internal Auditors.

- GTAG 1: "Information Technology Controls," 2005.
- GTAG 3: "Continuous Auditing: Implications for Assurance, Monitoring, and Risk Assessment," 2005.
- GTAG 11: "Developing the IT Audit Plan," 2008.

Glover, Hubert D., and James C. Flag. *Effective Fraud Detection and Prevention Techniques Practice Set.* Altamonte Springs, Florida: The Institute of Internal Auditors, 1993.

Goldsmith, Jim. "Using Audit Tools, Part 1, Audit Software Packages." *ITAudit,* August 14, 1999.

"Government Auditing Standards (The Yellow Book)." US Government Accountability Office (GAO), www.gao.gov/govaud/ybk01.htm.

Gray, Glen L. *Changing Internal Audit Practices in the New Paradigm: The Sarbanes-Oxley Environment.* Altamonte Springs, Florida: The Institute of Internal Auditors, 2004.

Guide to the Assessment of IT Risk (GAIT). Altamonte Springs, Florida: The Institute of Internal Auditors.

Hargraves, Kim, Susan B. Lione, Kerry L. Shackelford, and Peter C. Tilton. *Privacy: Assessing the Risk.* Altamonte Springs, Florida: The Institute of Internal Auditors, 2003.

Heizer, Jay, and Barry Render. *Principles of Operations Management*, fourth edition. Upper Saddle River, New Jersey: Prentice-Hall, 2001.

"How to Get Action on Audit Recommendations." Washington, D.C.: United States General Accounting Office, July 1991.

Hubbard, Larry. *Control Self-Assessment: A Practical Guide.* Altamonte Springs, Florida: The Institute of Internal Auditors, 2000.

Hutton, David W. *The Change Agents' Handbook.* Milwaukee, Wisconsin: ASQ Quality Press, 1994.

Improving Business Processes. Boston, Massachusetts: Harvard Business School Press, 2010.

The Institute of Internal Auditors, www.theiia.org.

"Integrated Auditing" (IPPF Practice Guide). Altamonte Springs, Florida: The Institute of Internal Auditors, 2012.

"Interaction with the Board" (IPPF Practice Guide). Altamonte Springs, Florida: The Institute of Internal Auditors, 2011.

"Internal Auditing and Fraud" (IPPF Practice Guide). Altamonte Springs, Florida: The Institute of Internal Auditors, 2009.

"Internal Auditor Competency Framework." The Institute of Internal Auditors, www.theiia.org/guidance/additional-resources/competency-framework-for-internal-auditors.

International Professional Practices Framework. Altamonte Springs, Florida: The Institute of Internal Auditors.

ISO 31000—"Risk Management." ISO, www.iso.org/iso/home/standards/iso31000.htm.

Jerskey, Pamela. "Automated Workpapers Made Easy."

Lanza, Richard B. *Proactively Detecting Occupational Fraud Using Computer Audit Reports.* Altamonte Springs, Florida: The Institute of Internal Auditors Research Foundation, 2004.

"The Laws That Govern the Securities Industry—Sarbanes-Oxley Act of 2002." Securities and Exchange Commission, www.sec.gov/about/laws.shtml.

"Managing the Business Risk of Fraud, A Practical Guide." The Institute of Internal Auditors, the American Institute of Certified Public Accountants, and the Association of Certified Fraud Examiners, 2008, www.theiia.org/media/files/fraud-white-paper/fraud%20paper.pdf.

Marcella, Albert J., Jr. "Preparing for the Digital Records Storm: ESI, the Law, and Corporate Vigilance." Unpublished manuscript.

Marks, Norman. "Auditing Governance Processes." *Internal Audtior (Ia),* February 2012.

McNamee, David. *Business Risk Assessment.* Altamonte Springs, Florida: The Institute of Internal Auditors, 2005.

"Measuring Internal Audit Effectiveness and Efficiency" (IPPF Practice Guide). Altamonte Springs, Florida: The Institute of Internal Auditors, 2010.

Nigrini, Mark. "I've Got Your Number: How a Mathematical Phenomenon Can Help CPAs Uncover Fraud and Other Irregularities." *Journal of Accountancy*, May 1999.

O'Gara, John. *Corporate Fraud: Case Studies in Detection and Prevention.* Hoboken, New Jersey: John Wiley and Sons, 2004.

Organizational Governance: Guidance for Internal Auditors. Altamonte Springs, Florida: The Institute of Internal Auditors, 2006. (As of February 2010, this publication is suppressed.)

"Organizational Guidelines." United States Sentencing Commission, www.ussc.gov/Guidelines/Organizational_Guidelines/index.cfm.

Public Company Accounting Oversight Board, www.pcaob.org.

Quality Assessment Manual, fifth edition. Altamonte Springs, Florida: The Institute of Internal Auditors, 2006.

"Quality Assurance and Improvement Program" (IPPF Practice Guide). Altamonte Springs, Florida: The Institute of Internal Auditors, 2012.

Reding, Kurt F., Paul J. Sobel, Urton L. Anderson, Michael J. Head, Sridhar Ramamoorti, Mark Salamasick, and Cris Riddle. *Internal Auditing: Assurance and Consulting Services,* second edition. Altamonte Springs, Florida: The Institute of Internal Auditors Research Foundation, 2009.

"Report to the Nations on Occupational Fraud and Abuse, 2012 Global Fraud Study." Association of Certified Fraud Examiners, www.acfe.com/ uploadedFiles/ACFE_Website/Content/rttn/2012-report-to-nations.pdf

"Revised Guidance for Directors on the Combined Code." Financial Reporting Council, www.ecgi.org/codes/documents/frc_ic.pdf.

"Risk Assessment in Practice." COSO, October 2012, www.coso.org/ documents/COSOAnncsOnlineSurvy2GainInpt4Updt2IntrnlCntrl IntgratdFrmwrk%20-%20for%20merge_files/COSO-ERM%20Risk%20Assessment%20inPractice%20Thought%20 Paper%20OCtober%202012.pdf.

"The Role of Internal Auditing in Enterprise-Wide Risk Management." The Institute of Internal Auditors, 2009, www.theiia.org/ download.cfm?file=62465.

Sawyer, Lawrence B., Mortimer A. Dittenhofer, and James H. Scheiner. *Sawyer's Internal Auditing*, fifth edition. Altamonte Springs, Florida: The Institute of Internal Auditors, 2005.

Sayana, S. Anantha, "Using CAATs to Support IS Audit," Information Systems Audit and Control Association, www.isaca.org/Journal/Past-Issues/2003/Volume-1/Pages/Using-CAATS-to-Support-IS-Audit.aspx.

"Skills for the New Internal Auditor" seminar. Altamonte Springs, Florida: The Institute of Internal Auditors, 2007.

Sobel, Paul. "Internal Auditing's Role in Risk Management." March 2011, www.theiia.org/bookstore/product/internal-auditings-role-in-risk-management-1561.cfm

"Tools and Techniques for the Beginning Auditor" seminar. Altamonte Springs, Florida: The Institute of Internal Auditors, 2007.

Warren, J. Donald Jr., and Xenia Ley Parker. *Continuous Auditing: Potential for Internal Auditors*. Altamonte Springs, Florida: The Institute of Internal Auditors Research Foundation, 2003.

Whitley, Jody. "Taking the Leap: Using Audit Software in Gaming Audit Shops." The Institute of Internal Auditors, February 15, 2005.

Woelfel, Charles J. *Financial Statement Analysis*. New York: McGraw-Hill, 1994.

Yau, Woon-Foong. "Embedded Audit Modules in Enterprise Resource Planning Systems: Implementation and Functionality." *Journal of Information Systems,* September 22, 2005.

Zhang, Charles. "The Art of Coordination." *Internal Auditor,* April 1998.

Index

D

E

F

G, H

I

J, K, L

M, N

O

S

T

U, V, W